T0227623

Dynamic
E-Business
Implementation
Management

E-Business Solutions

An Academic Press Series

Bennet P. Lientz and Kathryn P. Rea
Series Editors

Dynamic
E-Business
Implementation
Management

How to Effectively Manage
E-Business Implementation

Bennet P. Lientz
Professor
Anderson Graduate School of Management
University of California, Los Angeles

Kathryn P. Rea
President
The Consulting Edge, Inc.

Routledge
Taylor & Francis Group

LONDON AND NEW YORK

First published 2001 by Academic Press

This edition published 2011 by Routledge
2 Park Square, Milton Park, Abingdon, Oxfordshire OX14 4RN
711 Third Avenue, New York, NY 10017, USA

First issued in hardback 2016

Routledge is an imprint of the Taylor & Francis Group, an informa business

Library of Congress Catalog Card Number: 00-102787

International Standard Book Number: 0-12-449980-5

ISBN 13: 978-1-138-15825-2 (hbk)
ISBN 13: 978-0-12-449980-5 (pbk)

Table of Contents

Part I
Organize Your E-Business Effort

Chapter 1
Introduction

Chapter 2

Develop Your E-Business Implementation Plan

Chapter 3
Become an Effective
E-Business Implementation Manager

Chapter 4
Manage Your E-Business Teams

Chapter 5
Obtain E-Business Resources and Funding

Chapter 6
Use Technology Effectively to Support E-Business Work

Part II
Manage Your E-Business Implementation

Chapter 7
Coordinate Your E-Business Activities

Chapter 10

Manage E-Business Resources

Chapter 11

Manage E-Business Work

Chapter 12
Manage E-Business, Projects, and Regular Work

Chapter 13
Manage E-Business Contractors and Vendors

Part III
E-Business Issue Management

Chapter 15
Address E-Business Management Issues

Chapter 16
101 Specific E-Business Issues

Appendices

Preface

E-BUSINESS COMPLEXITY AND DYNAMICS

Implementing E-Business places substantial demands on the internal business organization and IT. There is tight time pressure. There are external influences in terms of the industry, the competition, and emerging software and network technologies. Complexity also arises from the use of consultants and contractors to support internal and E-Business activities.

Complexity exists because in E-Business you must implement changes in multiple related business activities. These span departments across the firm—making communications and coordination more difficult. Adding to this E-Business implementation means that you will have to cut out exceptions and workarounds. You will have to eliminate department grown shadow systems. Moreover, you may have to restructure current business activities to place them in synchronization with E-Business ones.

To put it in a nutshell, E-Business is complex because of the following factors.

- There are high management expectations. This means greater management visibility of the project.
- E-Business implementation can be quite disruptive to the business staff.
- Business organizations such as marketing, customer service, and other departments must change to adapt to E-Business.
- There is severe time pressure to implement.
- E-Business and e-commerce software are evolving and will continue to evolve during the project. New products may come out. These factors create opportunities and challenges.
- There is a need to involve many people in E-Business implementation.
- The work does not end with the initial implementation. Instead, E-Business work will have to continue and expand.
- There are competitive and management pressures that can surface during the work to change direction.

- There will likely be resistance to the E-Business effort from department staff and managers who see themselves in jeopardy.
- The current IT staff are often already stressed enough doing other work such as production support, maintenance, new development, and enhancement. Adding E-Business makes things worse.
- The IT infrastructure part of the project may be complex and much different than the technologies you currently have in place.
- There is substantial budget pressure. This is exacerbated since E-Business will seldom generate major profits initially. Like any other channel it has to be built up.

E-Business implementation is almost a soap opera. Management, technical, business activity, competition, and other factors combine to make managing E-Business a real challenge. Look at this list again. You can easily see why many E-Business efforts get into trouble. Often, the organization has to settle for either a limited function web site or no site at all. You can also understand why many efforts fail.

E-Business implementation is dynamic. Let's consider what some companies have experienced:

- Upper management changes direction, scope, or the schedule without consulting the implementation team.
- New software, hardware, or network technology arrives on the scene. You find it very appealing over what you are using now.
- Some competitor has come up with new ideas for their web site, promotions, and/or advertising. Your E-Business implementation effort could be in big trouble unless you respond—and fast.
- Suppliers or customers are changing their requirements or needs based on their experience with e-commerce transactions.
- You find that you have to fix more of the current business processes than you thought because of problems uncovered in designing the new E-Business activities.

These are examples of why the word "dynamic" is in the title. You have to respond to issues and situations in E-Business implementation more than almost any other type of work.

WHY TRADITIONAL MANAGEMENT METHODS DON'T WORK FOR E-BUSINESS

Traditional project management is not well-suited to deal with E-Business in particular and IT projects in general. Here are some characteristics of traditional and E-Business projects to offer a contrast.

Characteristic	Traditional Project Management	E-Business Implementation Management
Objectives	Narrow and fixed	Broad and changing
Scope	Narrow range	Wide range and tendency to grow
Staffing	Assumed to be full time	Mostly part-time; split with many other duties
Critical path	Focus on the longest path	Focus on tasks that have risk; the longest path is important, but not critical
Technology	Supporting role	Major role
Requirements	Stable	Dynamic and changing
Duration of initial project	One year or more	Less than one year for the first effort
Type of work	One time focus	Continuous, on-going focus
Project ending	Ends with the key milestones being attained	Achievement of milestones just leads to new work
Interrelation with other work	Limited	Intense through resource sharing
Structure of tasks	Many sequential tasks	Many parallel tasks
Attitude of departments	Supportive	May be resentful

This table is really the reason for this book. We have found that following traditional project management methods can get E-Business implementation into big trouble. Also, E-Business implementation is a continuous program rather than a discrete project. That is also why we are going to use the phrase "implementation management" rather than "project management."

Dynamic E-Business Implementation Management presents a step-by-step approach for successfully accomplishing the following:

- Define the purpose, scope, roles, and issues for E-Business implementation in a clear way to prevent scope creep and changing requirements.
- Get the E-Business implementation leaders and team members on board and working effectively and in a collaborative manner.
- Manage vendors, consultants, and contractors to support aspects of the implementation within the schedule and budget.
- Set up the E-Business project plan quickly with the involvement and commitment of the team and management.
- Present and market E-Business and the implementation plan to management and line organizations.
- Manage the work, quality, and results in the E-Business implementation.

- Address issues and opportunities that will arise during implementation.
- Measure implementation performance and results.
- Extract and use lessons learned for E-Business success.
- Expand E-Business after its initial roll out.

WHO CAN BENEFIT FROM THIS BOOK?

The individuals and organizations that have gotten value from this material include the following:

- Upper level business managers who are thinking about, who have started, or who have on-going E-Business efforts.
- Project leaders who are or wish to be involved in E-Business.
- Middle level business managers and staff who are involved or going to be involved in E-Business.
- IT managers and staff who have to support E-Business implementation.
- Consultants who wish to be involved or who are involved in E-Business implementation.
- Investment, accounting, and auditing firm managers and staff who want to assess how an organization is doing in their E-Business implementation.

ORGANIZATION AND FEATURES OF THE BOOK

The book begins with the implementation concept for E-Business. This leads to planning, identifying the team leader, defining the methods and tools, and getting the team assembled. With the work underway, there are chapters on how to manage the people, how to manage the resources between regular work and E-Business implementation, how to manage the work, and how to deal with vendors. There are two chapters dealing with communications—one with the team and one with management. There are also chapters that address measurement and implementation issues. Each chapter generally follows the same structured format.

- *Introduction.* background and definitions for the chapter
- *Milestones.* purpose of the chapter and end products
- *Methods for E-Business.* techniques for management and direction of the activities
- *E-Business Examples.* we follow the experience of four firms in their E-Business implementation efforts; not all of these were successful
- *E-Business Lessons Learned.* guidelines to help you manage the E-Business implementation better
- *What to Do Next.* specific steps that you can take

In addition, there is a closing chapter that gives you help in addressing 101 issues that you are likely to face in your E-Business efforts. There is also an appendix that provides you with implementation templates for E-Business to get you started faster. A second appendix provides something we have wanted in many books—a cross reference of all lessons learned and guidelines for E-Business (called with tongue-in-cheek—The Magic Cross Reference).

The techniques used in the book have been employed in a wide variety of E-Business implementations around the world, in different industries, and with organizations of different sizes. Each chapter contains detailed guidelines and action items to help you use the chapter material quickly and effectively.

Some of the features of **Dynamic E-Business Implementation Management** are:

- How to set up your E-Business implementation effort with minimal effort
- How to gain the involvement and commitment of the project team
- How to gain and keep upper management support
- How to address issues and opportunities that arise in implementation
- Specific checklists and guidelines for each implementation activity
- How to detect when the implementation is in trouble and what to do about it
- How to use project management software and other software tools to facilitate the work in the project
- How to manage resources that are shared between the E-Business implementation and regular work assignments
- How to instill a spirit of collaboration and teamwork in your E-Business implementation
- How to prevent problems in the implementation before they occur
- How to gather lessons learned from E-Business implementation for later E-Business efforts
- Get quickly to specific issues and guidelines through Appendix 2, the Magic Cross Reference

DIFFERENCES WITH OTHER BOOKS ON E-BUSINESS

Here are some key differences between this book and the other 1,000 or so other E-Business books.

- You won't find an emphasis on the "what" of E-Business. This is not an academic book on E-Business. It is a book on the "how" of managing the implementation.
- Some books rely on a "magic bullet" such as buying an ERP (Enterprise Resource Planning) system. This is usually infeasible. You might be broke or dead by the time you finish.

- Other books develop their own e-jargon. This is nonsense. What you need is common sense. This book is written in common language.
- Some books are technology based. This is a variation of the magic bullet. Technology changes and will continue to evolve. For us in E-Business it is simply a means to an end. E-Business should be business focused.
- Many books are general and vague. They sound good, but give you little tangible to use after you read them. We have over 250 specific guidelines in this book drawn from real life.
- Some books rely on specific examples of success. These are typically very specific and special situations. Don't you wish you worked for firms like that? In fact, we find that these tales of success often end up having problems and issues—just like real life. Moreover, you learn more from organizations that are partially screwed up—they are more real. Our examples are composites of the real world of business—they may be not pretty or elegant, but they make money and employ people.

About the Authors

Bennet P. Lientz is a consultant, teacher, and researcher in E-Business. He has advised startup E-Business firms as well as helped firms move into E-Business. He is Professor of Information Systems at the Anderson Graduate School of Management, University of California, Los Angeles (UCLA). Dr. Lientz was previously Associate Professor of Engineering at the University of Southern California and department manager at System Development Corporation, where he was one of the project leaders involved in the development of ARPANET, the precursor of the Internet. He managed administrative systems at UCLA and has managed projects and served as a consultant to companies and government agencies since the late 1970s.

Lientz has taught project management, information technology, and strategic planning for the past 20 years. He has created two E-Business courses. He has delivered seminars related to these topics to more than 4,000 people in Asia, Latin America, Europe, Australia, and North America. He is the author of more than 20 books and 60 articles in information systems, planning, project management, and E-Business.

Kathryn P. Rea is president and founder of The Consulting Edge, Inc., which was established in 1984. The firm specializes in E-Business, information technology, project management, and financial consulting. She has consulted with over 45 organizations in E-Business implementation and expansion.

Rea has managed more than 65 major technology-related projects internationally. She has advised on and carried out projects in government, energy, banking and finance, distribution, trading, retailing, transportation, mining, manufacturing, and utilities. She has successfully directed multinational projects in China, North and South America, Southeast Asia, Europe, and Australia. She has conducted more than 120 seminars around the world. She is the author of eight books and more than 20 articles in various areas of information systems and analysis.

Part I

Organize Your E-Business Effort

Chapter 1

Introduction

E-BUSINESS CHARACTERISTICS

What is E-Business? E-Business occurs when organizations perform transactions electronically with their customers or suppliers. In E-Business you have to modify your internal business activities to attain acceptable performance goals for the business transactions. E-Business employs e-commerce transactions and formats. In this regard, e-commerce is part of E-Business. Here are several common characteristics that you find on good E-Business web sites and in company operations.

- Transactions flow seamlessly across departments. Traditional processes have barriers and boundaries between departments requiring a handoff of the transactions.
- Exception transactions, workarounds, and shadow systems in departments are greatly reduced or eliminated. Traditional business processes tend to have many of these.
- There is a focus on providing the web visitor with information. Traditional business focuses on doing the transaction with less information.
- Policies and procedures are more formalized in E-Business. Many traditional processes rely on informal procedures that depend on critical employees with business knowledge. We will call these people "king bees" and "queen bees" because most junior employees rush up to these people with questions on their work. We also will use "business activity" in place of "business process" to indicate and reinforce the differences between a standard business process and a wider ranging E-Business activity.
- In E-Business there is a greater dependence on systems and technology than in much of traditional business. The systems must be highly scalable to deliver good response time during peak loads of work. Traditional systems have to address more predictable workloads. Also, traditional systems tend to handle more reports and exceptions.

Implementing E-Business successfully means that you will have the following goals.

- Business activities (which include the basic business processes) must be streamlined and made efficient. This applies not only to the core E-Business activities, but also to traditional work and supporting activities. E-Business and traditional business must be synchronized.
- The business activities must become knowledge based. That is, information to help customers and suppliers must be added to the web site. You will also be taking advantage of the vast volume of information that is available through web navigation and activity by customers or suppliers. This information helps to differentiate your web site from those of your competitors.
- Exception transactions, manual workarounds, and separate shadow systems in departments have to be eliminated through automation, policy change, or procedure change.
- Organization change is often necessary. Barriers between departments have to be eliminated. The marketing department has to be overhauled to support E-Business promotions, discounts, and other marketing.
- There may have to be infrastructure changes—in office location, office layout, and basic telephone and other services.
- Some standard work processes must be changed to support the E-Business activities.
- New systems and computer and communication components and systems have to be installed. A robust extranet network is necessary to support customers and suppliers.
- There is a flood of information from E-Business transactions. This creates a need and opportunity to create new activities to assess the competition, analyze the product and customer data, and do financial analysis.

E-BUSINESS IMPLEMENTATION IS DIFFERENT

We have highlighted differences with traditional project management in the preface. Nevertheless, project management methods can be used as is or with the guidelines that will be provided in these chapters.

... Versus Traditional Project Management

Project management started as informal guidelines and practices. As time passed, it grew more formal with information gathering, data analysis, and management reporting following sets of standard procedures. This reached extremes in many IT and engineering organizations where people were assigned full time to carry out the mechanics of project management.

Project management in some cases lost direction. The old standard formal methods of project management did not fit the nature of modern projects. The methods did not take advantage of new software tools and technology. Here are some differences that expand on the chart in the preface.

- *Structure.* Traditional project management is quite rigid. E-Business demands flexibility and the ability to address change.
- *Project leader.* In traditional projects the role of the project leader is to act as a project administrator using various project management tools such as GANTT and PERT charts. It is very different in E-Business. The leaders must spend much of their time addressing issues. In traditional project management there is one project leader; in E-Business you are better off with several.
- *Project teams.* Traditional project teams were composed of people who performed work on tasks in the project. It was assumed that these people worked full time on the project. Not so in E-Business. There is a need for a collaborative and participative approach where team members define and update their own work. There is a greater requirement for teamwork. Team members in E-Business have to do at least part of their normal work as well as work in E-Business implementation.
- *Technology.* Technology in standard projects is just part of the project. In E-Business, systems and technology play a much wider role.
- *Objectives.* The objectives in a standard project are defined at the start and are assumed to not vary much during the project. In E-Business you can be hit by new technology or the web site of a competitor that you cannot ignore.
- *Scope.* The scope of a traditional project is more narrow and focused than that of E-Business implementation.
- *Structure of the tasks.* Traditional projects have both parallel and sequential tasks. E-Business tasks tend to be more parallel due to time pressure. In traditional project management, people pay attention to the critical path. The critical path is the longest path in the project from start to finish, so that anything delayed on the critical path results in a delayed project. This sounds well and good, but in E-Business you have to pay attention to tasks that have risk. Tasks that have risk have issues behind them. Who is to say that these are on the critical path? Normally, they are not, and then addressing the critical path leads you in the wrong direction.
- *Lessons learned.* Lessons learned were significant, but were not a dominant feature of projects. In E-Business, gathering and using lessons learned and experience effectively are critical to your long term E-Business success.

. . . Versus Reengineering

Because you have to create new business activities and change existing processes, you may be tempted to believe that E-Business implementation resembles reengineering projects. However, there are some significant differences. First, E-Business aims at positive goals: to make the company more competitive, to reach new customers and markets, and to provide a wider range of products and services. In contrast, reengineering typically aims at process efficiency for its own sake. As a result many people think of reengineering as downsizing. In E-Business you may actually add people. You will continue to use some existing processes because of the time pressure to implement E-Business. This is a second difference. A third difference is that in E-Business implementation there is major time pressure put on the team to get "live" quickly, whereas reengineering appears sometimes to be almost leisurely.

. . . Versus Software Package Installation

For software packages you normally evaluate and select among a class of software such as Enterprise Resource Planning (ERP) software. You might select the package that has the best fit. Then you install it and try to get it to function in the business. This often requires that you change your internal processes to fit the system. Unfortunately, many software packages are quite rigid in responding to the demands of E-Business. Then you have to make substantial efforts at workarounds or custom programming. In general, software package installation tends to be more narrow than E-Business implementation.

Overall Focus of E-Business

E-Business implementation has a combination of themes:

- E-Business implementation often does involve buying and installing software packages, but it also involves interfacing with your existing software.
- E-Business implementation creates new business activities, changes some current processes, leaves others alone, and may replace yet other processes.
- Implementing E-Business involves changes to business organizations such as marketing.
- E-Business implementation is more than project management because of the size, scope, time pressure, flexibility, and nature of the work.

CRITICAL SUCCESS FACTORS IN IMPLEMENTING E-BUSINESS

There have been many E-Business failures and successes. You can note factors leading to success or failure to enhance your chances for E-Business success. Our examples in the book are not all successes by any means. Here are some critical success factors in E-Business implementation.

- *Upper Management.* Management involvement must be continuous, but noninterfering. Management can provide E-Business by supplying a vision for E-Business, providing resources for implementation, and also in addressing issues and problems related to change in business activities, policies, and organization.
- *Information Technology.* Many IT groups are typically not equipped and trained to handle E-Business. With the time pressure for implementation, the existing maintenance and support work, and other projects, there is just no time to come up to speed in many cases. Therefore, it is no surprise that you find vendor involvement and some outsourcing of the systems side of E-Business implementation.
- *Organization.* You cannot wait until after E-Business is in full production to change the organization. Signs of stress and strain will appear while you are trying to get E-Business established. This must be addressed during the implementation.
- *Business activities and processes.* Not only must some current processes be transformed into E-Business activities, but changes must be made to other processes as well. New business activities will have to be created to analyze information on transactions and competitors as well as to handle credit card transactions.
- *Policies.* Company policies must be changed to accommodate E-Business. Examples are stock levels, customer service performance, and credit review.
- *Vendors.* You may have to obtain additional vendors who can better support E-Business for product delivery and shipment. You may want to increase the range of your web offerings, requiring you to reach out to new suppliers. You may place new demands on existing vendors to reduce and eliminate back order situations.
- *Business employees.* The business employees cannot just lie back and let IT or consultants do the work for them. They have to actively participate in E-Business implementation. They have to be brought on board the E-Business project and bandwagon. They have to be willing to change their work practices. In addition, they can provide valuable information that can be placed on the web.
- *The E-Business implementation work.* You will have more success and fewer problems if you treat the E-Business implementation as a series of interrelated subprojects under the E-Business umbrella. That is how Appendix 1 addresses E-Business plan templates.
- *Customers and suppliers.* These are your audiences for E-Business. They are external and beyond your direct control. Remember this when you implement. Their experiences, needs, and knowledge may change dynamically to impact your implementation.

This is a rather daunting and intimidating list. Now do you see why many efforts fail? They treat E-Business implementation like some standard project they have carried out in the past. Our experience shows that chances for implementation success rise if you follow some of the implementation management guidelines and shortcuts that we will suggest. Consider the preceding list as dimensions for E-Business implementation. We will be using it often in this book.

While there is a natural inclination to center your attention on the initial rollout of E-Business, the work doesn't stop there. E-Business requires continuous attention—beyond standard system or process maintenance. You have to have ongoing E-Business work to expand the web site and to add more features, information, and capabilities. Here are some examples of potential sources for changes.

- Management decides to change the entire E-Business strategy.
- Suppliers or customers provide input on the web site and problems.
- Competition heats up.
- Activities that you thought you could leave alone are now causing problems and complaints in E-Business.

ALTERNATIVE E-BUSINESS VISIONS AND STRATEGIES

A company should have a vision of where it wants to go with E-Business. Less than 50% of companies surveyed have even the vision, much less a strategy for E-Business. The vision should encompass the following questions:

- How do you see the company changing due to E-Business? You might see E-Business as a major force for change and restructuring. Or you may see it as just another channel.
- Where do you want to go with E-Business? Do you want to make money, save money, expand, etc.?
- What is to be included and excluded for E-Business? What are the boundaries of E-Business?

Here are some examples:

- We want to move our company into E-Business so that web volume will constitute over $x\%$ of our business.
- We desire to establish a web site that will help draw additional customers into our stores.
- We want to change our business processes so that they are more efficient and lower cost through E-Business.

You first want to answer these questions. Then the next step is to figure out how to get there—your E-Business strategy.

How do companies approach E-Business? You can discern four basic approaches.

- *Overlay.* The company overlays E-Business activities onto its current business.
- *Integration.* The company creates new E-Business activities and then integrates these into its current processes.
- *Total separation.* The company creates a totally separate entity for E-Business.
- *Replacement.* The company replaces some of its current processes with E-Business activities.

Arguments can be made for each of these. Overlay may result in the fastest implementation, but it creates major long-lasting problems. Integration is probably one of the most effective long-term approaches, but it takes more time and effort. Total separation reduces the upheaval in the current organization, but it is very expensive and fails to take advantage of experience with and knowledge of the current processes. Replacement may not be possible in many organizations where the current processes must be maintained. This book discusses implementation through four examples. Each company followed a different strategy.

MANAGEMENT TRENDS

Modern management of large projects and work focuses on the following themes:

- Sharing resources among projects. This leads to a focus on managing multiple rather than single projects.
- Resolving issues and crises before they impact the project. Issues in projects are associated with tasks that have risk.
- Lessons learned about the project associated with the project tasks.
- Collaborative project management, in which team members share more information, participate in project management, and perform common tasks.
- Information sharing among team members, managers, and employees. Generally, information sharing helps to reduce the number of issues and problems as well as supporting collaboration.

The widespread use of computer networks has had a significant impact on the practical aspects of modern project management, along with the Internet, intranets, electronic mail, shared project management software, databases, and groupware. This will continue in the 21st century. Using networking and the Internet, people can share information and make decisions related to a project across thousands of miles. This electronic approach to project management will be a key theme of this book. You will be using all of the bulleted items listed above.

Why do problems arise in managing E-Business projects? One answer is that an E-Business project is different from standard work. A project is more focused. It generally gets more management attention because of this and because the goal is of direct importance to management. Risk is involved, and there is little opportunity to hide failure. Sometimes organizations attempt to carry out projects without calling them projects. Structure is lacking. If you are going to use project management, take it seriously and follow project management methods.

In general, project managers have not made an effort to apply lessons learned during the past decades of project management. Lessons learned are one of the cheapest and easiest things to implement in E-Business. This book will emphasize techniques learned as a result of E-Business experience. Directions are given on how to deal with commonly encountered situations. After all, without relying on lessons learned, people repeat mistakes needlessly.

E-BUSINESS EXPERIENCE

This book offers guidance on how to perform and manage E-Business implementation efficiently, effectively, and successfully. Experience shows that while there are individual differences among E-Business implementation efforts, there is also much in common. We want to exploit those common features here. The expertise of a number of E-Business managers worldwide is collected in this book to enable you to get a quick start and achieve success. This expertise was gained from implementation in the real world, where there are organizational conflict, dysfunctional operations, many issues and problems, cultural resistance to change, and many opportunities for E-Business. To this end, this book makes the following assumptions:

- You cannot change the organization overnight.
- You cannot replace all of your older, legacy systems. Experience shows that implementing new software packages tends to replace one set of problems with another since the underlying problems do not reside in the software.
- There is no magic software tool or method that you can throw at this.
- Most people are too busy in their regular work to spend time on E-Business.
- You cannot replace or change all processes for E-Business in the short time that you have for implementation.
- Change must be taken as a given.

RELATIONSHIP TO LINE ORGANIZATIONS

When you implement E-Business, you are obtaining and allocating resources to achieve a specific set of objectives using a planned and organized approach. The implementation should support the vision and be in line with the E-Business strategy you have selected. To get the work done, implementation teams are formed.

Resources are drawn from the line organizations, support organizations such as IT, and external firms. Here is a simple analogy. Putting a new sprinkler system in the back yard is project work. Turning on the sprinklers and maintaining the lawn and garden is routine work. Routine work is performed by the line and support organizations.

Line organizations have specific rules and procedures. E-Business implementation represents a separate structure outside of the line organization or functional departments. This puts the spotlight on the implementation and creates tension between the line organization and the E-Business organization. E-Business tends to accentuate the tension by placing very strong demands on the line organizations and their employees to participate in the work. Making the pressure worse, E-Business wants to change how the line organization operates. E-Business wants to change the culture. This is a three-pronged threat that many organizations find very threatening.

When line organization techniques are applied to E-Business implementation, the E-Business effort tends to stall or fail. Line organization techniques do not provide sufficient focus and support for E-Business. Attention goes mainly to routine work, and the best people are often kept doing standard work—away from the creative work. There is traditionally no real reward in being a whistle blower or agent of change in a line organization—just the opposite of E-Business.

ESSENTIAL IMPLEMENTATION MANAGEMENT CONCEPTS

Before plunging into developing the implementation plan, let's review some concepts to provide a common basis for understanding. These come from project management and are adapted here.

THE SCHEDULE

A plan, or *schedule,* for E-Business implementation consists of the following:

- *Tasks (detailed activities).* Each has a start date, an end date, and a duration.
- *Summary tasks.* A rollup of several detailed tasks (i.e., an outline format).
- *Milestones.* Deliverable items and end products of the work. A milestone is usually the last item under a summary task.
- *Dependencies between tasks.* Two tasks can depend on each other in a number of ways: head-to-tail (one task cannot start until another is completed), lag (one task must start five days after another task), or lead (one task must start 10 days before another task).

- *Resources.* Personnel, facilities, equipment, and other resources that are assigned to tasks. In E-Business we have to allow for all of these categories.
- *Calendars.* The project, tasks, and resources can all have separate calendars of work. Generally, we will stick to a standard calendar except when we are doing trade-offs in terms of overtime and additional resources.
- *Subprojects.* Subsidiary projects that can be rolled up into a larger project plan. We will create many subprojects for E-Business (see Appendix 1).
- *Responsibility.* Who is responsible for an area of the E-Business implementation?
- *Multiple projects.* There is not only the E-Business implementation going on, but also normal work and other projects.
- *Project management software.* The software for managing and tracking work in projects. Most project management software packages have at their base a relational database. In this book Microsoft Project will be employed as an example. However, the comments apply to just about any similar package. While there are other project management tools, this is the most popular.
- *Project template.* Consisting of high-level tasks, dependencies among these tasks, and general resources. There are no durations or specific resources assigned. A project template replaces the old notion of a work breakdown structure (WBS), which consisted of a detailed list of tasks.

In E-Business the overall implementation is a rollup of subprojects that address specific areas of the implementation. A key milestone is the live operation of E-Business. However, there are others that involve changes in business activities, system implementation, and so on. An E-Business plan is large—too large to be defined in one plan. Therefore, you should divide it up into subprojects based on function and accountability (see Appendix 1). Resources and responsibility are different. The department or person responsible may not be doing the work in the task. Tasks in the plan have dependencies—keep these as simple head-to-tail dependencies.

When we consider multiple projects, consider including normal work as projects. For example, maintenance and enhancement work on a system will be a project. Standard network support can be considered as an ongoing project. You will want to analyze data across these projects. Why? Because you and other managers will have to allocate staff and other resources among the projects and normal work. Technically, doing network support is not a project. However, if you don't make it into one, you have no way to combine the E-Business plans with normal work to allocate people's time and determine where you have resource problems. In order to perform multiple project analysis you have to be able to combine data from a number of project plans using the project management software. This requires compatibility. More specifically, you need the following:

- *A common resource pool.* If each project leader calls the same resources by different names, you cannot combine projects.
- *Common high-level templates.* Templates provide standardization across projects at the highest-level tasks. There are many other benefits to templates that will be explored later.
- *Standard customization of Microsoft Project.* If people use different customized data elements, the schedules are not compatible.

In your E-Business implementation you will want to retain many different sets of dates for your tasks. There is the baseline date, the actual date of the finish of tasks, and the baselines that were set before. Changes of dates occur in E-Business because of changing requirements. In one company we ended up with eight sets of dates. Retaining these dates allows you to do analysis and trace the history of the implementation over time—very useful politically, trust us.

A few words should be said about Microsoft Project. It is based on a database that has literally hundreds of data elements. Project allows you to customize the meanings of these data elements. You extract from the database to create tables. This is the "what." Next, you can query on the specific data through filters. This is the "who." Finally, you can customize the format and dialog boxes. This produces views. This is the "how."

THE TASK

For each task, generate the following:

- Task duration—elapsed number of working days to do the work
- Task constraint—how the task is scheduled (as soon as possible, must start on a specific date, as late as possible, must end on a specific date, etc.)
- Resources assigned to the task
- Task calendar—schedule that determines when work can be done on the task
- Resource and project calendar—working hours and days for each resource and the project overall
- Start and finish dates—when the task is supposed to start and end
- Duration of the task—difference between the finish and start date for a task

CRITICAL PATH AND SLACK TIME

If you trace a series of lines from the start of a project to the end, you produce a path. *The critical path,* or *mathematical critical path,* is the longest path in the project. It is important because if anything is delayed on the critical path, the project is delayed.

Any task can be on the mathematical critical path (even holding a meeting) if the durations, dependencies, and dates place it there.

Slack time refers to the amount of time that a task can slip before it becomes part of the critical path. The time a task can slip before it impacts another task is called free slack. The time that it can slip before the project slips is called total slack.

MANAGEMENT CRITICAL PATH

Some tasks have risks. You want to consider a path through the project that includes risky tasks. Such a path is called the *management critical path.* It is a path in the project that contains tasks with substantial risk. In E-Business you will be spending a lot of time on these risky tasks.

RISK MANAGEMENT AND ISSUES

You have heard people say, "This project has risk," or "This task has risk." They mean that there is a substantial likelihood that the project or task will run into trouble. The overall schedule may slip. The project may fail. To say that a task or project has risk is to indicate that underlying issues are associated with the task or project that must be resolved to prevent trouble.

You can associate tasks with risk with a list of issues. A task can have multiple issues; an issue can apply to several tasks. It is important to note that *managing risk means managing issues behind the risk.* If you don't resolve an issue, the tasks start to slip and the project falls behind. There can be political impact as well. The problem moves from managing problems and issues to managing crisis. Our experience is that dealing with issues is a key to successful E-Business implementation. That is why we address over 150 issues in this book.

Putting the management critical path with the discussion of issues, you can see that if you manage the issues, you can address the risks in the E-Business implementation. That is how we will manage risk. Conversely, you can use the tasks that have risk in the management critical path to point toward the issues that you should address in your E-Business effort. As a result of keeping the management critical path in control, you reduce your overall E-Business risk.

E-BUSINESS IMPLEMENTATION AND MULTIPLE PROJECTS

How do you deal with multiple projects? You can use either a tactical or a strategic approach. On a tactical level, there are three ways to combine a number of projects. If you define a number of different projects and save them in individual computer files, you can then combine them into a single schedule (merge the schedules). Or you can cut and paste from each into a general schedule. A third approach is to have a general high-level schedule reference the detailed schedules so that an individual task in the general plan rolls up to the entire detailed schedule (rollup).

Moving to strategy, the problem is how to manage the resources that are shared among E-Business implementation, other projects, and nonproject work. Where do you place the priority? How do you manage issues that apply to these multiple projects? How do you address dependencies among different projects? How do you get an overall view of the projects? These are all critical questions. If you don't have some minimal level of standardization among the projects, doing multiple project analysis is very difficult.

PROJECT TEMPLATE

When you start an E-Business project, you don't want to begin with a blank piece of paper. Instead, you want to have an E-Business template that can be fleshed out. Appendix 1 contains an E-Business project template.

Begin the construction of the template by identifying general and specific resources. Create as complete a list as possible. General resources are generic roles in the E-Business effort, and specific resources are individual people and other resources. Save these as a resource pool.

You will create high-level, outline tasks for the template. The lowest level of a task in a template is about one to two months. Then the individual project leader and team members fill in the details for the specific project. This brings detailed tasks down to one to two weeks. Follow this approach to ensure a greater degree of standardization.

Building on a template, you can construct a unique project plan for the specific project, define more detailed subtasks, allocate resources to the subtasks, define durations, and set schedules. These would then "roll up" to the summary tasks of the template.

There are many benefits in employing templates for E-Business projects.

- Time is saved in setting up a schedule by building on the template.
- A common base of knowledge is built through the templates.
- Standardization is provided at the higher level for analysis of multiple projects and at the lower level for detail.
- Lessons learned from previous projects are used to improve the templates.
- An issues database can be associated with template tasks relating issues and tasks with risk.
- A lessons learned database can be associated with template tasks so that when you begin to define detailed tasks, you can get some hints on both the tasks and the work itself. Without this association, it is difficult to relate a book of lessons learned to your E-Business work.

GANTT AND PERT CHARTS

A project uses two basic types of charts: GANTT and PERT. The GANTT chart is the most useful for E-Business. Here are suggestions for using a GANTT chart:

- Place tasks in outline form; detailed tasks are the most indented.
- Use symbols to stand for tasks and milestones in the chart.
- Use standard abbreviations for words in the tasks.
- Show three sets of dates—original baseline dates, latest baseline dates, and actual dates—to compare real and ideal.
- Number tasks so that it is easy to talk about them in a meeting without reading the task name. This allows you to add tasks within the same framework.

PERT (Program Evaluation and Review Technique) charts are best at showing dependencies. For E-Business this chart can drive you nuts since it emphasizes dependencies in people's minds. This can slow down the work. The lesson learned here is to stick to GANTT charts.

BASELINE PLAN

The created E-Business schedule is reviewed and approved. The dates will be established as targets. These target dates become the baseline schedule dates or planned dates. The plan is then the *baseline plan.* The start and finish dates of the baseline plan are locked in for later analysis. The actual start and finish dates move.

UPDATING THE SCHEDULE

How do you update the E-Business schedule? When you actually start the project and perform work, you will mark tasks as complete. Then you will be creating another series of dates—actual dates. You thereby create another schedule—the *actual schedule.*

ACTUAL VS. PLANNED ANALYSIS

If you compare the actual and planned dates, you obtain the *actual vs. planned analysis.* You could use yet another set of dates to model "What would happen if . . .?" This "What if . . .?" analysis is one of the benefits of project management software systems. You could get yet another set of dates if you add the dates that you promised the E-Business implementation.

THE E-BUSINESS IMPLEMENTATION PLAN

To be successful, you need more than a GANTT chart. Your E-Business project plan must include the following:

- E-Business project objectives—clearly and unambiguously state the purpose of the implementation
- E-Business implementation strategies—identify your approach for directing resources and handling issues
- A detailed E-Business project plan—the set of tasks, resource assignment, dependencies, and schedules
- Project resources—all personnel, facilities, equipment, and any other resources
- Project methods—techniques to be used in creating, maintaining, and managing the implementation
- Project tools—software or other products that support the methods
- A definition of what work will constitute the implementation
- Policies and procedures for developing, updating, and reviewing the work
- An approach for defining and resolving issues and opportunities
- Standard budgeting and cost methods
- Methods and tools to support the projects and project management
- A list of issues associated with the project and which tasks correspond to these issues (tasks that have risk)

SUCCESS AND FAILURE IN E-BUSINESS IMPLEMENTATION

CHARACTERISTICS OF THE SUCCESSFUL E-BUSINESS EFFORT

Successful E-Business projects have these factors in common:

- The E-Business effort has a regular flow of interim, measurable milestones. This allows management to ensure that the implementation overall is on schedule. People on the team can be given a pat on the back as they make progress. Each E-Business subproject should have a regular flow of milestones. Due to time pressure, this flow is usually 2 weeks.
- The implementation team can tolerate change and issues. The team is adaptive to internal and external change. In such projects the staff has a positive attitude toward change. If there is one thing to count on in an E-Business effort, it is change.
- Management avoids micromanaging and blanket approval. Management monitors progress and evaluates the milestones or end products of the project. Management should participate in resolving issues.

- Beyond the strategy, the E-Business purpose and scope are clearly defined at the start. Clarity of definition varies with the type of project. The scope can change during the work, but there must be a consistency between the purpose and scope at any given time. Lack of clarity leads to confusion. Confusion means you are more likely to miss your deadlines.
- The team works together in a collaborative way. Information is shared; there is no hiding of information. The team members participate in some management tasks, such as defining, estimating, and updating their own tasks.

UNSUCCESSFUL E-BUSINESS PROJECTS

Some common reasons for E-Business failure include the following:

- The original purpose changed, but the E-Business deadline didn't. The resulting work goes unused. An example is a continuing project for a weapons systems or nuclear power plant for which the original need disappeared.
- The organization opted for a magic bullet. In a number of cases, companies chose to implement an ERP—setting back the E-Business implementation by months.
- The work was mismanaged. Milestone dates were missed; morale dropped; people still produced PERT and GANTT charts. Issues and resources were not properly managed. Mismanagement can occur in any area and can affect the entire project.
- The E-Business scope changed too often. People get confused by changing requirements and sense chaos. Progress grinds to a halt.
- The E-Business goals were not realistic. Many E-Business efforts do not take into consideration the conditions of the organization, technology, and infrastructure. Another area sometimes ignored is the corporate culture.
- The elapsed time for the E-Business effort was too long. There was a lack of intermediate milestones. The project churned up resources and never delivered. This occurred in a large insurance project that cost more than $6 million over a three-year period.
- Management failed to address E-Business related issues in a timely manner. Another problem is that management attempts to micromanage the E-Business implementation.

THE ORGANIZATION OF THIS BOOK

This book is organized to reflect the new project management environment. Part I addresses the development of the E-Business plan; Part II deals with managing the implementation work; and Part III focuses on dealing with E-Business–related issues. The chapters address the key managerial, technological, and organizational areas of E-Business management. Each chapter also addresses issue management. (Chapter 15 covers this topic in detail.)

Each chapter is organized in the same basic manner. The introduction and milestones for the subject of the chapter are followed by the section "Methods and Techniques" for the specific topic. This material is organized around actions you can take. You will need this organized approach in E-Business to reduce the amount of time spent in doing management. Four E-Business examples are discussed in each chapter. Later in the chapter, lessons learned from E-Business work are given. These are specific ideas and recommendations for reducing risk and ensuring that your project has a competitive advantage over other projects vying for funding and management attention. Each chapter presents specific things to do next. The appendix provides you with a project template for E-Business in terms of high-level tasks.

If you are using this book in a project, you might want to select the chapter that fits where you are in the project. You might also start with the index, which is organized by topic or issue. For a class or seminar in E-Business, you can proceed through the book sequentially. The flow of the chapters follows that of an E-Business implementation. By taking a case or a sample project, you can apply the lessons learned in the chapters to a realistic situation. This has been done with a combination of group and individual projects. You can also gather stories of success and failure from the web.

E-BUSINESS EXAMPLES

We will draw upon four examples of companies that were successful in E-Business. While the names of these firms are hypothetical, they are based on combinations of real-world firms. In implementation each faced a series of major decision points and crises. All were successful in dealing with them.

- *Ricker Catalogs* was a standard producer and distributor of paper catalogs. They had a loyal customer base. In their catalogs, they sold their own products as well as those of other suppliers. At the start of E-Business implementation, there was no internal experience. Ricker was drawn to E-Business for both negative and positive reasons. Management saw E-Business as a chance to reach new customers and gain new suppliers. They also were aware that the catalog business as they knew it could well shrink due to E-Business. On the other hand, by embracing E-Business, they could become one of the darlings of the e-stock market hype. They chose the wrong strategy first and then had to change. You may view this company as dysfunctional, but it is real life and not untypical of many others. Ricker's strategy for E-Business was overlay.

- *Marathon Manufacturing* is a major manufacturer of machines and components for metal fabricating products. Marathon had concentrated on reaching customer firms that had at least 50 employees. Management decided to enter E-Business to reach the hundreds of thousands of smaller firms. They decided to take the time and do the web site right while changing their internal processes. Their strategy toward E-Business was integration.
- *Abacus Energy* is a major international oil company. At first, its management did not see the opportunity or need for E-Business. Their problem was a lack of vision as to the potential of E-Business. They were focusing on their customers to whom they sold gasoline, other petroleum products, and food products. Finally, they decided to consider their suppliers. The E-Business implementation here consists of the replacement of the processes for purchasing and contracting by E-Business activities. Although this implementation has a narrow scope, it will be useful to us as an example.
- *Crawford Bank* is a major domestic bank that is considering using the Internet and Web to offer installment loans. Its management hoped to build new business and reach new customers through E-Business. Using these customers, they hope to build an entirely new company. They decided to start small and then grow. Their approach was to establish a separate entity for E-Business.

E-BUSINESS LESSONS LEARNED

Lessons learned (key strategies) appear in each chapter. Each is stated in a succinct manner and then discussed in more detail. Each is intended to reduce project risk, deal with issues, and ensure that you have a competitive project.

- **Clearly delineate the ground rules regarding when work becomes a formal E-Business effort.**
  You don't want to start an E-Business effort informally. Too much is at stake. If you begin work and get partway through, you have set a pattern. If you then decide to label the work a project, you would apply project management, methods, and tools to the work—retroactively. Progress will slow while this is being established. it will also mean that the work will be redirected into a more formal approach. These are two reasons for determining that a project is a project early in development. If you wait, your risk increases, along with the likelihood of failure.
- **As a project leader, maintain a low profile of the E-Business work.**
  There is already enough attention given to E-Business. Don't make it worse. Visibility can breed interference and envy at the resources you are consuming.

- **Focus on both the details of the E-Business implementation and the wider view.**
  Management of the E-Business effort involves concentrating on the detail of the work as well as having a wider perspective on what is going on and why. A good manager should be capable of doing both and not focusing too much effort on one of the two extremes.
- **Be aware of the impact E-Business has on the organization and direct the change and impact, rather than having it direct you.**
  E-Business efforts create their own dynamics. The end product of an implementation can transform an organization. However, success or failure can change the balance of power between managers of line organizations and upper management. A failing manager is less likely to do well when he or she returns to the line organization.
- **Insist that the E-Business project involve people from multiple departments.**
  Don't leave out departments, even those that play supporting roles. These departments may have a major role in E-Business transactions.
- **Align the purpose and scope of the E-Business plan.**
  When you present the plan for an E-Business project, you raise people's expectations. They form a mental image of what E-Business will do. As time passes, this may change and expectations may rise as progress is reported. Reinforce the original purpose and scope of the effort at each progress or issue meeting.
- **Inject humor and a sense of being a team through the sharing of experiences.**
  Humor is important given the time pressure. Remember or reminisce about project experiences to capture the humor and joy in a project. E-Business efforts are dynamic and charged with deadlines and issues, but they are also fun. Thinking about past project experiences can also help to lighten the stress in your current work.
- **Keep the E-Business project team as small as possible, regardless of organization size.**
  Many E-Business failures can be traced to large project teams. Large teams involve too much coordination and communications. These activities take time away from solving issues.
- **Gather the team together and share lessons learned during the E-Business implementation.**
  If you wait until the end people will have disappeared. Memories will have faded. People won't want to talk about the implementation. They are tired of it.
- **Make sure that E-Business success supports the organization.**
  You want the organization to feel that it has a stake in the E-Business project and that they have "skin in the game." Project success does not equate to

organization success. Even if the E-Business effort is successful, the end product and the work itself can tear the organization apart.

- **Know who gains and who loses from the success of the E-Business implementation.**
  There will be middle managers and some departments that lose power when E-Business is implemented. In the work you can identify potential winners and losers. If the project succeeds, the backer of E-Business gains. If it fails, the reverse may occur. The goal is to have the implementation appeal to the self-interest of many managers. This will increase their stake in the support of the work.
- **Enforce accountability.**
  Lack of accountability for poor E-Business leadership can increase failure rates. Sometimes a poor manager is transferred to another project. No one acknowledges that management problems existed. The manager carries the problems to the new position. If you enforce accountability, at least others will have some sense that failure or problems occurred.

WHAT TO DO NEXT

Here is a set of tangible actions you can take to implement the materials of the chapter. These apply to projects in general. However, if you have an E-Business effort going on, you can obviously include these.

1. Here are some basic questions to answer that relate to the culture of projects and project management.
   - Does the project you are working on have a clear objective and scope? Have these changed since the project was started?
   - Is there an established process in your organization for setting up and running projects?
   - For a project that was less than successful, was an effort made to develop lessons learned and apply these to other projects?
   - Are your projects managed in a traditional way—project administration and management handled by the project manager—or are they based on collaborative project management where duties and information are shared with the team?
2. Projects and project management have been discussed. A first suggestion is that you assess the projects around you by reviewing the following statements. Answer each on a scale of 1 to 5, in which 1 means that you strongly disagree with the statement, 2 means that you disagree with the statement, 3 means that the statement is sometimes true, 4 means that you agree with the statement, and 5 means that you strongly agree with the statement.

- Our company allows project leaders to use their own methods and tools in doing their projects.
- Our projects take many good resources from the line organizations.
- We do not have many tools or defined methods in general.
- There is no organized training support for the tools and methods that we have.
- We do not collect lessons learned from our past projects.
- We do not have standardized project templates for projects. Each project starts from scratch.

Use your responses to assess the current problems with project management in your organization.

3. Assuming that your organization has multiple simultaneous projects, how does the organization cope with multiple project management? More specifically:
   - Is there an overall project summary?
   - How are resources shared and managed among projects?
   - How are issues that cross multiple projects identified and resolved?
   - How is the mixture of project and nonproject work managed?

Chapter 2

Develop Your E-Business Implementation Plan

INTRODUCTION

You are now ready to begin developing the E-Business implementation plan. In the old methods, you would probably have been told to start making lists of resources and tasks. Such an approach forces you into detail and you lose sight of the overall E-Business picture. This doesn't work for E-Business for a number of reasons.

- You have to think about the structure of the overall implementation. Don't you want to break up the implementation into manageable chunks?
- You have the ingredients of an E-Business implementation template in the Appendix. Don't you want save time by using this?
- You will be spending a great deal of your time as a manager or team member addressing issues. Wouldn't it be nice to get these out on the table sooner rather than later?

You will first develop the big picture of E-Business implementation—the implementation concept. Then you will relate it to both the E-Business vision and the E-Business strategy. An implementation concept includes the following:

- *Business and technical objectives of the E-Business implementation.* You need both because you want these understandable and interrelated for all.
- *Scope of the implementation—what is in and what is out.* Emphasis here is on what is out.
- *Organizations that will be involved and how they will be involved (the roles and responsibilities).* Emphasis here is on how and the extent of involvement.

- *Technology direction for E-Business.* Here you identify what new systems and technologies you will procure and what of the current stuff you will keep and interface with.
- *Issues that are likely to be faced in E-Business implementation.* Divide these up into categories as we have done in chapter 16. You should have over 50. Use the list in chapter 1 as a guide.
- *Business benefits and costs of the E-Business effort.* The emphasis here is on tangible benefits. Forget the fuzzy benefits unless they can be turned into tangible benefits.
- *General schedule for the implementation.* Include dates for major milestones.
- *Template for the E-Business implementation.*

Why does all of this work? Why not just get down to the detailed tasks? Because you want to gain consensus and support for the E-Business effort. It is easier to do this at the start than after the implementation has been started. Some additional benefits of the implementation concept are:

- You can perform trade-offs between the scope, purpose, and alternative E-Business strategies.
- You will be able to align the elements of the implementation concept with each other so that they are consistent. This is important because if they are not consistent, experience shows that you will have a higher likelihood of failure.
- You will get agreement from business line managers about the roles of their departments and gain commitment to participate.
- A better understanding of E-Business is gained by everyone.
- You raise the awareness of issues that the E-Business effort will face.
- A common sense of E-Business effort is gained that is more tangible than a fuzzy business vision since it focuses on implementation. This also handles the problem wherein everyone has a different idea of what e-commerce is.

The elements of the implementation concept must align with the E-Business strategy. After the implementation concept has been approved, you will then develop the detailed tasks and milestones and other elements of the plan. It will be easier to obtain review and approval for these because of the early work with the concept.

After you have the implementation concept nailed down, you can develop the E-Business plan, make management presentations, and gain approval and funding. You will also identify the initial players on the implementation team.

MILESTONES

The end products of this chapter are the following:

- The implementation concept for E-Business.
- The project plan and schedule.
- The anticipated benefits from E-Business implementation.

- Consensus by departments to participate in the E-Business implementation.
- A wider understanding of the E-Business effort overall.
- The E-Business budget and costs.
- The implementation team is identified and ready to go.
- The methods and tools to be employed in the E-Business effort.

Overall, work on the E-Business implementation can begin. Don't even think about starting before these milestones are met. Starting work too early can make people angry and stir resentment.

METHODS AND TECHNIQUES

ACTION 1: DETERMINE THE IMPLEMENTATION CONCEPT

Creation of Alternative Implementation Concepts

You begin with the E-Business strategy. In the previous chapter, four alternative strategies were identified. For each strategy, the potential effects on your purpose and scope can be determined.

- *Overlay strategy.* The company overlays E-Business on top of their current business activities. The purpose of the E-Business effort is to implement E-Business so as to have minimal negative impact on current processes and the revenues generated. The scope of the implementation project is quite narrow since the current processes tend to limit what can be done for E-Business.
- *Integration strategy.* The company creates new E-Business activities and then integrates these into their current ones. The purpose of the E-Business effort is to implement new and modified business activities for both E-Business and traditional business. The scope of the implementation is broad in that it covers both new E-Business as well as traditional architecture, organization, and processes.
- *Total separation strategy.* The company creates a totally separate business for E-Business. The purpose is to implement E-Business activities that are as complete as possible. The scope here is very narrow and limited to the few key activities that you need to get up and running.
- *Replacement strategy.* The company replaces some of their current processes with E-Business activities. The purpose of the implementation is to replace and eliminate some of the current business processes. The scope is also narrowed to these processes.

Of the four strategies, the last (replacement strategy) is probably the narrowest, followed by the total separation strategy. The integration strategy has the widest purpose and scope since you must touch many parts of the current business and

you are aiming for improvement and not replacement. Figure 2-1 gives a table
with comments for each area of the implementation concept.

Each of the other elements of the implementation concept are impacted by the
E-Business strategy that you select. Some general comments are:

- Roles and responsibilities of organizations. Generally, the number of organizations in the company and the extent of their involvement are related to
  the range of the purpose and scope. However, even in the case of total sep-

Concept Element	Overlay	Integration	Separation	Replacement
Purpose	Narrow based on some processes	Widespread since you must pick up supporting processes	Reduced since you can be more selective as to which processes to do	Selection of several related processes
Scope	Limited	Moderate since you must include more processes	Have to set up entire organization and processes	Narrow
Roles and responsibilities	Some business debts will be heavily involved	Widespread involvement will be needed	Key business managers will likely be involved	Some business depts will be heavily involved
Technology direction	Minimal new technology	Potential new technology	New technology	Limited new technology
Issues	Issues will arise as you go	More issues are predictable at the start	Many issues will surface as you implement	Narrower range of issues
Schedule	Schedule may slip as new issues arise	Integration requires major process changes—more time	May take longer than you think with major setup	Controllable
Benefits/costs	Benefits may be less than you think; costs may be more	Major benefits and substantial costs	Cost of infrastructure and organization often underestimated	Significant, but narrow benefits and reasonable costs

Figure 2-1:   Project Concept Elements versus E-Business Strategies

aration, you will want to involve experienced employees and managers to draw upon their knowledge.

- *Issues to be faced in the E-Business effort.* Some issues tend to be general and apply to all four strategies. Many of these are discussed in Chapter 16. Others are more specific. Some of the most common that you are likely to encounter are given in Figure 2-2.
- *Benefits and costs of the E-Business implementation.* Figure 2-3 gives a table of benefit areas versus each of the strategies. The table entries are comments on the relevance of the benefits to the specific E-Business strategies.
- *General schedule for E-Business implementation.* The schedule is not only governed by the strategy chosen, but also by overall deadline imposed by management for E-Business operation.

The last element of the implementation concept is the template. In Appendix 1, a modular approach to templates has been taken so that you can select which sub-project templates are most appropriate for your E-Business strategy.

Assessment and Selection of the Implementation Concept

How do you evaluate specific objectives and scope? Here are some tests you can use:

- Do the objectives and scope fit with the organization? Are the purpose and scope aligned with each other in terms of both business and technical types?

Sample Issues	Overlay	Integration	Separation	Replacement
Education of business mgrs. In E-Business	High impact	High impact	Limited impact	Some impact
Existing IT legacy systems	Major impact	Major impact	Limited impact	Some impact
Cultural change to E-Business	Some impact	High impact	Limited impact	Some impact
Channel conflicts	Some impact	High impact	Some impact	Positive impact
Trained IT staff	High impact	High impact	Some impact	Moderate impact
Priorities of staff	High impact	Moderate to high impact	Minimal impact	Moderate impact

Figure 2-2: Sample Issues versus E-Business Strategies

Benefits and Costs	Overlay	Integration	Separation	Replacement
Modified business model	New and old models exist side by side	New model	New and old model exist side by side	New model
Competitive position	Risky, but can improve position	Major benefit	Possible, but cannot leverage off of current business	Not really impacted since this tends to be reflected in costs
Customer satisfaction	Uncertain as customers cope with two channels	Major benefit	Possible	More with suppliers
Employee productivity	Some benefit	Major benefit	Not a factor	Major benefit
Increased profit margins	Major benefit	Major benefit	Major benefit	Major benefit through cost savings
Increased market share	Major target	Major target	New markets	Not really a target
Increased employee communications	Some benefit	Major benefit	Not a factor	Not a major factor
Knowledge of markets	Major benefit	Major benefit	How to use this with regular business is a puzzle	Some benefit

Figure 2.3: Benefits and Costs versus E-Business Strategies

- Are the objectives too broad or too focused?
- Are potential resources available for the objectives and scope you have defined? Have you already defined an E-Business effort that is not feasible?
- Where are the areas of risk—both technical and managerial? This ties in with the issues.
- Are the benefits and costs reasonable, given the purpose and scope? In information technology, if the purpose is to install a system and the benefits are to increase productivity and make E-Business operational, you are not likely to achieve benefits because the purpose is too narrow. It does not include the process change the system has installed. Is it any wonder that many IT efforts are completed successfully without tangible benefits? The business activities were not changed.

You will be selecting and using templates as discussed earlier. However, you have several possible ways to create subprojects within the overall E-Business implementation. Here are some approaches. Each of these has pluses and minuses. Given the wide scope of many E-Business efforts you will probably end up using several of these. For example, you may divide the overall project by time and then by function. Within function you may divide by project leader or organization.

- *By general organization.* This ensures greater accountability for each subproject but may make coordination between the subprojects a nightmare. This is typical when installing large financial software systems.
- *By project leader.* This approach starts with the people and divides up the work according to their skills and experience. This is a good approach with the right people. However, if you have gaps with no leader or if a leader moves on, you could be in trouble.
- *By function.* Here you would partition the implementation into parts that apply to specific functional activities. An example is the infrastructure and construction subproject, which has electrical, plumbing, and carpentry subprojects.
- *By geography.* This is the historic approach to managing large projects where authority was delegated to specific regions. This is probably not a good choice since E-Business is not location-dependent within a country. Between countries it makes more sense to reflect the different cultures of the countries.
- *By time.* This is also a traditional approach. You divide a project into phases. Each phase follows another. Each phase is a subproject of the overall project. The problem here is that it forces the implementation to be sequential. It is difficult to establish a parallel effort if only one or two phases are active at one time.
- *By interface.* Here you begin by assuming that risk lies in interfaces between parts of the implementation. Therefore, you organize the implementation to concentrate on interfaces at the start.
- *By line organization.* A typical setup for failure is to divide E-Business implementation by line organization. The line organizations will not get along. The issues and problems will not be resolved at the interfaces between organizations. The implementation will likely fail even if the parts in each organization succeed, which is doubly frustrating. Dividing the implementation this way will tend to reinforce the barriers among departments.

Some additional questions to ask are:

- How will you gather data across the subprojects to get a sense of what is going on overall?
- How will you identify issues that cross multiple subprojects and get them resolved?
- Is the risk spread among the various subprojects, or does it fall into one subproject?

- Are some subprojects too small to be viable and likely to fall within another subproject?
- Have you ensured accountability? Or, have you set up a situation in which project leaders from different subprojects may blame each other?
- Can resources be moved and shared between subprojects?

Now you are prepared to move up to a more general evaluation of alternative implementation concepts. Note that you will likely have multiple concepts for each strategy that you are considering. You should consider all of the strategies now because it is cheap. Management needs to know the problems with strategies that were rejected. You don't want to reject a strategy out of hand.

To undertake the evaluation, identify the evaluation criteria. Here are some that the four example firms used.

- Cost of E-Business implementation
- Tangible benefits of E-Business implementation
- General impact and risk to the business
- Attraction to suppliers and customers
- Overall schedule of implementation
- Potential and likely resource conflicts
- Long-term benefit contribution to get your firm into E-Business for the long haul
- Ease of E-Business expansion later

You can prepare a table of these elements as rows and the alternative concepts as columns. You can also graphically portray these using a spider or radar chart.

After doing this analysis, you can use the table and chart to perform trade-offs with management. What is the normal result that you can expect? The basic result is to bring management expectations down to earth. Next, you lock into an integrated set of elements for the concept so that you can proceed with the rest of the plan.

ACTION 2: DEVELOP A STRATEGY FOR YOUR E-BUSINESS IMPLEMENTATION

A strategy will be your approach for attaining the objectives within the scope and the environment. The strategy provides focus for the "how" of the project, just as the implementation concept provides the focus for management. A strategy must address all parts of the scope. Thus, if the scope includes political factors, you must have a political strategy—even if you don't advertise it. A political strategy is an approach for dealing with potential political problems, for advertising and marketing the project, and for getting support. You may have a stated strategy and several unstated strategies. For example, in a reengineering project the stated strategy might be to improve process and design and implement a new computer system at the same time. The unstated strategies might be to rightsize and restructure the organization while you are implementing E-Business.

What should your strategy address? Here are some questions to answer.

- How will you organize the effort?
- How will you select the leaders and team members?
- What will be the role of the team in the implementation management?
- How will you manage risk and address issues?
- How will work changes and change control be handled?

If you choose to ignore these, then you will have problems later because you will have to respond to each item as it arises. You will not have established a pattern to address them.In order to develop a strategy, define your approach for each of the above items. Consider political, organizational, and technological factors to refine the strategy. Prepare another table in which the questions are rows and the factors are columns. The entries are how you will address the types of factor for the questions.

ACTION 3: IDENTIFY YOUR MAJOR MILESTONES AND INITIAL SCHEDULE

A milestone in the plan is a task that has no length or duration. It must be capable of being evaluated or tested to see if it has been achieved. You can see a list of milestones in the templates given in Appendix 1—this will get you started. Draw up at least 10 to 20 milestones for each subproject.

You must be centrally focused on the relationship between milestones of the E-Business subprojects. Logically relate the milestones between the subprojects in terms of dependencies. If you have a dangling milestone that you know should relate to another subproject, you are probably missing a milestone. You will likely need to add some milestones.

Next, take a piece of paper and lay it out sideways (landscape). The long side of the paper is the timeline and the short side is for the subprojects. Draw a horizontal line for each subproject. Put the milestones on each line for the corresponding subproject. Draw lines between the milestones to show dependencies. You can also use graphics software to create this.

Make several copies of this chart. On one, start backward from the target date for completing the overall work. This will tell you when things will have to start so as not to delay the end date. On another chart, start at the beginning and estimate as you go. On a third, take a colored marking pen and highlight the milestones for which you perceive risk in their underlying tasks. Which milestones are these? They are the ones in which you have the least experience, the ones in which you really don't know how the work will be done, or the ones in which problems have occurred in the past with similar projects. Define the schedule based on these risky tasks.

An alternate approach is to move from the start of the implementation to the end by estimating earlier tasks first. However, this approach tends to lead to unacceptable dates. You could get too focused on near-term milestones and lose sight of the big picture.

Put all the charts side by side and create a fourth chart that reconciles these three. You can use the computer to do this. However, using manual methods gives you greater flexibility.

ACTION 4: DEFINE THE INITIAL BUDGET, USING THE MILESTONES

Think about what resources will be necessary to achieve each milestone. List four or five key resources for each milestone. Now develop an initial budget by milestone for each subproject. Always develop your initial budget bottom up. If you do it top down, you will miss part of the plan and resources. After you have completed this, you can estimate overhead and other resources as a group. Include facilities, supplies, and equipment as well as personnel.

For your E-Business implementation, begin with the areas that are easiest to estimate first. This might be hardware, network, and facilities work. Then you move onto the estimation of software, vendor, and personnel-related costs.

Here are some common mistakes that people make in budgeting and planning.

- Failure to adequately consider downtime waiting or rework.
- Failure to allow for some change of scope in the project.
- Failure to consider potential additional tasks and work, resulting in underestimation.

In doing your budgeting, plan on holding onto resources only as long as needed. In E-Business work you seek to release resources as soon as possible to reduce costs. Remember that the critical people you need are also needed by other projects and nonproject work.

For personnel costs, use a high average cost for an employee. Add the overhead cost in as well. For facilities and equipment include the setup time and teardown time, if applicable. If you are involved in new technology or methods, include training costs along with potential travel costs. Many E-Business efforts have two budgets. Since the implementation plan cannot detail all of the costs, use a spreadsheet to develop the realistic budget. This second budget will reflect the work performed by the resources. When you perform budget analysis, you often will extract this second budget from the project management software and then incorporate it into the spreadsheet.

ACTION 5: IDENTIFY WHICH GROUPS AND ORGANIZATIONS WILL BE INVOLVED IN THE IMPLEMENTATION

Get out an organization chart and a piece of paper. Draw two vertical lines about 1/3 and 2/3 of the way across the page. Write down the organizations on the left and their roles in the implementation in the middle. Write down how important their involvement will be in the project in the right column using words that describe how they are important. Define a role for almost every organization—even if you indicate no role. Any that you omit can come back to haunt you. Include outsiders as well.

ACTION 6: DETERMINE THE METHODS AND TOOLS TO BE EMPLOYED IN THE E-BUSINESS IMPLEMENTATION

In many projects people begin the work and then select tools and methods as they go. The homeowner, doing repairs around the house on the weekend, is an example of a person who starts a project and ends up running to the hardware or lumber store many times. This can spell disaster in E-Business implementation with so many players.

Get two sets of methods and tools identified early, one for the actual implementation work and the other for the management of the implementation. Doing this identification at the start will help you identify where you have holes or gaps of knowledge.

ACTION 7: IDENTIFY AREAS OF RISK AND ASSOCIATE THEM WITH MILESTONES AND TASKS

Recall that risk management in E-Business implementation involves managing issues associated with implementation tasks. Risk and therefore issues can arise from a number of causes. You may not know exactly what is needed to produce the milestone. Perhaps, the organization has never implemented E-Business. You may have to rely on unknown internal staff or external contractors to do the work. The milestone may be more complex than first perceived. Another factor is lack of definition of the tasks. Sometimes you just don't know what an acceptable milestone is. New technology and lack of direct control are other sources of issues.

Label the tasks and milestones that have substantial risk. Now attempt to define some additional, more detailed milestones within each of these. If you can divide a major milestone into smaller milestones, you might be able to reduce the risk, or at least isolate the risk to smaller milestones. Now remember that a task has risk if there are one or more issues behind the task. Issues associate with risk. You have now identified issues from risky tasks.

From the work so far, you can start with the list of issues that may impact the implementation as defined in the implementation concept. Use the list of issues at the end of the book in chapter 16 as a start. With the list in place, scan the tasks in the plan. Identify any tasks to which an issue pertains. Label the task with the issue. You now know these tasks have risk. Go through the list of tasks. You will find some that have risk. For each task that has risk, go to the list of issues and find the associated issue. There are two situations you will face in addition to matches. First, there will be issues that have no tasks. However, these issues are valid. Therefore, tasks are missing. There may be tasks that are risky but have no associated issues. This means that you have missing issues.

This action is valuable in validating the tasks so that you can feel that your plan is complete. It also helps you to identify tasks that have risk and the source of the risk.

ACTION 8: REFINE THE E-BUSINESS SCHEDULE AND BUDGET

Refine the estimates of budget and schedule. If they don't change, you are either a good estimator, or you have missed something. Perhaps, you might have someone outside who has implemented E-Business several times check to see if these numbers are reasonable.

ACTION 9: IDENTIFY THE IMPLEMENTATION LEADERS

Think about candidates for managers for the implementation and for the subprojects. Identify several alternatives, if possible. Think of availability and the potential of not having them throughout the effort. You will need a backup plan for leaders as well. This subject will be discussed in detail in the next chapter.

ACTION 10: IDENTIFY AND ESTABLISH THE IMPLEMENTATION TEAM

This is addressed in detail in Chapter 4. In this initial stage of the work, identify a few key people that you need for the core of the team. Decide how many team members you will need, then determine who you will choose to be the other team members by evaluating skills and knowledge. You can use the results of your budgeting and scheduling effort to help you here. Don't rush out and get team members just to fill up slots—the later you select team members the more knowledge you have of the project and the specific staffing needs. Guiding phrases here are "just in time" and "as late as possible".

ACTION 11: DEVELOP THE DETAILED IMPLEMENTATION PLAN

For each subproject identify the tasks that will have to be performed over the next three months. These will be broken down in detail and estimated by the team members and the team leaders. The tasks that are further out will be estimated at the template level.

The second action is to assign template tasks to team members for estimation and detailed definition. To build confidence start with the near-term tasks. Have each member come back to the team leaders with a list of detailed tasks under each of their template items. A detailed task is typically one to two weeks in length. You as the team leader can now probe as to how the work would be done. Determine if there are any missing issues.

After the tasks are nailed down, have the team members proceed to dependencies and resource requirements for tasks. These should be reviewed with the team leader. The following action is to estimate dates and durations of the tasks. During the review here, the reasoning behind the estimation of dates can be reviewed.

For the tasks that go beyond three months, have the team members estimate at the template level. For some tasks they will be unable to define estimates. What do you do? Divide up such tasks into smaller parts and estimate these. Eventually, you will be able to estimate all parts or you will have one or more parts that you cannot estimate. Why can't you estimate? Aha! You now have identified more issues—reasons behind the estimation problem. That is good. Identify the issues and then estimate as best you can.

You have developed an overall implementation plan that may have dates further out than your earlier high-level plan. What can you do to move the dates in? Here are some suggestions.

- Look at the tasks that have no risk or issues and see if they can be done in parallel to a greater extent.
- See if you can reduce the elapsed time of the nonrisky tasks.
- Now move to tasks with issues and risk. Examine the underlying issues and determine if they can be resolved. Then determine the impact on the schedule.

There are a number of benefits to this approach. First, you are involving the team members in the planning for the E-Business effort. They will be more committed. Second, you are now more aware of issues and how the work will be done. Third, you are more assured that the plan is complete and that there are no hidden risks.

Setting Up Tasks in Project Management Software

Here are some suggestions for setting up tasks so that they will be easy to use and work with.

- Keep the task description simple—less than 30 characters. This will allow you to print the GANTT chart.
- If the task name is compound or complex, split the task.
- Start each task with an action verb for consistency.

- Use a field in the software database for responsibility for the task. This is different from resources since the person responsible may direct resources in the performance of the work.
- Each detailed task should be from five to ten days long (shorter tasks mean too much detail; longer tasks mean that the task is too general and cannot easily be monitored).
- Use standard abbreviations wherever possible (e.g., Dev for Develop).
- Number all tasks in an outline form (e.g., task 1100 is the first task under task 1000).
- Establish categories of resources (personnel, equipment, facilities, etc.).
- Keep resource names to less than 10 characters.
- Use a field in the software to indicate which tasks have substantial risk (e.g., a flag field that is either yes or no in value).
- Use task outlining and indenting.
- Group the tasks with appropriate milestones.
- Label milestones as such (e.g., "M: Foundation completed" and "M:" indicates a milestone).
- Use a field to indicate the number identifiers of the issues that pertain to a specific task.
- Use a field to indicate the number identifiers of the lessons learned that pertain to a specific task.
- Use a field to indicate the date that the task was created.
- Use a field to indicate if the task is part of the template (another flag field).
- Use a field to indicate why the task was created (rework, bad estimate, etc.).

Let's amplify some of these suggestions. The reason for short names and abbreviations is to have more readable GANTT charts and reports. The numbering of tasks makes it easier to follow later when tasks are added or changed. Resource categories are useful in filtering and reporting by type or category. Most software has the capability of customized fields in the database. The flag to label tasks as risky allows you to extract only these tasks for evaluation and review. You can also define all paths that pass through these tasks. Define any of these paths to be a management-critical path. The reason for not having names as assigned tasks is to provide flexibility if the assignment changes for individuals, but the same person is performing the task. The reason for the use of a separate field for accountability is to distinguish between who is accountable and what resources are required.

IMPLEMENTATION DOCUMENTATION

Obviously, documentation depends on the size and complexity of the E-Business effort. Here is a list of items recommended for most E-Business efforts.

- Implementation concept
- Implementation project plan
- Specification of the current architecture
- Specification of the new technology architecture
- Documentation of current business activities
- Definition of the new E-Business activities
- Requirements for the new activities
- Benefits from the new business activities and systems
- Design of the E-Business software
- Operating procedures for all business activities (including policies, procedures, and systems procedures)
- Procedures for suppliers or customers
- IT procedures for the network, hardware, system software, and application software
- Training materials for the new processes for internal staff
- Testing scripts and results
- Integration approach and results
- Program maintenance documentation
- Documentation of any changes in requirements along with reasons and impact on schedule
- Post implementation evaluation and assessment

EVALUATE YOUR E-BUSINESS PLAN

After you have developed the working plan or the initial version of the plan, evaluate it yourself. Be your own worst critic. Put the plan aside for several days and work on other activities. When you reopen the plan, ask the following questions:

- Are the objectives and scope consistent?
- Is the scope reflected in the range of tasks?
- Is the E-Business strategy borne out in the tasks?
- Have you identified the areas of risk?
- Have you defined the key resources?
- Have you associated tasks that carry risk with the list of issues?
- If you were assigned the job of attacking the plan, what would you see as the major weaknesses?

E-BUSINESS EXAMPLES

RICKER CATALOGS

Ricker Catalogs was in a big hurry to implement a competitive web site. They considered all of the alternative strategies and thought that the overlay strategy would be the fastest. However, in their scope, purpose, and schedule they did not include changing the current processes at all. This later blew up in their faces.

The goals of E-Business for Ricker were:

- Protect the customer base from competitors and expand the market base;
- Offer new products and items that were not in Ricker catalogs.

The scope included sales and accounting processes. It was felt that the existing customer service, fulfillment, and other processes could remain unchanged. This turned out to be false.

MARATHON MANUFACTURING

Marathon had all of the time they needed. They thoroughly evaluated alternatives and decided on the integration approach. The purposes of E-Business for Marathon were:

- Attract smaller machine shops as customers through the web.
- Integrate marketing for all market segments.
- Provide state-of-the-art software tools for customers.
- Utilize information both internally and from the web to provide lessons learned to customers.

The scope included all major sales, marketing, accounting, manufacturing, and distribution processes.

ABACUS ENERGY

Abacus wanted to use E-Business to reduce costs. As a major petroleum company, Abacus decided to center their focus on supplier relations. Abacus wanted to make relations more efficient, obtain goods and services at lower prices, and standardize on a smaller number of suppliers. The scope included all procurement and contracting processes. Their strategy was replacement.

CRAWFORD BANK

Crawford Bank decided to center their attention on lending products for E-Business. So as not to affect their current business and consumer customers, they decided to offer lending through a new bank exclusively targeting the web. The purpose was to gain marketshare on the web. The scope started with all lending processes from application processing through servicing.

E-BUSINESS LESSONS LEARNED

- **Build your E-Business plan with great detail on the near-term tasks but less detail for tasks that are further out in the future.**
  This will allow for flexibility in working with those future tasks. Also, team members will then have the opportunity to participate and fill in details as the work progresses. On the other hand, if you build a detailed schedule for the entire plan, this schedule will have to be revised often, based on actual results. It may be too restrictive and may lead to disruption later.
- **Take a large E-Business effort and divide it into phases.**
  In a given phase, identify the major tasks and milestones to see if you could increase effort and move tasks up in the schedule. Be careful how you do analysis across the subprojects.
- **Consider how much time you have to spend on updating the plan when you design it.**
  If you design a complex and detailed plan, you will have to spend more time updating the plan. For example, if the lowest level of detail is two to three days, you can update the schedule twice a week. If you go down to tasks of one day or less, you may have to update the project daily.
- **Look at the implementation plan's external appearance to learn about the past and present of the project.**
  Examine the project from the outside. What are the perceptions of managers outside of the implementation? How has the planned budget and schedule tracked against the actual? Have people left the project? Why?
- **Use a spider chart to create a picture of the E-Business effort.**
  An E-Business implementation can be characterized by an eight-dimensional figure—project plan/schedule, project manager, management, user, staff, purpose, scope, and methods/tools. Construct a bar chart or a radar chart with each bar or line signifying one dimension. You can use this to compare different subprojects in each of the eight dimensions. Charts such as this give a picture of the implementation without plunging into detail. You can also consider alternative purposes, scopes, etc. for the same subproject.
- **Start E-Business implementation based on a fiscal year to avoid resource conflicts.**
  If you start an E-Business effort in the middle of the year, you will likely have to rob resources from other previously approved and active projects. This can have a dramatic negative impact.
- **Try to keep the E-Business schedule limited.**
  When you consider the relative hardships of long E-Business efforts that are also large in scope, you can start to see that long is worse than large. A long project can transform the implementation team into a pseudo line organiza-

tion. Watch that the team does not get caught up in the process of the implementation as opposed to the actual work.

- **Remain sensitive to the E-Business environment throughout the work.**
  The environment of the implementation was covered earlier. Implementation not only must be planned with these factors in mind, but also assessed during the life of the implementation for changes in the environment.
- **Understand what not to do in the E-Business implementation.**
  Start the implementation with tasks that you know have to be performed. If you start adding tasks that might be needed, you could escalate the cost and work. You will divert attention from the important tasks.
- **Hold one person accountable for each detailed task.**
  If you have to identify two people for a task, then split the task into two parts.
- **Minimize documentation.**
  In the implementation, you and team members can devote your time to doing either project work or to administrative tasks. Documentation is an administrative task. It may be necessary to produce the documentation. However, working on documentation may mean spending less time on the project itself.
- **Perform risk management at the start.**
  This reinforces doing extensive analysis and planning prior to and at the start of the E-Business implementation. If you understand the risk areas, then you can give them proper attention.
- **Choose longer elapsed time over greater effort.**
  Time is usually your E-Business enemy. If you ever have an opportunity to choose between more time and more people, choose the time. Also, introducing more resources will likely impede the project. If you are offered more resources, do not accept these at face value. You may discover hidden costs in the politics of procuring the resources.

WHAT TO DO NEXT

1. Here are some basic questions to ask about your organization relative to general project management.
   - Does your firm follow an established sequence of actions in developing project plans? If so, are these clearly distributed and supported by training?
   - How are small projects handled differently from large projects in your company? What happens to projects that are in the middle?
   - If you were to develop a new project plan, what guidance, templates, and other support are offered in your organization?
   - In what areas of project management are your company's greatest strengths and in what areas are the greatest weaknesses?

2. Look over several projects and attempt to define the objectives, scope, and strategies for the projects. Create a table in which the rows are the projects and the columns are objectives, scope, and strategies.

3. For a simple E-Business effort, develop a template using the following steps:
   - Identify 10 to 15 highest level summary tasks.
   - Identify the same number of major milestones. Put these into a task list. You now have a very high-level work breakdown structure.
   - Identify dependencies between all tasks and milestones. Note any cases in which you are having trouble deciding if there is a dependency. Later, you will be able to determine such dependencies when you create more detailed tasks.
   - Now, for each major task, write down the detailed tasks. Put these under the summary tasks.
   - Identify several key resources for the work. Assign these to the detailed tasks.

You have now created a template.

4. Take the template you have just created and add more detailed tasks for the work to be done in the next month. Define the duration of all detailed tasks. Determine the starting dates for all detailed tasks that do not have predecessor tasks. You have now created a schedule. Flesh out the tasks one month in advance on a regular basis.

Chapter 3

Become an Effective E-Business Implementation Manager

INTRODUCTION

E-Business implementation and expansion are complex in that they involve many areas of the business, technology and systems, E-Business vendors, customers, and suppliers. Now, you can try to have one person manage the entire effort. However, this is not a good idea for several reasons.

- Successful E-Business implementation requires a range of skills and knowledge areas. These are not likely to be found in one person.
- Different skills are needed as the E-Business implementation proceeds. At the front end the project leader must be creative and market driven. At the back end the project leader must be an implementation driver and task master.
- Different personalities are needed to cope with the variety of E-Business issues that will surface.
- Due to the elapsed time of E-Business implementation, you will want continuity to manage the expansion of E-Business. Having several leaders achieves this goal.

Here are some ideas related to E-Business leaders.

- Have two overall E-Business managers during the implementation. One serves as the primary leader at the start and is supported by the implementation-oriented leader. The roles are then reversed as implementation occurs.
- Within the E-Business effort, consider having several leaders who report to these two and direct the individual subprojects of the E-Business implementation.
- The group of E-Business team leaders can be constituted as a project steering committee.

There are a number of benefits of this approach.

- The approach allows E-Business to draw upon the different skills of different people.
- You have a backup if one of the leaders departs from the E-Business work. As a result, you reduce the risk.
- Different people have different abilities to get along with people. This helps in addressing the many audiences of an E-Business effort.
- Two project leaders can play the roles of "good cop" and "bad cop". That is, one person can be strict and the other can be understanding—very useful in E-Business.

Many successful E-Business leaders share the following attributes:

- Problem-solving capability to identify and to resolve issues associated with the E-Business effort;
- Ability to communicate effectively with business units, vendors, IT staff, and management;
- Steadfastness to see the work and tasks through to completion;
- Ability to work successfully with the team, management, and other employees and outsiders.

Notice what is *not* on the list—being clever or being an E-Business technical genius. Notice also that the characteristics described above can be developed. Good E-Business leaders are not born, they are made. Most successful project leaders grew into the role by necessity. Even if you are not in charge of E-Business implementation, you can use the material to build your skills and better prepare yourself to be one.

MILESTONES

The purpose of this chapter is to explore the most significant parts of an E-Business leader's duties. Your success will rest on your ability to deal with people, to address issues, and to analyze and demonstrate leadership, so these attributes will be emphasized. Administrative responsibilities will also be examined.

The milestone here is that you understand the role of an E-Business leader. You will also understand situations which you are likely to confront. The scope extends from the start of the effort to the completion, and perhaps beyond to E-Business expansion. Sometimes you are thrown into the middle of an ongoing E-Business effort. This situation will also be covered.

METHODS AND TECHNIQUES

One might say that an E-Business leader's role is to direct the implementation and completion of E-Business. However, this is the narrow version of the scope of the job. A wider view is that the role is to work toward leaving a management process in place for people to use after the project is completed; since E-Business is ongoing, it can be employed in subsequent E-Business efforts.

People sometimes fail as leaders because they never clearly define their role. A leader who embraces the role in a broader sense can create a more aggressive approach to the entire E-Business effort, while a leader with a narrow mindset may be defensive and weaken the effort.

E-BUSINESS LEADER SELECTION

Unfortunately, many times the choice of a leader for E-Business implementation or expansion is made on an ad hoc, spur-of-the-moment basis. Often, the people are selected based on availability and a general experience fit with E-Business. In projects that are routine and of low risk, this will probably work. This fails in E-Business which has greater risk than an ordinary project.

What is a better approach for selecting leaders for E-Business? Here is an organized method:

- Have managers maintain a list of people who appear to be potential leaders for E-Business. Scour the organization to find these people. The benefit of this list is that it gives management a reference point from which to begin.
- When E-Business is being considered, round up all other project ideas that are likely to turn into projects in the next three to six months. Identify the degree and source of risk in each E-Business subproject. Sources include organization coordination, systems and technology, and external organizations. Construct a table where the rows are the subprojects and the columns are the areas of risk. In the table, rank each project according to the specific area of risk on a scale of one to five where one is low, or no risk, and five is very high risk. This table indicates what skills you need for each subproject to minimize risk.
- Take the list of leader candidates and add the names of project managers who will be available during the period. Construct a second table in which the rows are people and the columns are areas of risk in E-Business. Some areas of risk in E-Business are political problems, change in direction, meeting a tight deadline, and dealing with changing requirements. Enter a one to five in the table, based on the degree to which the person can deal well with that type of risk. This shows the most suitable areas for each candidate to handle.
- Now you can compose a third table of leader candidates (rows) and subprojects of E-Business (columns). The entry is the extent to which each person is suited to the specific subproject. Note that you cannot just put the previous two tables together. The table here reflects knowledge and familiarity with the subproject as well as with handling risk.

Errors in this approach come mainly from misunderstanding E-Business and its risks, not from misunderstanding the people. Often, there is insufficient analysis of the project before leaders are selected. Carry out the pre-project activity as presented in Chapter 2 before you use this method of selecting the leaders.

E-Business Leader Responsibilities

Consider the table in Figure 3-1. The columns are the phases of implementation from startup to after completion activities. The three rows are for major duties, administrative duties, and background duties. Major duties are where you should spend the most time. Administrative duties are overhead tasks that are necessary. Background duties are things that you can do to help yourself be a better project manager. At any given time, have several of these activities in process with one getting primary attention. Give primary attention to the major duties rather than to administration. Also, gradually work at improving yourself through the background duties.

- **Major Duties at the Start of the Work**
  - *Define the E-Business concept and gain consensus.* As discussed in the preceding chapter, setting and getting agreement on the E-Business objectives, scope, roles, issues, and other parts is crucial to eventual E-Business success.
  - *Obtain the team members and define the E-Business plan.* Take the time to develop the plan using the templates. It will be important to make the issues with the tasks in the plan to identify the areas of risk.
  - *Market the E-Business project.* Prepare a presentation on E-Business. Be prepared to answer the following question: What is in the E-Business effort that appeals to the self-interest of the organizations and individuals involved? There is an additional benefit here—by doing marketing and , sales, you force yourself to consider the work from points of view other than management's and your own.
  - *Coordinate vendor selection.* In many E-Business efforts you will require outside help from the start.
- **Major Duties During the Work**
  - *Identify and address issues.* Keep on this subject constantly. If you let up, you risk the entire effort. Act as a constant problem-solver. Look for issues. Make sure that the issues that have been resolved do not resurface under a different guise.
  - *Monitor the actual work.* Go out and actually see what is going on in the work. Do not take people's word for it even if they are good and truthful team members. By visiting them while they are working and showing an interest you also show that you care.

Type	Start of Implementation	During Implementation	End of Implementation
Major duties	• Define alternative implementation concepts • Get approval for one concept • Develop the plan • Define and gather the team • Market the effort	• Identify and address issues • Interact with line managers and the team • Monitor actual work • Control the interfaces between subprojects • Review the milestones • Deal with E-Business changes	• Identify new opportunities for E-Business • Gather and use lessons learned • Measure results of the implementation
Administrative duties	• Setup implementation files • Establish project reporting	• Update status • Perform budget vs. actual analysis • Revise schedules	• Clean up and store E-Business implementation files • Follow up on loose ends • Create a final budget vs. actual analysis
Background duties	• Conduct casual marketing • Line up staff for later in the implementation	• Track what is going on in other projects • Coordinate the leaders of the subprojects	• Apply lessons learned • Place team members on new subprojects

Figure 3-1: Duties of an E-Business Leader

- *Make decisions and do marketing.* You have to do marketing to convince someone that the decision is needed, that the timing is important, and that the form and structure of the decision are correct.
- *Interact with line managers and the team.* Keep line managers informed of what is going on in the project and how their organization is contributing.
- *Review the work.* This is not a background task. Actively set aside time for analysis and perspective.

- **Major Duties at the End of the Work**
  - *Construct lessons learned.* As the project winds down, develop a list of lessons learned with the tips provided. These demonstrate the added value of E-Business to the organization, as well as showing that you really do care about more than a single project.
  - *Measure the results of the E-Business implementation.*
  - *Determine and recommend how E-Business should expand.*

- **Administrative Duties at the Start of the Work**
  - *Set up the files.* This means not just paper files, but also electronic files, templates, forms, and all of the support required for the work. If you take the time to do this with care at the start, you will save yourself grief and problems later.

- **Administrative Duties During the Work**
  - *Update the project status.* Keep track of status and keep management informed. *Don't assume that if you tell one manager, other managers will be told.* Inform people one-on-one of what is going on.
  - *Perform a budget vs. actual analysis.* Get in the habit of routinely looking at the budget so that you constantly know the status of the budget.
  - *Revise schedules and budget.*

- **Administrative Duties at the End of the Work**
  - *Document lessons learned generated during the work.*
  - *Clean up and store the files.*
  - *Follow up on any loose ends in the project.*
  - *Create a final budget vs. actual analysis with assessments of variations.*

- **Background Duties at the Start of the Work**
  - *Conduct casual marketing of E-Business and plan.*
  - *Line up staff for future work later in the work.*

- **Background Duties During the Work**
  - *Track what is happening on other projects that have interdependencies with yours.*
  - *Exploit common ground, issues, and opportunities with other project leaders.*

- **Background Duties at the End of the Work**
  - *Build ties with other project leaders.*
  - *Try to apply the lessons learned.*

THE IMPACT OF TRENDS ON E-BUSINESS LEADERS

The basic role of the project manager has not changed throughout the years. Some trends have made the work easier and some have made it harder.

- Availability of software for electronic mail, groupware, and project management has eased some of the administrative and communications aspects of the E-Business effort.
- Corporate downsizing and reorganization have made projects leaner and more accountable, making E-Business efforts more challenging.
- The availability of new technology and project successes has increased management expectations for E-Business.
- Improvements in technology and their business impact have increased pressures for projects to succeed.
- Resources have to be shared among projects and with nonproject work, creating a coordination challenge.
- Fewer resources are dedicated to an individual project, producing a management challenge.

Overall, projects are more challenging than they were 20 years ago due to tight schedules and limited resources. The upside of this is that in many organizations you can more readily advance in the organization by succeeding with a project. The trend is moving towards more projects and, consequently, towards more project managers. Projects appeal to management in many organizations because of the accountability and visibility. As one manager said, "Projects can generate revenue; line organizations generate costs." This is especially true with E-Business.

THE POSITIVE ASPECTS OF BEING AN E-BUSINESS LEADER

Managing a successful E-Business implementation is a major career milestone given all of the projects that fail or run into problems. Such talent and skills can often be recognized in immediate compensation increases or through a job change.

However, there are some basic reasons why E-Business management is rewarding. For younger people it is an opportunity to gain the recognition and attention of management. E-Business is visible. The leaders are visible. A leader may have more opportunities for advancement than an employee stuck in a line organization. Here are some additional reasons to become an E-Business leader, beyond the potential of advancement:

- E-Business may be a chance to learn new skills and methods.
- Being a leader may be your best shot at breaking into management.
- The role of leader may be more challenging than your current position.
- Being a leader will increase your range of contacts and personal network.

Becoming an E-Business Leader

If you are a project manager with a known track record, you can wait to be called. Otherwise, how do you get started? Consider the old-fashioned approach of volunteering. Read up on E-Business using the web. Even if you are turned down for a particular project, people will see that you have an interest in the company. Second, you will have shown initiative. How many people around you are doing that? Third, you are alerting people to your interest in E-Business and project management.

What should you do before volunteering? Do the research into E-Business. Scout the project out. Determine what you could add to the effort. Don't stress the negative things in the work that you could fix. Focus instead on the opportunities you could support and the strengths you could bring to the table. Next, determine what you would do with the duties of your current job. You definitely don't want to say that these can be left undone. Instead, show that you can piggyback the E-Business tasks on top of your normal work, even if this means extra work.

What if you want to volunteer to replace a current leader? Do not undermine the current leader. How do you propose your services? The best technique for taking over a subproject or the whole thing is to volunteer to address the outstanding, unresolved E-Business issues. Never emphasize administrative or communication skills unless there is a known problem there. You want to show that you care and want to help.

When you make your proposal to management, use the words "volunteer" and "assistance," and ask them to think about it. To avoid pressuring them for a decision, indicate that you will check with them in a week or so to see what they might suggest.

Characteristics of Successful E-Business Leaders

Here are some of the most common characteristics of successful E-Business leaders:

- **They know what is going on in the effort at any time.**
  Be ready to answer any reasonable question about the work from anyone. This will show that you are in touch. It will show the team that you care.
- **They work on communications with line managers**.
  Stay in touch with the line managers who are responsible for your team members. This way, they will know about the contributions of their people to the project and will be less likely to remove them.
- **They are aware of the trade-off between the needs of the organization and the needs of the work.**
  Many times both the project and organization have a common interest. However, sometimes a decision is made one way for the organization and another way for E-Business. When you press for a decision, point out this

trade-off so that all involved can see how the decision will affect the work if they decide in favor of the organization.

- **Keep up-to-date on E-Business trends and what other firms are doing.** You don't want to be too internally focused. This can hamper your perspective. Remember too that you don't want unpleasant surprises.
- **They can address resource allocation among multiple projects dynamically.** A modern project manager must often compete for resources for the project on an on-going basis. This is true even if the project is recognized as critical.
- **They are able to evaluate and criticize themselves.** Be your own worst critic. However, also pat yourself on the back when you succeed. That is part of the evaluation.
- **They have a sense of humor.** Look at the humorous side of projects. Consider how ridiculous all of the red tape and bureaucracy are. "Dilbert" cartoons often point out the absurdities of organization life and sometimes give a humorous view of project management.
- **They work with team members one-on-one to understand their needs and frustrations.** This includes working with the people who are part-time players in the work as well as with your core team. It may be casual conversation away from the project. Treat the team members evenhandedly. This is difficult since certain people at any given time are more critical to the project than others. Also, some people in the project may be taken for granted. When the pressures of the project build up, this continues. The E-Business leader is the one who can most easily get such people recognized in their own organizations or with management.
- **They are always on the lookout for ways to improve the work and the environment.** Listen to the team members for their ideas. Solicit suggestions as to what could be done to improve the work. Don't mention budget or schedule. This will just increase pressure. Ask the question, "Do you have any thoughts on how the work might be accomplished in a better or easier way?"
- **When decisions are made, they act immediately.** Prior to the management decision, map out a plan of action assuming that the decision goes the way you anticipated. Be ready to act when the decision is made. This is not just to show action. You wanted that decision; you had said how important it was. If you sit on your hands after you have the decision, you may lose credibility.
- **They become adept at the methods and tools.** The purpose of this is to be self-sufficient. You do not want to have a critical deadline come up and then have the person on whom you depend be unavailable. While you cannot be an expert, you should know enough about most tools to get by.

- **They practice fire drills in project planning**.
  Be ready for emergencies. This will also help you deal with the unexpected. For example, you show up for work on Monday and a manager comes in and says that someone is being pulled off the team for a high-priority task. Or management asks you to determine whether and how the project could be accelerated. Think through these and similar scenarios and formulate plans, both to have the plans ready for possible use and to practice thinking through problem situations.

E-BUSINESS LEADERS WHO FAIL

Here are some common reasons an E-Business leader may fail:

- **They treat E-Business as just another IT project**.
  This is very dangerous since you have already noted many differences with standard projects.
- **They focus on one or two subprojects in E-Business that they are most familiar with—neglecting the interfaces and interrelationships among the subprojects**.
  The subprojects are typically where you will have the most risk.
- **They avoid being involved in the actual work**.
  This is a sure ticket for trouble. You risk losing touch with both the work and the team. Also, if you roll up your sleeves and do some of the work, the team will respect you more.
- **They try to micromanage the work**.
  This can irritate the team members. The project manager might cruise the area where the work is being done and direct people in the smallest task. People notice the project manager's presence and start to ask, "Doesn't this person trust us?" or "Why can't we do the work ourselves?" Instead, delegate tasks and then follow up on tasks that have risk.
- **They attempt to deal with issues one at a time without analysis**.
  As will be discussed in a later chapter, issues tend to link together. Some issues may continually resurface due to political factors. Sit down and analyze these issues and then attempt to resolve a group of them at a time.
- **They leave project administration alone or delegate it**.
  Administration is downplayed compared with other work, but you still should do the reporting and analysis of the project yourself. If you rely on others, you may not be able to answer questions when asked casually by managers in a meeting or in the hallway. Any hesitation may be viewed as a sign of weakness.

- **They spend too much time schmoozing with upper management rather than spending time in the E-Business effort**.
  The more time you spend with management, the less time you have for the E-Business work. It is a zero-sum proposition. Balance your time. Also, do not wear out your welcome with management.
- **They spend excessive team meeting time on status**.
  Get status one-on-one before the meeting. Use the meeting time to address issues and opportunities.
- **They become obsessed with how many tasks have been completed and the percentage of work completed towards a milestone**.
  If this occurs, you are becoming a bureaucrat. A milestone is only complete if you validate that the work is of high quality and fulfills its purpose. Percentage complete means nothing if you cannot validate it.
- **They leave issues, especially old issues, unresolved**.
  Issues left unresolved tend to fester and get worse. On the other hand, you might want to allow an issue to mature until you understand its ramifications.
- **They make too many changes at once or minor changes too often to the schedule**.
  This can irritate team members because the effort then appears to be adrift. Make several changes at one time with an umbrella reason for the changes. Then leave it alone for awhile.
- **They become focused on either the tools of project management or the tools used by the team**.
  Tools are often technology-based. They are impressive and captivating. Don't be sucked into this trap. Tools support a method. Pay attention to the method. Let others worry about the tools. Your main concern is whether the tools support the method and are being properly used, not the internal workings and features of the tools.

How to Measure Your Performance as an E-Business Leader

How are you doing as a leader? To make the most of your experience and come up with lessons learned, use this checklist to evaluate yourself:

Checklist for a Project Manager

- How aware are you of what other firms are doing in E-Business?
- How much time are you spending in administration vs. management? Is the balance good or does it need adjustment?

- What is the actual state of the work in the right now? What are the problem areas?
- Do you communicate informally with upper management? Do you need to communicate more often?
- List the key issues that remain unresolved. How long has each remained so? What is the age of the oldest unresolved issue?
- Is the plan and schedule up-to-date? If not, what areas need to be brought up-to-date?
- Do you communicate with members of the team one-on-one frequently enough?
- What is covered at meetings? Do the meetings last too long? Are the meetings rushed?

Your team members will benefit from periodically evaluating their own work on the project as well. Use the following checklist with your team members. Discuss with them areas that need to be improved, either with more effort on your part or on theirs.

CHECKLIST FOR A TEAM MEMBER

- Do you have an adequate picture of the overall project status?
- Have you taken care of issues assigned to you for analysis and resolution? Are you unsure about how to proceed with any of the assigned issues?
- How much time are you devoting to the E-Business work vs. other work? Is the balance good or does it need adjustment?
- Are you using the methods and tools correctly and effectively? Do you need more training?
- Do you volunteer to do additional work?
- Have you had any problems getting along with the leaders?
- Do you communicate what is going on in the project with your line manager?

E-BUSINESS EXAMPLES

RICKER CATALOGS

Ricker Catalogs decided to treat the E-Business effort as an IT project with an IT project leader. They appointed a senior systems analyst who had been the project manager in implementing the customer service system. This system was developed by a vendor so that the leader spent most of his time dealing with vendor-business coordination issues. He was not familiar with e-commerce or E-Business, but thought it could be treated like any other project. He formalized a plan that focused on the system implementation side and not on the organization or business processes. As time went by, it became clear that these pieces were missing. The leader was delegated down to the IT subprojects. A marketing business manager was placed in overall charge of the E-Business implementation.

MARATHON MANUFACTURING

Marathon management knew that going into E-Business was a complex undertaking. They decided to appoint a steering committee of three leaders. One was drawn from manufacturing. One was from marketing. The third and last was from the systems organization. This approach gave them flexibility to deal with the many issues and subprojects that had to be faced. Problems were decided by a majority vote of the steering committee. The losing member of a vote also had the capability to make an appeal to management.

ABACUS ENERGY

Abacus decided to appoint the purchasing manager as the overall leader. She was supported by an IT project leader as well as a project leader from a vendor organization. The three functioned similar to that of Marathon. Since Abacus' E-Business efforts were narrowly focused, this approach was probably overkill. Eventually, the vendor leader dropped out and the two internal managers shared the duties of the manager.

CRAWFORD BANK

At Crawford Bank, management wanted someone who knew E-Business rather than endure the learning curve for one of their internal managers. Remember too that Crawford wanted to implement E-Business for lending as a separate entity. The overall project leader was hired from outside. A technology project manager was also hired. A team of four people was identified to serve and support liaison between the new entity and the existing bank organization. These people were from IT, lending, general consumer banking, and auditing.

E-BUSINESS LESSONS LEARNED

- **To encourage the team having a wider view, have team members bring in E-Business examples and articles into team meetings**.
  Build the data base of lessons learned from these examples.

- **Check out any project before joining or taking over**.
  If you are considering volunteering for E-Business or are a potential draftee, do some scouting about the status of the work. Ask some basic questions about the issues, status, and past events. Then you can answer the important question, "How will I make a difference and contribute to the work?"
- **Play many roles, but not that of a specialist**.
  If a leader is also a specialist, the team has to consider the leader as having two non-complimentary roles—leader and expert. This can lead to confusion when issues are being addressed. In some cases, the leader should consider suppressing knowledge of his or her expertise to the team and center attention on leadership.
- **Learn about yourself from the way you manage the work**.
  E-Business applies stress and presents a variety of situations to you. You then respond. Sit back and review what you do. How are you holding up? Use the scorecard presented earlier.
- **Motivate the team throughout the work**.
  E-Business is not for sprinters. It is for marathon runners. Coping with issues over time and dealing with management and organization are constant challenges for the leader. The key here is to avoid being overwhelmed and to motivate the team throughout the work.
- **Control your administrative time**.
  This reinforces the earlier discussion of duties. Gather the information you require to accomplish these tasks along with a list of things to do. When you are not likely to be disturbed, sit down and dedicate yourself to the work.
- **Re-evaluate the E-Business work often**.
  Concentration refers to giving attention to issues, resources, and work. However, unless the project is short, if this is your major activity, you may be tripped up on some underlying problem or issue that you had ignored or not thought about. This means that on a regular basis, you should sit back and think about what is happening overall.
- **Drive the work**.
  Don't just monitor the work—drive the work. This includes the work of all consultants and contractors as well as internal staff. This also reinforces the benefits of a team approach.

WHAT TO DO NEXT

1. Address the following questions.
   - Does your organization have a standard approach for becoming a leader or remaining as a leader?
   - How are project managers evaluated in your organization? Do the criteria involve motivation of staff, addressing issues, and dealing with crises?

2. Using stories of success in the magazines, define attributes of successful E-Business leaders. How did they become leaders? Where did they learn about E-Business?
3. Assess the state of the project management process in your organization. Are standardized templates and procedures in use? Are projects with different levels of risk managed differently? Or are differences based on size, cost, or duration?
4. Evaluate yourself in terms of the following:
   - How much exposure do you give team members in reporting to management?
   - How much time do you spend individually with team members vs. group meetings? Spend more time individually.
   - Do you involve team members in addressing issues? Or, do you present the issue and the recommended action for their feedback? This gets at the heart of the question to what extent the team is involved in decision-making.
   - How do you inform the team of changes? Do you change the schedule and assignments each time some new item emerges? Or do you implement larger scale changes?
   - Do you know how the team members will react to an issue in advance? How much time do you spend thinking about what the team will think?

Chapter 4

Manage Your E-Business Teams

INTRODUCTION

Implementing E-Business requires the skills and knowledge of many different people. Unfortunately, these same people are going to be the ones who are heavily in demand for their normal work. Even though E-Business has a priority, it is not the only game in town. The likelihood that you can get people full-time on E-Business for an extended period of time is low. In addition, if some of these people are assigned full-time, they are likely to be pulled off the project later due to emergencies, business peak periods, etc.

This situation presents a dilemma for E-Business leaders. The following questions have to be answered:

- Who are all of the players that may potentially be needed in E-Business?
- At what point in the work are these people needed? Also, when can they be released from E-Business?
- Which roles and responsibilities can be shared among people from the same department?
- What roles require full-time involvement over an extended period of time?
- Which specific people should be involved in E-Business?
- When should the team be formed?

Beyond these items we must address how to bring on or discharge team members as E-Business continues through implementation.

E-Business is different than standard IT projects in terms of teams because it involves more people with typically greater time pressure. IT projects in general differ from standard projects because you must involve people part-time and not full-time. You tend to involve vendor staff as team members as well. Business complexity, downsizing, and mergers have contributed to the fact that few people understand the new technology and also have in-depth business knowledge. They will probably not be dedicated to and consumed by a specific project. These factors have also increased pressure on the capable people employed in a company.

There are other differences as well. People needed by E-Business are shared among project and nonproject work. Many team members also still have to perform their line organization duties. Now more outsiders are involved—consultants, suppliers, partners, and customer firms involved in projects. The projects are more widespread geographically. Also, technology has enabled team members to communicate in a wider variety of ways at faster speeds. This chapter addresses the new team environment.

The goal here is to examine some of the key questions and issues related to managing an E-Business team. Within this goal, the purpose is to help you assemble and maintain a cost-effective team. The scope includes all aspects of team management.

MILESTONES

The major milestones associated with the E-Business team are:

- Develop the strategy for managing the E-Business team.
- Assemble the initial E-Business team.
- Get new team members on board.
- Ensure that team members participate actively in management and issues resolution.

METHODS AND TECHNIQUES

YOUR E-BUSINESS TEAM STRATEGY

The elements of an E-Business team strategy are the following:

- General approach for timing to get team members
- Approach for how you will work with line departments and other business units
- Activities that the team members will be involved in during the E-Business work
- Approach for bringing new team members on board the project and releasing other team members

We cover the review of work and specific personnel-related issues in later chapters.

Timing—When and How Should the Team Be Formed?

The traditional argument is that you should form the team as early as possible. However, there are some disadvantages to this in E-Business, including:

- The E-Business effort may still be fuzzy in scope.
- You may not know what exact personnel requirements you have for the work.
- People who are volunteered to E-Business may not be a good fit with the requirements.
- You lose flexibility by committing to people early.
- You have limited knowledge of requirements at the start of E-Business—this knowledge improves as the work proceeds.

Therefore, our first guideline is to identify some of the people early. The second guideline is to have them join the project as late as possible or just in time. In this way you minimize the drain on the department in terms of loss of skills and knowledge. Have the people committed only for some near-term tasks related to process analysis, data collection, and definition of the new E-Business transactions. This gives you flexibility later for replacement. It also means that you will not be placing undue demands on the departments—they will tend to be more supportive of E-Business as a result.

Here are examples of what can go wrong.

Example: Banking

In a large E-Business banking project, the team was formed early. It consisted of 10 people. The project scope and direction were set. Work was started. Within a week it became clear that there was not enough work to keep ten people busy. Rumors started flying about waste. Some team members worked on other assignments. Morale started to sink. The project had to be reconstituted with a smaller number of people. Time and money were lost.

Example: Insurance

In a case involving an insurance firm, the plan called for staffing to be built up. The project manager feared that if he did not hire the people according to the plan, the budget of the project would be cut. Instead of preparing a revised staffing plan, he hired the people and the same problem occurred as at the bank.

Guidelines

Team formation will continue to change throughout the project. Different needs will arise and requirements will change. Teams today are much different than teams of 20 years ago. You are unlikely to be able to keep a large team intact. Your team will resemble a play or movie in which the cast changes as the plot progresses. Here are some more suggestions regarding timing:

- *Identify requirements for a small core of the team that will persist in the effort.* Get these people on board early in the work.
- *Determine requirements for other team members, but add them to the team as you go.* Get team members as late as possible to minimize the drain on their time, increase flexibility, and reduce costs.
- *Develop the mindset that most team members will be working only part-time on the work doing specific tasks.*
- *If the requirements of E-Business are fuzzy, delay forming the team.* Wait until the objectives, requirements, and schedule become clearer.

CHOOSING THE PEOPLE FOR THE E-BUSINESS EFFORT

In E-Business you will have to have two sets of skills from most departments. On the one hand, you want people with in-depth knowledge of the department processes. On the other hand, you want people who question the current processes and want to support change in the processes. These are in general different people. We suggest that you start with energetic junior people whose loss from their departments will not present a major problem.

Prior to management approval, contact a few people to determine their level of interest in E-Business. Choose people whose work habits and patterns you are comfortable with, who have skills that you think you will need, and who perform tasks well.

Here are some additional guidelines:

- *You want to have long-term team members who have a proven track record in E-Business.* The reward for people doing good work in the project is that they can continue.
- *You want to rotate several people from a department through the E-Business work.* This will accomplish several goals. First, it will give the work different points of view. Second, you will draw upon different skills. Third, you will generate more support for E-Business through the involvement of several people.
- *You want to have a core of nearly full-time members on the E-Business team.* This provides stability. The core team will have many part-time team members who will come and go.

The core team should consist of one person from the IT group, at least one from the business areas, one from marketing, and one from the major consultant or vendor firm that you are using. Some of these may be subproject leaders in the E-Business effort.

Keep the core of the team small—usually no more than two to four people. Why so small a number? First, it is difficult to attract good people to projects, given all of their other commitments. Second, it is easier to manage a smaller number of people.

Other specific reasons for a small core team are the following:

- A smaller core team is easier to coordinate.
- It is possible to devote more individual attention to the team members.
- The members will feel more accountable since the team size is small.
- The chances of having underused resources are reduced.

Example: Marathon Manufacturing

In Marathon Manufacturing firm, the team started with three people and kept this number for six months. As the system moved into implementation, more part-time people were acquired for installation and training. The total team at its peak was more than 20 members.

Watch for these disadvantages of a small team so that you can compensate for them:

- Any person who leaves the core team leaves a big gap to fill.
- Small teams can be more difficult to manage if the members do not get along with each other.
- In some organizations, power flows to larger projects with more team members.
- What if you take over a team and it has too many members? After you take over, start moving some of the people to a temporary status. When people leave, don't rush to fill the slots. Let attrition take hold. Morale might fall, but you can compensate by reassigning the work and getting rid of less critical tasks which can be deferred or eliminated. This might be a good time to review the plan structure for excess tasks.

WHO SHOULD BE ON THE TEAM?

The core of your team should be people who have good general skills, but who also have a specific skill area that will be required in many phases of E-Business. The remainder of the team will consist of part-time and temporary members who enter to perform a specific task or set of tasks and then exit.

An insurance firm had an E-Business project in which the manager was an insurance executive. He felt weak in his knowledge of information systems. He then staffed the team with several systems people. However, it later became clear that the team had too many of these and suffered from a lack of people with insurance experience. The manager had to do double and triple duty by filling in for several team members. The manager had to train the entire team in insurance procedures. The team was not as efficient as it could have been due to lack of diversity.

Here are some questions to ask when choosing people to make up the core of the team:

- *Where are the areas of fundamental risk and uncertainty in the E-Business work?* This is where you want help.
- *What are the types of tasks that lend themselves to a "jack-of-all-trades," generalist type of person?* You want one person like this who is flexible and can be given a wide range of tasks.

Notice that you did not need to ask what technical or business skills were significant. The skills will become evident over time and they will change. However, if you know in advance that a specific business or technical area will have a major role, then at least indicate this to management. Do not even attempt to get someone committed to the project full-time, since it's not likely this person would be released for such a period. What you will want is to have them work on the project intensely for a specific shorter period.

APPROACH TO WORKING WITH LINE ORGANIZATIONS

In E-Business you will have to gain the cooperation and involvement of departments that link to the critical processes that will become "E." In a traditional project this is much more limited since typically only one or two departments are involved. However, in E-Business you will involve marketing, accounting, order processing, inventory control, shipping, and customer service, just to name a few. Why? Because the E-Business processes cross these departments. Leave one department out and you risk screwing up a key business process.

How do you approach working with all of these departments? One answer is that you will have to spend more time working in coordination with the managers of these departments. A second answer is that you must carefully orchestrate how these departments will be involved.

HOW DO YOU GET TEAM MEMBERS?

Make some initial informal contacts to determine availability and desire. The next step is to approach the managers of your candidates. If the people you seek are very good, their managers will be reluctant to let them go. Also, people will be hesitant to leave a secure line position or other project for a more uncertain future in E-Business.

How do you cope with factors such as these? First, describe to management what makes the work interesting and important. Second, indicate what steps you have taken to ensure that only a reasonable amount of risk exists. Finally, be willing to settle for part of an employee's time. If people join the team, become interested, and understand that their work is critical, they sometimes become full-time on their own.

You will seldom get all of your first choices for a team. Rather than settle for mediocrity, consider leaving a position unfilled. This offers an opportunity to use volunteers as the project takes off later. Base this decision on how crucial the missing role is at this time.

E-Business offers the opportunity for team members to gain exposure with management. This often offers employees a greater career opportunity than they would have in a line organization. This appeals to the self-interest of the team members. Use this approach to attract junior staff to the team.

Temporary team members enter the team to perform a specific set of tasks. When their task is completed, they are either released or they may perform other E-Business tasks. These people can be contract workers or employees. Often today you deal with contract or consultant people on projects. In one large government project, more than 75 percent of the total team was composed of non-employees. How can this be managed effectively? Employ the old strategy of divide-and-conquer. That is, manage the work by task area. In the government project, any given area had only one or two contract people, which made it easy to track and manage the work. Temporary team members must be given an understanding of the beginning and end of their work at the start of the assignment. It is here that milestones must be well defined. Lack of clarity is an invitation to overrunning the budget.

Instead of recruiting the top workers, go after more junior people at the start of the work. If you choose team members who are critical to their line organization and other projects, you could cripple their other work, especially if you use them full-time. Also, early in the project you don't know exactly what you need. Thus, it is better to recruit junior workers for a limited time. This gives you greater flexibility and a chance to evaluate their fit with E-Business. It allows you to buy time so that you can return and ask for additional people on a part-time basis later.

TRAINING OF TEAM MEMBERS

Of course, the team members know their areas of specialty. However, they are not familiar with E-Business. This is one area of training. Collaborative work and project management is a second area. Specific software tools and related methods are another area. Team members should be trained in the following:

- General concepts related to E-Business
- How processes are changed through E-Business
- Examples of firms in implementing E-Business

- How departments are involved in the work
- The E-Business project template
- Defining tasks and estimating durations
- Updating their tasks
- Identifying E-Business issues and opportunities
- Collaborative work practices

Activities for Team Members

In E-Business team members participate in the project beyond their assigned tasks. Here are some of the major activities of team members.

- Keeping their department managers informed of the progress and work
- Spreading the word in their departments about the need and benefits of E-Business
- Helping to analyze issues and suggest solutions
- Participating in joint tasks with other team members
- Helping new team members get on board
- Obtaining knowledge from team members whose work is wrapping up

Why are these important? Because the E-Business leaders cannot do these things alone. Another reason is that the more people participate, the more they will become committed to E-Business. A greater commitment can increase support from their respective home departments for E-Business.

Getting New Team Members on Board

It would be ideal for any new person to receive a briefing on the project at the time they join. This is often not accomplished, however, for many reasons—too much work, deadlines, the person already knew people in the project.

Orientation in E-Business is very beneficial. It can move the person into the right perspective. It can reduce the learning curve. It prevents the new member from plunging in and trying his best with misdirected efforts. That person may then need to be redirected, which wastes time and money.

Guidelines for Managing the Team

When managing a team, get in the habit of holding "issue meetings." These are much more important than status meetings or general project meetings. When the issue meeting involves a specific tool or method, use the meeting as a way for more seasoned members to discuss their views and experience.

Get feedback and suggestions from the team. Ask each person what he or she needs and what would be helpful to carry out the work. If an individual provides information, be prepared to act on ideas or problems. Do more than just thank team members for their views. Get back to them with specific actions. Test new ideas. If you use someone's idea, give the person credit.

How should you assign work to people? Some managers assign a few specific tasks to each person—like piecework. They think that this approach will keep a person focused. However, this can lead to boredom. Instead, assign groups of tasks that must be addressed in parallel. At a given time, a person will work on one of these tasks, but he or she will work on all of the assigned tasks over the period of time, such as a week or a month. An example of this method is found in a computer operating system. An operating system works on foreground (high-priority) tasks as well as background (lesser-priority) tasks. Help employees balance their time between foreground and background tasks by using the issue meetings to clarify which tasks are very important to E-Business.

In the case of people who bring up personal problems, move them to a flexible work schedule, if possible. This will free them up for a few weeks to address their problems.

Here are some ideas for managers that will work to keep team members involved for the long haul.

- *Involve people in the implementation and resolution of issues.* Give the group specific praise for the issue. This shows that you value results and contribution over just hard work. They become more committed if they see that their role is important.
- *Minimize the hassles of management.* Help the team members by meeting with their management when needed. Reduce status reporting to a minimum.
- *Keep the team informed of upcoming issues.* Give them some insight into the world of politics. This will capture their interest and give them some idea of what is going on in the bigger world.
- *Try to keep a sense of humor.*
- *Give examples and "war stories" of past projects to show perspective.*
- *Keep the administration of the project low key and invisible.* If you keep stressing administration, you will lose the team's respect.
- *Never compare E-Business with any other specific current project.* However, you can compare your project with other projects generally. Stress why your project is different.

What do you accomplish by doing these things? First, you convey to the team members how much you value their contribution and how much you want to have them involved in the project. Second, you provide them with a view of what you do as a leader. This will tend to increase understanding. Many team members who have never been project leaders mistakenly categorize the job as administration.

How to Solve Specific Team Problems

Observation over the years shows a number of problems that recur again and again in different types of projects. Here is a list of these, with suggestions on what to do when you encounter them.

Problem #1: You have absorbed a team member you do not want.

Upper management may stick you with a "turkey." What do you do? Instead of acting in a way that will show your attitude, look at the problem in a positive way. Determine the person's strengths and assign a noncritical set of tasks. Involve the person in meetings on issues. If this person proves to have valuable skills, continue to assign tasks and increase the responsibility involved in the tasks.

Problem #2: You have to replace someone.

Focus on having team members produce some milestone every two weeks. This will build momentum for the project and morale. If team members attempt to stretch the work out, get into the detail and narrow the scope of their work. Convey a sense that the project is changing and in transition. This is easiest to do with a part-time member of the team. Replacing a full-time member is a major issue. Divide up the member's work among a number of part-time people. This will avoid the team member resenting an individual replacement.

Problem #3: You have an enemy in your camp.

This is a team member who reports what is going on to managers and staff who are hostile to your project. This is very dangerous. How do you counter this? First, work to disseminate correct information to all team members, including those who are hostile. Second, establish direct contact with the line manager to whom the problem employee reports and have regular meetings to go over the project. Third, make the effort to meet with the employee and find out the source of these problem symptoms and get them resolved.

Problem # 4: A team member is not what you thought.

Suppose you thought that a certain team member was someone who really knew the technology and systems that were to be used in the project. But it turns out that the team member lacks in-depth experience. If this happens, what can you do? Cover the missing skills. Look for a part-time person who can perform the work. Try to have the team member work with this new person. If this fails, consider moving the team member to other tasks.

Problem #5: Two or more team members don't get along.

This problem is often encountered. Keeping the team small prevents some of this because there are fewer combinations of human relations. However, it can still happen. You want people to be individually responsible for work, then get together to work on issues. It may be that hostility surfaces at these meetings. Don't gloss over this or ignore it. Take a direct approach. Here is one: "We know that some of you don't get along and we recognize that this is part of human nature. This project is not going to solve problems with interpersonal relations. However, we have to tolerate each other to some degree to get the project completed. So let's make the best of it." In the meetings don't take sides on a personal basis. Keep the focus on the issue. Another action to take is to assign a task jointly between the two members who do not get along.

Problem #6: People become burned out.

Deadlines are tight in E-Business. Resources are limited. The same people are called upon to sacrifice their personal lives and work overtime and after hours. What you can do is take an active role in managing the overtime and extra work. Do not allow it to continue for an extended period. People will start to disappear. Absenteeism will increase. Productivity will plummet. Intersperse periods of heavy activity with forced periods of normal work. Do this even if the schedule has to suffer. As the manager, consider what can be done with the structure of the schedule to make up for the time. Build sympathy for the team with management so that they are aware of the heavy contribution being made. A rule of thumb is that the periods of heavy work should not exceed one or two weeks. Then there should be a two-week period of normal work.

Problem #7: Team members want to work on more interesting, but less important work.

If you force team members to work 100% on the important work, they will become resistant and will not work at all. Instead, go to them individually and ask what percentage of time they would like to spend on each activity. For the interesting work assignments, define precise, deliverable milestones that can be measured. This problem can sometimes be headed off by assigning a range of work at the start or by making weekly assignments.

Problem #8: Work is reassigned.

During any substantial project period, issues arise and changes occur. The project team must be flexible in responding to these new demands. At the start of the work, indicate to the team that assignments can be changed. The direction of the project may change. Indicate that you will warn people of impending change as much as possible within the bounds of your knowledge. Also, inform team members that you will have fewer, larger changes instead of many small changes. Many small project changes or continuous change can unnerve the team members and make them feel that the project is adrift.

Problem #9: The fate of a substantial part of E-Business rests on the shoulders of one employee, who is overwhelmed with critical tasks.

This problem is common and often occurs in cases where only one person has certain critical technical or business knowledge. This occurred, for example, in a natural gas distribution firm where only one person knew how the gas distribution system at a plant was designed and why it was designed that way.

Can this problem be prevented? At the start of the project, ask yourself what critical business and technical knowledge will be needed. Then try to find several people with these skills.

However, it may still happen that one person is critical. What do you do? Sit down with the person and indicate the bind the project is in and that his or her knowledge is critical. Ask the team member what help can be given by others. Ask what else is required to facilitate the job. Your objective here is to have the team member participate in working out a solution, based on the team member's unique knowledge and background. You can assign junior team members to work on tasks with senior team members. This "apprentice" approach has been successfully used throughout history.

Problem #10: Management wants to change the team in the middle of the work.

Management wants to remove a key person from your team. How do you respond? First, anticipate that this might happen when you are selecting team members at the start of the project. Assume the worst—that a member will have to leave at a critical time. Plan ahead by having team members do critical work in the early stages of the project, if possible. Second, when the request comes in, don't argue. Instead, develop a constructive transition plan.

Problem #11: Staff productivity is low.

Ask yourself why the staff is not productive. Go beyond the emotional and political areas. Consider what else they are working on in the project. Consider competing projects as well as nonproject work. Also, consider whether they have the entire set of skills needed to do the work. They may be trying to learn and to do the work at the same time. Spend time with the staff to find out what is going on. Your last resort is to restructure the work and narrow the tasks that they work on. Identify more near-term milestones.

Problem #12: New skills need to be taught to the team.

Don't feel that you have to train everyone at once. The effect would be to lower productivity overall. Instead, have two people learn the tool or skill. Then have them apply it immediately after they get the training. Set up a meeting in which they give their lessons learned to the rest of the team. If people know that the skill will be used immediately, they will absorb more during training. If they know that they will be discussing it with the team, they will be motivated to master the material and present it clearly. The learning curve for the other team members will then be reduced.

Problem #13: The people working on a subproject have difficulties.

In many projects, several people on a team are assigned to work on a specific set of tasks together (forming a subteam). These efforts often get off to a rocky start and have to be redirected later.

Here are some suggestions. First, get the members of the subteam together. Go over their roles in the subteam. What will each person do? Who has overall responsibility? How will they work together? Why were they put together? All of these questions should be asked and answered. Then get the subteam back together when an issue appears involving them. Use these meetings as opportunities to observe and ask how the subteam is working.

Problem #14: Task interdependence delays work.

The result of one person's task is required by another before he can begin his work. This is a recipe for trouble. Head this off in advance, if possible, by trying to eliminate these strict dependencies. If you must have dependencies, ask team members to plan what to do if another member is late. Get together with the dependent team members. Ask what one member can turn over to the other now so that he or she can start their work. Have them work together to become familiar with what the other is doing. If one encounters an issue, get the other involved in the process of resolution.

E-BUSINESS EXAMPLES

RICKER CATALOGS

At Ricker, each team member had specific tasks to perform, which were monitored. When an important issue arose involving scheduling, technical problems, etc., everyone met for no more than an hour and a half to discuss the issue. Individuals were praised who contributed to issue resolution as well as to milestone achievement.

This approach worked because people understood the importance of the issues and got an opportunity to see why the solution was important and what the implementation steps for the solution would be. People gained a sense of common purpose. After the meeting they went back to their desks and worked on their specific tasks.

MARATHON MANUFACTURING

Marathon followed the approach discussed in this chapter. By not involving many people early they gained more support from departments for E-Business. The project leaders made it a requirement that each team member brief the manager and some staff in their departments during the work on a regular basis. A number of the issues that surfaced in the project (over 40%) were handled by team members and not management. This increased the degree of the relationships among team members.

ABACUS ENERGY

Abacus was moving to replace their purchasing and contracting processes by E-Business. This naturally created a great deal of fear and trepidation among people in the department. Team members from the affected departments presented this as an issue. As a result, an early effort was made to identify future jobs for the employees assuming that the E-Business project would be successful. This calmed down departments and helped to involve the human resources organization in the work.

CRAWFORD BANK

Crawford Bank had to in essence form two teams. One team was within the subsidiary. Almost all team members there were full-time. The second team involved selected employees from the standard bank. Crawford project leaders faced the same challenge as Abacus. However, the threat was viewed as remote. There was also the fear that the bank was behind in E-Business.

E-BUSINESS LESSONS LEARNED

- **Look for achievement, rather than experience, when choosing team members.**
  You receive a resumé from a candidate with seven years of project experience on five E-Business efforts. All projects were completed. The candidate

looks good on paper, but remember: Project experience does not equate to project wisdom and learning. Find out how the person changed over those five projects. Some people repeat the same errors again and again. Also, the projects may not have had crises, so the candidate existed in a sea of calm. It is not the number of projects or the years of experience that are important. What counts is the demonstration of achievement and the ability to deal with issues.

- **Consider apprenticeship**.
  Junior staff are often intimidated by senior staff. Most projects and firms have no apprenticeship program where junior people are assigned to senior staff. The apprenticeship idea does work and should be considered. To handle this, consider sharing of ideas and experiences, as well as apprenticeship. Asking senior people to talk about a particular tool or method is a way for the sharing of experience and lessons learned.
- **Consider asking for only part of someone's time**.
  The people assigned to projects are often those with the fewest current duties. When a line manager is asked to assign someone to your project, he or she might first ask who is available, instead of figuring out who is the best person for the work. Remember, many line managers will get little credit for work on the project. If you ask for only a part of someone's time, you might get a better person than the one most available.
- **If you inherit the wrong people on your team, make the best of a bad situation**.
  Have you ever wondered, "How did these people get on that project?" You might attribute it to project change or just bad luck. Sometimes line managers put the least experienced and least valued people on the team by intent. If you inherit this, don't spend too much time or energy fighting it. Instead, try to make the most of the situation.
- **Before choosing a method, think about the skills needed**.
  Any method presumes that the people using the method have certain skills. This applies to basic language skills as well as to complex production systems. When you are considering a method, think about what type of person can successfully use it. If the method requires a star player, and you have few stars, the method is elitist and inappropriate.
- **Assign responsibility, then give team members the latitude of defining how they are going to work**.
  Many managers direct their team members like line managers directing hourly employees. How much time was put in? What was the hourly output? In most projects this is a portent for disaster. Managing the team by the clock will yield presence, but probably not results. Instead, be flexible. In one project, a team member worked on the project on weekends. She participated in meetings and worked at a slower pace during the week. This worked out well since it fit her lifestyle. The team was able to accommodate this.

- **Hold one person accountable for a detailed task**.
  Some managers like to assign a task to several people. They write on the project management form or in the software all of the resources involved in the task. The first problem with this is that you can never identify all possible resources required for all tasks. Second, the manager is not differentiating between assignment to the work and responsibility for making sure the work gets done. This act of delegation is very important. Assigning responsibility to one person is best.
- **Clarify team roles**.
  Do not assume that an experienced employee knows what his or her role is when he or she is assigned a task. Define the roles of each team member in front of the entire team. This will minimize misunderstandings later.
- **Eliminate excessive team communication**.
  Excessive communication among small groups can waste time and impact a team's effectiveness in a negative way. Watch for this to occur especially in E-Business.
- **Recognize that the risk and importance of E-Business lies in more difficult work**.
  Some people prefer to work on easy tasks to build volume. This is human nature. Be aware of this and tolerate it to some extent. The dividing line occurs when team members spend too much time on these small tasks at the expense of the larger tasks. To gain control, ask team members how their critical work is doing. Never ask about the small tasks. This will indicate that the reward structure favors the critical tasks.
- **Avoid polarization of the E-Business team**.
  This can be a byproduct of untreated issues. If you leave a critical issue unresolved, it may fester. People individually and collectively share their opinions. The team starts to polarize around the issue into opposing camps.
    Spend time in issue meetings on discussing the issue rather than the solution. If you are correct in analyzing the issue, then the solution is usually more direct. If you don't take any action after several meetings, the team senses a lack of management. If the issue awaits management approval for action, say so. Move on to other issues. Don't beat one issue to death.
- **Avoid giving financial bonuses and rewards for work**.
  This can backfire. For example, a software firm was missing deadlines for development. Financial bonuses were awarded to the key people on the team who were working on the critical tasks. Others saw what was happening and felt that their work was not valued. They slowed down in the hopes of getting a bonus. The project fell apart. The firm collapsed and was acquired by another firm. The software product never made it to the marketplace.
- **Vary project meeting dates and times to increase the level of awareness**.
  Routine weekly or biweekly meetings can lure team members into complacency. Often, the timing of a meeting does not fit with the issues at hand. At

other times, a lack of issues encourages team members to revert to small talk. Dump these meetings, as they are generally a waste of time. Consider more frequent meetings when there are many issues and less frequent meetings if things are calm.

- **Review test and evaluation results to raise morale**.
Most projects have milestones that have to be tested and evaluated. Many project managers lose out on a good opportunity here. They downplay this effort to concentrate on the development or design. But testing and evaluation are very important. They show the team what is passing and what is failing. They also provide a forum for sharing lessons learned. If the test results are negative, you can go over the reasons for this in an issue meeting and how this could be prevented in the future.

- **Focus on progress**.
Treating staff like children will produce amateurish results. When a manager badgers staff members for status and work results, he or she is like a teacher who checks students' work every day. What is the alternative? Since people are working toward milestones for their tasks, give attention to what has been done in working toward a milestone. What will come next? This provides indirect pressure on the person to get the work done. Also, you will obtain status by listening to a team member's statements in regard to how the work will be used.

- **Don't ask what you should have done; ask what you should do**.
Don't waste time looking back except to gain insight for the future. Learn the lesson from the past and then apply it to the future. Don't dwell on the past.

- **Work together to build a common vision of E-Business and the work**.
Doing work individually results in the whole being only the sum of the parts or worse. Underlying this point is the conflict between individual and group work. This will be an issue for centuries to come. It is probably a good idea to have a mix of both types of work to develop a common vision of what has to be done as well as to encourage individual initiative.

- **Keep in touch with team members who exit**.
Drop by to see team members who worked on the E-Business for months and now are no longer involved. Find out how they are doing. Let them know how the project is going. If you throw a party at the end of the work, make sure that they are invited. Tell management about the credit they deserve for their work.

- **Beware of team members who are very hard workers**.
Everyone tends to think of hard work as positive. It is, if it goes in the right direction. A team member who works too hard and fast can go far in the wrong direction quickly. They can become burned out.

- **Detect indirect resistance by team members through observation**.
People who do not agree with you often show this through physical appearance and body language. They may look down at the table. They don't look

you straight in the eye. They are noncommittal when you ask for their opinions or commitment. They are often silent in meetings. They do not seek you out to discuss problems and issues.

- **Consider involving as many people as possible from one department.**
  Widespread involvement will mean greater support and understanding of the project and its goals. It will also increase support for project results.
- **When people disagree, depersonalize the situation.**
  People who disagree strongly in a team can harbor this hostility throughout the project. E-Business and the team are hurt. How do you deal with this? Never allow emotions to get out of hand and personal. Instead, focus on issues. Indicate that many different approaches, tools, and methods are acceptable. Also, never announce that one side of an argument is a winner. This will just make the other side angry. Instead, think about how the solution can be presented as a compromise.

WHAT TO DO NEXT

1. Answer the following questions about teams.
   - Does your organization provide any rules, guidelines, or suggestions on roles and duties of team members on projects?
   - What is the mix of full-time and part-time team members on projects? Is an effort made to keep the size of the core team small?
   - Are lessons learned shared within the team on a project? Are they shared between project teams?
2. For the project you defined in earlier chapters (or a project selected as an example), identify the team members and their duties. Separate these into core team members and part-time members. Assign responsibility for the detailed tasks of your schedule. What skill areas are you missing? Where do you have gaps? The answers to these questions will provide information on the additional people you will require for the project.
3. If you are currently involved in E-Business, take this opportunity to assess the project team in the following areas:
   - Do some members of the team have too much to do while others are not busy? This is a sign that the team was not thought through or adjusted for workload.
   - Have you had many part-time members on the team? How are they treated? Is too much time spent getting them on board and later getting them to leave?
4. Sit down with the current schedule and task plan. Compare it with the first approved version of the plan. What are the major differences? How many differences can be attributed to changes generated by team members?

Chapter 5

Obtain E-Business Resources and Funding

INTRODUCTION

Negotiating for resources and transitioning them in and out of E-Business efforts are major roles of management. Resource management ranks in importance right up there with managing issues in E-Business. In this chapter we will look at some strategies for managing resources effectively.

Resources can be divided into the following categories:

- People—the project leader, the project team, support, and part-time players
- Equipment and services—machinery, tools, computers, telecommunications services, etc.
- Facilities—general and special purpose buildings and rooms, utilities, parking, etc.

Each of these is significant to E-Business. The people are obviously important. Equipment and services typically have to be upgraded and new computer equipment and network services installed for E-Business. Facilities are important, and in many cases the warehouse may have to be reconfigured to support smaller trucks since you must move the goods faster to the customer.

The last two chapters focused primarily on people—human resources. The extent to which equipment, supplies, and facilities play a role in a project depends on the industry. In a company, E-Business projects must compete head-to-head with other projects and normal, nonproject work for these resources and funding. You can be successful in getting an E-Business project approved, but then lose out in the battle to get money.

Equipment and facilities can require more management attention than staffing. In many cases, equipment and facilities have to be set up. The equipment may have to be calibrated. Staff may have to be trained to use the equipment. Support may be required during use. When the tasks have been completed, the equipment and facilities have to be moved or reconfigured.

E-Business may require many types of resources at different times. Critical resources cost money, affect multiple subprojects, and require meticulous planning in deployment and use. If you hold on to resources too long, you risk overrunning your budget. You may also be denying the resources to others, instilling resentment. If you are late in receiving resources, you may fall behind schedule. If you fail to obtain suitable resources, the project can be slowed and quality compromised. If you are not politically astute or careful, you can get the wrong resources assigned.

To think of managing all resources across the entire E-Business life cycle is overwhelming. Instead, center your attention on resources in each of the categories that are scarce, significant to critical tasks, or of special importance to you.

Here is a list of questions you can pose when considering a resource. If you answer yes to any of these, you are looking at a resource you will want to manage.

- Is the resource directly critical to multiple tasks?
- Do multiple subprojects and other outside projects require the same resource?
- Is the resource scarce and difficult to procure or build?
- Is the resource complex to use or apply?
- Is the resource part of a kit or collection that is critical to certain tasks?
- If the resource is a person, does the person possess significant skills and knowledge?
- Are resources being used and shared with nonproject work?

Surprises are bound to happen during E-Business efforts of substantial duration and scope. Resources that are needed through procurement may take longer to receive than anticipated; people are not available when you want them. To prepare for these contingencies, go back to the list of issues in the project concept and estimate what the impact would be of those issues not being resolved quickly.

MILESTONES

The purpose of this chapter is to help you reach five goals for E-Business.

- Define resources required for the E-Business subprojects.
- Determine the budget for E-Business.
- Schedule all aspects of resource management.
- Acquire the necessary resources.
- Determine when to release the resources.

METHODS AND TECHNIQUES

ACTION 1: DETERMINE WHAT RESOURCES ARE NEEDED AND WHEN

When the E-Business plan development was covered in Chapter 2, generic resources were listed in the E-Business template. More detailed resources were defined and associated with the detailed tasks to generate the specific schedule. The information in the template will provide the basis for what you are going to do in this chapter.

Consider each of the types of resources.

- *Human resources.* First determine if the people and skills are available internally in your organization. If they are, you may have to attract their interest and then negotiate for their participation. If you recognize that you require external support due to technical or engineering skills or specific knowledge, then you will be involved in the procurement process.
- *Equipment.* Consider commonly available tools and parts as well as any e-commerce software, hardware, network systems, and other equipment and services that E-Business requires.
- *Facilities.* Consider both general facilities, such as office space, and specific facilities, such as test facilities or special storage areas. Included here are utilities, telephone, parking, and other support associated with the facilities.

In all cases in which procurement is involved, be sure to define and place procurement steps in your schedule. The lead time for resources can be 90 to 120 days if you have to generate a Request for Quotation or Request for Proposal, receive and evaluate proposals, and negotiate with the selected winner.

Resource consideration fits in with financial management. Many cases of budget overruns result from keeping resources too long, having resources lie around unused, or mismanaging the resources during the work. In your budget planning, allow for some of these events.

ACTION 2: ESTABLISH THE BUDGET FOR E-BUSINESS

Begin with estimating the easy part of the budget. This usually includes facilities, equipment, and supplies. These can be estimated from previous experience. Save for later the more difficult part of the budget, which is to determine the personnel resource requirements. Then carry out the following tasks:

- *Task #1*: Use the project plan to develop a first cut at resource requirements. Get a resource spreadsheet view within the software. The rows are the resources and tasks and the columns are time periods. Export this into a spreadsheet for easier manipulation. Now look at the summary totals for each resource by month. Do these make sense? Are they too low? Often they are. Don't adjust the numbers in the spreadsheet. Instead, go back to the plan and project management software and modify your resource loading on the tasks. You may even encounter missing tasks. Continue doing this until you are satisfied that you have the major resources.

- *Task #2*: Now take the spreadsheet from Task #1 and add the resources for facilities, supplies, and equipment by task area. This will allow you to determine when you will be needing these resources. Another approach is to include these as resources in your plan.
- *Task #3*: You are now reasonably close, but you probably want to add some slack or padding to the budget for safety. Do this in the spreadsheet. If you do it in the plan, the schedule may be too unrealistic.

Even though you may be tempted simply to create a spreadsheet and put the budget items in, avoid this because the plan will not match up to the budget overall. Moreover, the budget will not match up to the requirements of when money is needed. If you link it to the plan, you have not only obtained a more credible budget, but also a more credible plan.

Budget for large E-Business efforts using a bottom up approach. That is, start with subprojects or individual projects, then aggregate these to get an overall picture.

ACTION 3: CREATE PROJECT OVERSIGHT

Unless your E-Business effort is small in budget, resources, and time, you should have management oversee the work in an organized way. This will provide a basis for dealing with issues and opportunities as well as a communications mechanism for management relations. It is best to consider a small steering committee—this will be easy to create.

Many managers are already overworked and overcommitted. It will be difficult to attract good managers. Look at the project and determine which departments are going to be involved. Go to the department managers with high-level tasks and milestones identified. Indicate the reasons they should be interested in the project. Point out that the committee will meet only for major milestone reviews and for issues that could not be solved at lower levels. This will show that you respect the various demands on the employees' time.

After getting some interest, hold your first informal steering committee meeting. Give the members of the committee an overview of the project and budget. Present the list of issues from the project concept. Do not ask for any decisions. The initial meeting should take no more than one hour.

ACTION 4: INTEGRATE THE RESOURCES INTO THE SCHEDULE

When you have identified the resources needed, schedule the following tasks in your plan for each resource:

- *Task #1*: Determine and document specific resource requirements.
- *Task #2*: For internal resources acquisition—
    - Identify resource candidates and determine their availability.
    - Negotiate for internal resources.
- For external resource acquisition—
    - Prepare necessary requests for external procurement in terms of schedule, duration, and requirements.
    - Procure external resources.
    - Negotiate for external resources.
- *Task #3*: Prepare resources for use in the work after acquisition.
- *Task #4*: Determine the release date for each resource.
- *Task #5*: Prepare the resources for release.
- *Task #6*: Release the resources.
- *Task #7*: Follow up on open items after resource use.

List these tasks in your schedule for each type of resource, even those that are not readily available, to avoid missing tasks as the work progresses.

Adding all of these tasks to the schedule serves a political purpose as well as an organizational one. Management will be aware of the effort required and they can provide support if the procurement hits a snag.

ACTION 5: DEFINE YOUR RESOURCE STRATEGY

This may sound like a vague action. However, most of the problems encountered in getting resources can be traced to a lack of thought and consideration early in projects. Don't assume just because the budget was approved that resources will automatically be assigned. These are two different steps involving decisions.

What should your resource strategy be? The first part of a strategy is to concentrate on resources required over the next three-month period. This will get you started. Don't ask for resources further in the future. Commitments may be meaningless since you haven't yet shown results. During the first few months, the project should begin to show results as initial milestones are achieved. Momentum will build. With this progress you can move to the next part of the strategy. With results in hand, approach management after the first month to begin seeking approval for resources in the next four to six months. These time frames are flexible, depending on the specific project. Continue with this pattern. You are seeking a rolling commitment based on continued results. This is much easier to accomplish than wholesale commitment at the start of the project. Management will also feel more comfortable because they will have greater control. At this point, establish priorities for trade-offs. Will you take a less desirable resource as a trade-off for lower cost? Are you willing to not have the resource when you want it in order to get the desired vendor? Get your priorities straight.

Prepare to position the project in terms of the techniques needed in negotiation and whether you get access to the best resources. Do this by answering the following questions:

- Who is responsible for the resources that you require?
  - Find out both who has direct responsibility and who has political responsibility.
  - For internal resources, begin contacting managers who control the resources at the start of the project or very early in the project. If you fail to do this early on, you will upset the plans of these managers when you require the resources.
  - For external resources, contact purchasing to determine the process for acquiring the resources, the various steps, and the schedule. Start building rapport with the staff in purchasing.
- What other projects and work are demanding the same resources? Remember that your project will be going on for some time. If your plan calls for a resource from the second to the fifth month of the project, consider any project that requires the same resources from now until the end of the sixth month or longer. Allow for slippage.
- What are the benefits of E-Business to management and their organizations after the project is completed? What is their self-interest in giving the resources to you? What are their objectives and goals?

You may already know people in upper levels of management. If possible, talk to them about the potential problems of getting the resources. Maybe they can introduce you to the managers of the needed resources, so you do not have to make a cold call.

ACTION 6: WIN THE COMPETITION FOR RESOURCES AND COMPLETE THE PROCUREMENT

With downsizing and rightsizing, many organizations do not have spare people, equipment, or facilities lying around. You may have to compete with other projects for resources. If you are the manager of the key project in the company, then you get priority. However, this is clearly the exception. The general situation is that you head up one project among many and the world will not end if the project is not completed. How do you compete?

A first guideline is to make sure that you have developed a realistic minimum requirement for resources. Tell managers that this estimate is truly a minimum and is realistic. You will have to be willing to negotiate for resources. Be ready to trade off.

A second guideline is to employ the E-Business team as part of a sales force to obtain the resources. This approach is preferred to appealing to upper management to force a line manager to release equipment or people to you. That approach will breed hostility because you will have removed the resources from the control of the line manager.

A third guideline is to follow your resource strategy. Aim at incremental commitment. You will tend to attract more support and resources with the momentum of success.

Let's turn to procurement. Provide purchasing or the line manager with the resource requirements, a copy of the project plan and schedule, the specific tasks that you desire to be performed, and the milestones or end products that you seek from the resources. Indicate how the tasks affect the overall schedule. The more information you provide, the more comfortable the managers and staff will be in trying to help you. The more vague you are and the less information you provide, the less likely you are to receive timely cooperation and support. Nail down your agreement in a memo of understanding that can help resolve any problems later.

ACTION 7: PLAN FOR THE TRANSITION OF RESOURCES INTO THE E-BUSINESS EFFORT

If you are bringing people on board, establish some kind of orientation for E-Business. Don't expect people to jump in without some sense of priorities, tasks, and the plan. Never assume that they were prepared or briefed by their own management in advance. Cover basic issues such as where they will work, how they will access the building, what telephones are available, and how parking will be handled.

If you are moving equipment in, make sure the necessary support (utilities, space, support staff, etc.) is in place. Often equipment arrives on time just to sit in a loading dock for several weeks because the organization was not prepared to receive it. The transition may also include training personnel in the use of the equipment.

Facilities can present challenges. Visit to see if the facilities are ready for your use. If additional work is to be performed to get the facilities ready, who will manage the work? Who will do the work? Who will pay for the repairs or cleanup?

ACTION 8: TRANSITION THE RESOURCES INTO E-BUSINESS

This is the actual transfer to the E-Business effort. It is possible that you may find problems immediately with the resources. The right people were not sent. The equipment does not work. The facilities have power problems. If this should occur, contact purchasing, management, or the vendor. Stop using the resource. Do not use the person on the project. Do not employ the equipment. Do not move into the facility. Usage can be interpreted as acceptance.

ACTION 9: DETERMINE WHEN TO RELEASE THE RESOURCES

Even as the resources are beginning to be employed in the work, define how and when resource usage will stop. Make sure that this is in your schedule. Develop a turnover approach for the release of the resources. In most cases this can be a simple checklist. Never allow the core project team members to accept these temporary resources as permanent. Also, reinforce the temporary nature of the work with the people who are brought into it so that there will be no misunderstandings.

The release of resources should be announced to the team. You will want to debrief people and get their lessons learned. For all resources, obtain feedback from the team on how the resources could have been put to better use and the lessons learned.

In your budget analysis, consider what percentage of the time the resources were effectively used. This can help pin down any budget variances. It can also make clear to the team the cost for resource waste.

If you have an opportunity to release a resource without significantly harming the work, then do it. Remember: in general, the fewer resources you have the better.

HOW TO COPE WITH CHANGING REQUIREMENTS

Here are some reasons that the resource requirements on a particular subproject may change after the E-Business work begins.

- *You find new information as you progress in the subproject.* This may alter the resources needed.
- *Management shifts requirements or direction.* Management decides on new requirements that the project must address. This can change the nature of the project entirely, including which resources are suitable. Changing requirements may occur in software systems, engineering, or marketing projects, for example.
- *A change in resources results from external information.* A competitor is about to introduce a product better than the one you are building in the project. Your

team is sent back to the drawing board for a new product. This may mean new resource requirements. Another external source of change is government regulation. A rule can change, impacting the underlying assumptions of a project. The same is true with new technology, which may replace technology currently in the project. This change may call for different staffing and skills.
- *You have alterations in timing of requirements and the amount or extent of the resource needed.*

How to Take Advantage of Resource Opportunities

An opportunity in this context occurs when a resource that is potentially useful to the work suddenly becomes available. To take advantage of this situation, do the following:

- *Keep an eye out for resources at all times.* Alert managers and your project team that you are always looking for resources—"A few good people."
- *When you hear about potential availability of a resource, analyze your plan to see what benefits you could reap from this.* Also, assess the financial impact on the effort.
- *Be ready to sit down and negotiate for the resources immediately.* Cut a deal.
- *Put the additional resources to work immediately.* You will not only appear organized, but you will also attract more opportunities later.

E-BUSINESS EXAMPLES

Ricker Catalogs

At Ricker, resources were given by management to E-Business along with funding at the start. There was no struggle for support. Things looked bright. However, no one thought about the fact that a number of the people assigned to E-Business would be needed back in their departments. No protest to management would have worked. It was essential for these people to return to their departments to work—to generate sales. This impacted the schedule of the project. Could anything have been done in retrospect? It was possible to hire additional people to handle the daily non–E-Business work. However, this was not done.

Marathon Manufacturing

Marathon assigned priority to E-Business and made resource allocation a major management activity throughout the life of the effort. This helped raise the level of interest and involvement in E-Business. Management also indicated to all employees that E-Business was going to be a key factor in their future. This approach generated employee support that continued due to management providing signs of commitment on an ongoing basis.

ABACUS ENERGY

The people who had to interface with suppliers for E-Business implementation were also the people necessary for negotiation and procurement. This conflict was evident from the start. Abacus decided to hire several temporary managers to support the daily work. This slowed the progress on E-Business initially as these new managers had to be trained by the current managers. However, the approach paid off later when E-Business implementation took up most of the managers' time.

CRAWFORD BANK

Crawford did not have any resource problems in the E-Business subsidiary. The problems with resources lay in getting management and key staff in the regular bank operation to support the E-Business project. Eventually, separate teams and plans were established to monitor and direct the involvement of these people in the E-Business implementation.

E-BUSINESS LESSONS LEARNED

- **Identify at the start as many resources as might be needed**.
  The more comprehensive your list, the lesser the chance you will be surprised later with a new requirement. Review your resource list once a month and update it.
- **Develop a transition strategy**.
  Not only must you have a good understanding of the resources required, but you must also be able to transfer resources skillfully and take advantage of opportunities. You must be able to come up with creative substitution approaches.
- **Seek incremental commitment from management**.
  Don't request too much over too long a period. Also, keep management up-to-date on the work and maintain their interest in E-Business.
- **Make sure that your approach to resources is integrated**.
  Consider resources in groups necessary to perform and support specific tasks. This is an integrated approach. If your approach is on the basis of in-

dividual resources, you will be more likely to miss some resources. You will also lack focus during negotiations.

- **Think, plan, and take small actions when a resource is added.**
  Often this is wiser than precipitous, decisive action. Employ the new resource on a trial basis to see the results. If the resource is a person, for example, and you take decisive action and hand over a task area to the new resource, the person may fumble around for weeks and hurt the effort.
- **Do not treat all subprojects equally.**
  Equality produces mediocre results. In considering resource assignment the first thing to discard is fairness. Subprojects have different levels of importance and benefits. No two are alike. Therefore, it doesn't make sense to treat them the same.
- **Keep infrastructures small.**
  Every project has an infrastructure. Included are files, methods, policies, procedures, and tools that are used in the work. In addition, all projects have a project manager, a project organization, and project support. It follows that many times more infrastructure means more control and structure. More structure may mean that decisions and action in the project take longer. Smaller infrastructures are more efficient.
- **Take on and manage some unsuitable people to contribute to political success.**
  In an ideal world, you could assume that only the best and brightest will participate in the work. In real life, you run into mediocrity. Also, E-Business may be the place a manager unloads an unwanted employee. Your first reaction might be to fight it, but at what cost to E-Business and your career? Keeping that team member may be politically beneficial. Look over your subprojects and see if you have any slack where this person could do some useful work.
- **Structure the work so that you will not need the best people.**
  E-Business progress can stall under internal competition for resources. Even large organizations may have only a few highly experienced and qualified people. In your plan never assume that you will get the best.
- **Work with fewer resources.**
  Can you do the work with less in terms of resources? This is one of the questions you should always ask during the work. Ask it of yourself before someone asks you. In an era of downsizing and efficiency, making do with less is essential. Remember, fewer resources means less to manage. It is also true that smaller projects get more done than large projects due to less need for coordination and a simpler chain of command.
- **Do not try to hold on to resources.**
  Do not hold on to resources that are not being used. You will become known as a person who hoards and wastes resources. Later, when you make new requests, it is more likely that you will be turned down.

- **Understand why people are motivated to be on E-Business.**
  It is important to understand why someone is on E-Business. Obviously, many possibilities exist—attention, risk, the desire to do something different, the desire to learn, etc. Even if a person is assigned to the project and has no choice, you can still probe for what that team member would like to get out of it. What do you do with information? You use it to your project's advantage. Structure the project so that the work gets done and people get some of what they want. It pays off.

WHAT TO DO NEXT

1. Answer the following questions about resources.
   - How long do people stay on projects in your organization?
   - Are efforts made to release resources as soon as possible?
   - Do your projects have resource strategies?
   - Are efforts made to get management to commit resources too early? Are many resource changes needed? Is there often a mismatch between the resources you have in the project and those that are needed?
2. For the project you developed in the first chapters, make a more complete list of people, equipment, and facilities that you require on the project. For each category of resource, identify the manager or vendor who can provide the resource. Identify alternatives to be used if the selected resource is not available.
3. Using the information from the list in Question 2, develop a GANTT chart in which the tasks are resources arranged or sorted by type. The schedule is the time that the resource is needed. This GANTT chart is a useful tool to help you plan resource transitions.
4. Return to your plan and insert the resource-related tasks that were identified earlier in this chapter.

Chapter 6

Use Technology Effectively to Support E-Business Work

INTRODUCTION

You must consider how you will use technology to support the management of the E-Business implementation. The proliferation of software tools that support workgroup and collaborative management have given a major boost to E-Business implementation. Some of the benefits are:

- Increased sharing of information among team members and with people outside of team
- Opportunities for team members to participate in defining and updating tasks and addressing issues
- Greater visibility of E-Business information that can support faster resolution of issues

However, if you manage E-Business without modern tools and methods, you will not receive any of these benefits and will likely have surprise problems come up. This happened at Ricker Catalogs. They had the tools, but the E-Business leader and team felt that they did not need them. Using them, they said, "would take too much time." When things started to fall apart, they then started to use the tools.

Let's define a few terms. A method in E-Business management is a defined technique for carrying out specific management tasks and activities. So a method is a step-by-step approach. You already saw a method in how we defined building the E-Business plan step by step. Methods are often easy to understand, but clumsy to implement and use without tools to help you out. Automated software tools provide the assistance to the method so that it becomes feasible to do. For example, at Marathon Manufacturing, upper management wanted widespread employee participation in E-Business lessons learned and other areas. Given the hundreds of employees, this would have been totally infeasible and impractical without software tools. Tools are essential for E-Business. An E-Business effort typically requires a great deal of collaborative work between IT staff, consultants, marketing, and other parts of the organization.

The above discussion shows that if you have a method, then you search for software tools. It also works in the reverse way. If you have identified a tool to employ in your E-Business work, then you must have rules and guidelines for using the tool. This is the method. Methods and tools go hand in hand. It is critical that everyone in the E-Business effort employs the same methods and tools for management. If they don't, then you will end up spending a lot of time reconciling the different results from the incompatible methods and tools.

There are both benefits and pitfalls to using specific methods and tools in E-Business. This points out the need for an overall strategy to make and support good choices. Pick some arcane method or tool and you could doom the E-Business effort—which has happened many times before. Let's list some benefits of having a strategy and using common, standardized methods and tools in your E-Business effort.

- Since you have a strategy, people don't have to waste time trying to fill in gaps in methods or tools.
- E-Business is a continuous program. Using the same methods and tools again in later efforts will add to your experience, lessons learned, skills, and knowledge of the methods and tools.
- The learning curve is reduced because you are using standardized methods and tools. People can help each other.
- Management information can be aggregated and analyzed more easily since everyone is working with the same stuff.
- There are more opportunities for collaborative effort since people are using the same methods and tools.
- There is an opportunity for greater predictability in future E-Business efforts. The same methods and tools reduces uncertainty.

Watch for these potential pitfalls with the use of methods and tools:

- If the methods and tools are not synchronized, benefits are reduced.
- People tend to be dazzled by a new tool. They adopt it without thinking of the method. Everyone adopts the tool a different way. Chaos reigns. Since E-Business is a long-term proposition, new tools will emerge and require careful evaluation.
- People can become too comfortable with a set of methods and tools. Without thinking, they apply the methods and tools to projects of all sizes and

shapes. The result is overkill and small projects become swamped with overhead and process.

- People resist new methods and tools. This is natural since many people feel most comfortable with the things that they know now.

Here is an example of failure. A retail firm had 12 different projects going on simultaneously. The firm was trying to implement E-Business, and EDI, store point-of-sale, conduct video training, perform scanning, and handle management controls, all at the same time. While all the project leaders followed the same method, they used a total of four different project management software tools. They also had set their schedules and plans up differently so that it was impossible to get an overall picture of what was going on. One project failed and dragged down two other projects. It was like dominoes. When the firm attempted to standardize its tools, it was too late.

MILESTONES

This chapter will identify the major activities where methods are needed. These will then be matched up with the appropriate software tools. Guidelines for both methods and tools for E-Business will be covered. In the end you will have developed a method and tool support strategy for E-Business management. The scope for the chapter includes all management activities.

Let's look at the downside if you just select methods and tools ad hoc without a strategy. Here are some specific situations we have encountered.

- A method for collaborative E-Business work was defined and mandated, but no tool was specified. It was then impossible to use the method. Management lost credibility.
- A project management software tool was identified. However, no guidelines were given for its use. Contractors and internal groups involved in E-Business set up their subprojects differently in the software. It was then impossible to combine the schedules into one overall schedule. The E-Business leader had to re-key summary data into yet another schedule. Isn't it great to reduce an E-Business manager down to the level of a clerk?
- There was no method or tool strategy at one firm. The firm was attempting to implement E-Business at three locations. With no strategy, each location picked their own mix of tools and methods. Some had methods and tools. Others only had tools. Can you guess the outcome? The schedule impact was later estimated at five months in slippage.

There are also political milestones. By enforcing the use of common methods and tools, the E-Business managers exert more direct control over the work. If people are using the same tools, there will be fewer opportunities for arguing about which tools are better.

METHODS AND TECHNIQUES

Let's identify a series of steps for methods and tools in E-Business management. Note that we are not considering the technical software, statistical, and other tools of the work itself—just the management.

- *Action 1*: Identify the management areas of E-Business where methods and tools are needed. This provides the scope of what you have to work with.
- *Action 2*: Define the method and tool strategy.
- *Action 3*: Evaluate and select specific methods and tools. This obviously fits the strategy in action 2 to the areas in action 1.

You might now be expecting the fourth action to be use the methods and tools. You would be wrong. Typically, there are gaps among the methods and tools. People may not agree on what to use. The software tools in a particular area may be viewed as undesirable by the team. This is real-life E-Business where people from different backgrounds come together to work—for the first time.

- *Action 4*: Identify and address any gaps in methods and tools for E-Business management.
- *Action 5*: Establish a support structure for the methods and tools for E-Business.
- *Action 6*: Rollout the methods and tools and enforce their proper use; measure the results of use.
- *Action 7*: Evaluate and implement a new method or tool.

Why go through all of this work when you are under so much pressure to get E-Business going? Because it provides the benefits stated earlier. It also will gain political support from the team because you are following an organized approach. Let's now examine each of the actions.

ACTION 1: IDENTIFY APPROPRIATE E-BUSINESS MANAGEMENT AREAS

Here is a list of management areas to address. Consider adding more for your specific E-Business effort.

- **Set up the E-Business schedule and plan initially.**
  The method should include a project plan template (see Chapter 2), along with lists of tasks and resources. Guidelines in the form of a step-by-step

approach should be given. The review method for the first version of the schedule should be identified.

- **Analyze and improve a schedule.**
  Support this with guidelines and examples. In addition, the availability of an "expert" helps. Look at the wording of tasks, split up long or compound tasks, reduce dependencies, and perform a specific "what-if" analysis.
- **Update and maintain the E-Business plan.**
  Support this with a formal method in which the E-Business schedule and plan are maintained on a network at all times so that they are visible. Update plans at least twice per week. Label detailed tasks as either "not started," "in process," or "completed." Summary tasks that are a rollup of several detailed tasks will have a percentage completely based on the detail underneath.
- **Modify and change the E-Business plan.**
  Changing a plan in a significant way in terms of schedule, resources, and deliverable items should require management approval. Changing task structure and assignments without impacting the schedule in a significant way does not require such approval. Support this policy with a detailed set of procedures on modification and updating.
- **Address issues and communicate within the E-Business team.**
  Draw up a common, standard set of procedures for handling and tracking issues. These can be supported by guidelines on how to identify issues. Also provide lists of issues.
- **Communicate and work with management and other people and organizations outside of the team.**
  Communication is often a matter of style. Different managers have many different styles. Without intruding on personalities, provide information on what organizations outside of the project can expect from the project team.
- **Assess benefits, costs, and risks associated with E-Business.**
  Have a standard set of rules for defining benefits and costs for each E-Business subproject. Don't deal with fuzzy benefits. Deal only in tangible benefits. The same philosophy applies to costs. How costs are applied to a project is unique to the specific subproject as well as to the organization.

Let's turn to tools that are candidates in E-Business management.

- Project management software
- Database management systems
- Groupware
- E-mail software
- Calendaring software
- Presentation software

Not everything is included. We did not include personal information management (PIM) devices or voice mail, for example. Both would be candidates for general use.

Next you can match up the areas with the tools. You can do this in a table where the rows are the areas and the columns are the tools. The table entry can contain the specific software and any comments of how the tool supports the methods for the area. Figure 6-1 contains an example for Marathon Manufacturing. You will use this table to identify gaps. If the team and leaders cannot agree on a tool in a specific area, then they can indicate this in the table.

ACTION 2: DEFINE YOUR E-BUSINESS MANAGEMENT STRATEGY

You seek an E-Business method and tool strategy that achieves the following goals:

- The first goal is *scalability*. That is, you want to be able to apply the method or tool to small as well as large projects. Also, plan for use with single or multiple projects.
- The second goal is *collaboration*. You want the method or tool to be compatible with having multiple people work with it on the same or different projects at the same time.
- *Modernization* is a third goal. You want a strategy that will accommodate new methods and tools in a smooth manner.
- *Measurability* is another goal. You want to be able to measure the effectiveness of the method or tool so that you can be assured that you are employing it effectively.
- *Formulating lessons learned* and improving at project management over time are also major objectives.

Use these elements of your strategy to evaluate and select the methods and tools. A method and tool strategy goes beyond selection; it includes support and direction on how to increase skills on a cumulative basis over time. Your strategy should indicate, generally, how the following will be addressed:

- Who the E-Business team will go to with questions
- How lessons learned in using the methods and tools will be gathered and then used later
- How to disseminate guidelines and lessons learned to the team and others
- How to enforce and measure the use of the method and tools

ACTION 3: SELECT THE METHODS AND TOOLS

You should select the methods first and then the tools that support the methods. If you do the reverse, then you are likely to end up with an incomplete method. When evaluating and selecting methods and tools, you must keep in

| | Tool | | | | | |
Area	Project management software	Database management systems	Groupware	E-mail	Calendaring	Presentations
Setup plan	Microsoft Project; standard templates; collaborative work	Uses issues and lessons learned data bases in Microsoft Access	Issues data base with Lotus Notes	Microsoft Exchange	Microsoft Outlook	Microsoft Powerpoint
Analyze/improve plan	Microsoft Project		Lotus Notes	Microsoft Exchange	Microsoft Outlook	
Update plan	Collaborative use of Project		Lotus Notes	Microsoft Exchange		
Modify plan	Organized changes		Lotus Notes	Microsoft Exchange	Microsoft Outlook	
Issues	Customize project	Archive issues with Microsoft Access	Lotus Notes	Microsoft Exchange	Microsoft Outlook	Microsoft Powerpoint
Communications	Shared files on network		Lotus Notes		Microsoft Outlook	Microsoft Powerpoint
Benefits/Risks	Microsoft Project with customization		Lotus Notes			Microsoft Powerpoint

Figure 6-1: Area and Toole Table for Marathon Manufacturing

mind what the rest of the organization is doing, what your contractors, suppliers, etc. are using, and the trends in the industry. You cannot afford to select in isolation.

Examine large and complex projects that were successful. This will give you ideas about methods. You should also be able to expand on the methods presented in these chapters. Here are more specific method selection guidelines:

- **Consider methods that use everyday language.**
  A method that employs arcane words is too much work and effort without the additional payoff. People will not use the terminology anyway since it is not familiar.
- **Pick all methods at the same time.**
  For each of the method areas listed earlier, identify a specific method. Then sit down and determine how someone would work with the total set of methods. Or, do they overlap so that their use becomes counterproductive?
- **Evaluate scalability and flexibility.**
  Here is a test. Choose three projects of different sizes. These can be in the recent past or present. Next, choose several projects that are very different from each other. Apply the method to all of these. How do they scale up?

Now return to the table in Figure 6-1. Review each of the tools in the table to see if these are the ones that you really want. If they are, fine. If there are several candidates, then you must select now. For example, you can store issues and lessons learned in either or both groupware and a database management system. Which do you choose? Here are some guidelines.

- The default is usually to select what your company currently uses. This eliminates training, software costs, and lead time for setup. However, there are cases where the current tool is not satisfactory. It might be, for example, an old version of a software tool.
- Pick the most popular software tool for the type of software. This will probably be accepted easily and save you from receiving heat politically.
- Select the tool that your team members know.

ACTION 4: IDENTIFY AND ADDRESS ANY METHOD OR TOOL GAPS

Using the previous work, you will find cases where you have a need for a specific method or tool and there is nothing from the previous action that meets the need. You can have the method without the tool, the tool without the methods, or be lacking both. For each gap, consider the importance and urgency of filling the gap now. If you wait, what will you lose and how will E-Business suffer? Time is somewhat on your side in that new methods and tools may appear later.

Now you are left with gaps that must be filled. Begin with identifying the potential tools to fill each gap. Evaluate the tools first to eliminate ones that are too expensive, have long learning curves, and lack compatibility with other tools, hardware, and software. This process of elimination will narrow the field. With the finalists identified, then you can select based on the quality, goodness of fit, completeness, and learning curve.

This approach should handle most if not all of the gaps. However, there may be a case where you really need something, but there is nothing available. What do you do then? Go for the method, and implement manual methods or ones that use the acceptable tools. This is not ideal and is a forced fit, but it does support your strategy.

ACTION 5: ESTABLISH A METHOD AND TOOL SUPPORT STRUCTURE

Here is a list of what you need to address to support your strategy:

- Method and tool experts
  - Who are these people?
  - How will their time be paid for to provide help?
  - How can you motivate them to provide the help and not turn people off?
  - How can you extract their knowledge and convert it into guidelines?
- Guidelines and lessons learned
  - How will you initially construct guidelines?
  - How will the guidelines be validated?
  - How will the lessons learned be interpreted, organized, and used to improve the guidelines?
  - How will training in the guidelines be performed? Will there be any training?

ACTION 6: ROLLOUT THE METHODS AND TOOLS AND UNDERTAKE ENFORCEMENT AND MEASUREMENT

As preparation for initiating the new methods and tools, answer these questions:

- How will exceptions to the general methods be addressed? Will people improvise, or are additional procedures necessary?
- Will the methods and tools be applied to all subprojects? If so, how will they be retrofitted onto existing work? Who will pay for the learning and familiarity time? How will they be applied to very small and very large E-Business subprojects?

- Who will serve as the tool expert? Will this person be involved in training others? Is the expert going to be easy to reach when help is needed?
- How will the methods and tools used be monitored to ensure proper use? What constitutes proper use?

Here are three steps to use as you implement methods and tools:

- *Step 1*: Start small. Begin with several small subprojects. Learn from these subprojects to build lessons learned and guidelines. Document and use these guidelines and step up to larger E-Business subprojects.
- *Step 2*: Build the E-Business schedule with multiple parts and do a cross-project analysis. This demonstrates the added benefits of standardized methods.
- *Step 3*: Analyze and perfect the methods and tools. This way, many more people will be able to use the revised methods and tools successfully.

Here are a few words of caution:

- Keep management fanfare and endorsements to a minimum to avoid bad feelings.
- Do not implement the approach on the entire E-Business implementation or on large subprojects where work is far along. This will slow progress as people attempt to learn and use the new tools and methods.
- Test methods and tools so that you have experience with them before asking others to implement them.

Once you have rolled out the methods and tools for use and work has started, the questions that arise are:

- Are team members using the methods and tools properly?
- What are the benefits and other characteristics of use?

The first question deals with enforcement. The second addresses measurement. You can try heavy-handed enforcement with the team. However, this is very likely to fail given the intense pressure to deliver on E-Business. An alternative is to use these lessons learned.

- Monitor the use of the methods and tools through results and milestones.
- Orchestrate lessons learned sessions to share experiences with methods and tools.
- Have the team members make comments about the existing guidelines and methods.

You can then update the guidelines. This approach is more passive, but we have found it to be more effective.

Here is a list of what you might look for in measurement.

- How many different schedules exist? Are they being tracked for the same work? If there are many, then a common effort will reduce redundancy.

- Are many project meetings consumed in getting exact data on the status of a project and resolving discrepancies between different plans? If so, then issues are not being addressed.
- How long does it take for an issue to be resolved after it has been identified? If the answer is "Too long," time is probably being wasted while people spin their wheels waiting for decisions.
- What comments do people make concerning the current process? Solicit and collect comments from team members.

Here is a list of questions you can ask about your methods and tools.

- Is there consistency between subprojects of E-Business? This refers to structure of the plans and whether they follow similar templates.
- Can you assemble an overall schedule composed of the detailed schedules? Will it make sense?
- Have the E-Business managers identified issues and are these being addressed?
- Is there a table of issues vs. projects to see what different subprojects have common issues?
- Are people asking for help in using the methods and tools?

Prepare an evaluation report of current methods and tools and circulate this to lay the groundwork for introducing change. In E-Business this is important because it helps you build consensus. Here is an outline for such a report:

I. Introduction—purpose and scope.
II. Overview of current project management process, methods, and tools, describing what is being done today.
III. Issues with the current methods and tools. List the issues and describe their impact on the organization and projects. Use specific anonymous comments from staff.
IV. Summary—the cumulative impact of all of the problems.

ACTION 7: EVALUATE AND IMPLEMENT A NEW METHOD OR TOOL

E-Business work continues indefinitely. New software tools and methods appear. In general, when something new appears, you follow the actions that you have just read. Here are some additional guidelines.

- Be open to new methods and tools. The appropriate and most suitable new ones can save time and money.
- Be skeptical of any new method. Compare it to what you have in common English. Kill off the jargon if there is any.

- For any method specify what tools are needed and vice versa. In this way, you are considering a complete solution.
- For new tools think about the learning curve, the conversion from the current tool, how you will drop the old tool, and how the new tool meshes with the ones that remain.
- Trade off the benefits with the risk, cost, and effort to implement and use the new method or tool.

How long should these actions take? Not long. The elapsed time in our experience is about several weeks for actions 1–4. Action 5, the setup, takes time because it includes training, software installation, customization, etc. Action 6 is dependent on the situation. Action 7 follows the same earlier actions.

GUIDELINES FOR E-BUSINESS MANAGEMENT TOOLS

The most current generation of project management tools provides some or all of the following:

- Standard project management features
- The capability of sharing project information, a plan, and a schedule in a network
- A means to delegate tasks in the project to staff
- A way for staff to update management and communicate with management regarding the staff's tasks
- Consolidation and tracking of all work

Such a software package combines a database of project information, project management software, electronic mail, and groupware. It offers the benefits of an integrated approach for tools. It is simpler than having a grab bag of tools.

If such a tool is not available, assemble a unified set of methods that draws upon specific tools. Integration is provided through the methods and not the tools. Take every item in the plan and define the procedures and tools. You could then expand on this with specific guidelines for small, medium, and large subprojects, as well as for multiple subprojects. The manager and team members can now work together with methods for identifying and resolving issues. They can track progress and identify areas of risk.

Here are some guidelines to help carry out E-Business management tasks.

- **Project management software can have data resident on a network to allow sharing of the files.**
  Establish the basic project plan on the network with the baseline plan (agreed-upon plan), the actual results, and an estimated plan for the future. They can add more detail to their part of the plan. Encourage people to review and update their schedules once a week and maintain their own tasks. The danger is that people make mistakes, so save the file frequently during the week.

The project plan has fields for the person responsible, whether the task is management critical or has risk, and the issues that pertain to the task. These are put in individual text fields associated with a task. These fields are then searchable.

- **Electronic mail software supports attaching project files.**
  Electronic mail can also be used as a vehicle for sharing and routing information. The limitation of electronic mail is that it lacks the database elements of groupware. It is freeform, which will cause problems later when you want to do analysis. It is often better to use the electronic mail within the groupware to add structure.

- **Groupware or a shared database tracks issues and action items.**
  Groupware allows you to carry out a dialogue for managing a specific issue or updating the plan. Groupware has been employed for several international projects. It was found that the elapsed time to obtain decisions and resolve issues is cut by more than 50 percent.

  The issues database contains all of the information pertaining to an issue or opportunity. The database is stored on the network so that people can update the issue information. Data related to status, assignment, resolution, description, category, and tasks that relate to the issue are all in the database. You can now put the issues and project plan together. You can search the project plan, filtering the plan to obtain only those tasks that relate to an issue or are dependent on other tasks. Alternatively, you can search the database for all issues pertaining to a specific task. Establish a similar database for both lessons learned and action items. If you employ standardized templates of high-level tasks, the results are even better, since anyone who employs the template can access the lessons learned for specific tasks.

- **A spreadsheet can be used for project analysis.**
  Spreadsheets can help overcome some of the limitations of project management software. Most project management tools allow you to assign costs through resources. You can input standard and overtime rates and vary the calendar for specific resources. Some project management packages support earned value work and financial calculations. However, this is often too inflexible. Establish a table of data from the project database and then export the table to a spreadsheet. The spreadsheet can then be manipulated and analyzed to obtain cost and resource reports.

Begin with project management software that supports customization of data elements and views such as GANTT charts as well as sharing of E-Business data on a network. The software should support rolling up subprojects into an overall project. An example is Microsoft Project, but there are other software packages that are Internet based as well.

At a minimum, employ a database management system (dbms) for issues and lessons learned. This dbms should be compatible with the project management software so that data can be shared by people on the team.

In terms of methods it is important to customize both software tools for not only E-Business, but also for other projects and regular work. Why? Because you will need a method to allocate staff between working on E-Business and other projects. Recall that many of the people on your E-Business team will be working on other things. We suggest a regular allocation method to be used weekly or on a two-week basis to do staff allocation for the next period.

What does the future hold? It is evident that the tools are becoming more supportive of collaborative work. This bodes well for project management. It will eliminate some of the concern that people have for using project management. As it becomes easier to do, you will be able to use the tools for smaller projects. The use of the Internet provides standards for data sharing between firms and supports compatibility. Thus, you should see more effective projects between companies—very good for future E-Business. The availability of collaborative tools will also mean good project managers can take on more work if their time is freed up. This should encourage more parallel effort.

The Cost of Method and Tool Implementation for E-Business

Implementing modern collaborative scheduling and tools is neither inexpensive nor easy, possibly involving hundreds of people and requiring a tremendous time commitment. Using a multiphase implementation approach will help by spreading the cost over a longer period.

Some of the major cost elements if you have to implement new methods and tools are as follows:

- Hardware, software, and network upgrades
- Application software licenses
- Training and documentation costs for the new tools
- Staff time to learn the new methods
- Learning curve and coordination effort to get everyone to use the methods and tools in compatible ways
- Management time to measure and evaluate the new tools and methods
- Potential customized software development to provide additional features
- Conversion effort to move current schedules and data to the new tools
- Negative impact on the E-Business work due to the diversion

Potential Problems and Opportunities

Even with analysis, organized planning, and necessary support, problems arise with the implementation of new methods and tools. Here are some common problems encountered, along with suggested remedies.

- *Resistance to new methods and tools.* This is natural since some team members may have used the previous methods and tools for years. Concentrate on winning over the younger staff members who are less resistant. As an E-Business leader, be a strong advocate of the new methods and tools through the methods of tracking the project, resolving issues, and maintaining communications.
- *Complaints that the new methods or tools take too much time.* Review how the team members are using the methods and tools that they are complaining about. Hold a meeting specifically to address how to use these. Have team members demonstrate how these methods and tools would be helpful.
- *Resistance to formal methods and tools.* Perhaps you are asking for more detailed methods and tools than the team members are accustomed to using. To counteract this attitude, show the team members that the more formal methods and tools free up time that can be better spent dealing with issues.
- *Team members raise new ideas on how to do management.* Don't discard these. Try to get them reviewed and, if feasible, adopt them. This will show that you care about your team members and their ideas. And, of course, exceptional ideas can come from any team member.
- *A new software release appears.* Team members are enthused and want to use it. Always be ready to carry out a pilot effort to evaluate new tools. Retain project information on an old project and use this to test the new tool. Always consider possible hidden costs of using something new.

E-BUSINESS EXAMPLES

RICKER CATALOGS

Ricker decided to employ project management software for the overall planning, but decided to use a spreadsheet to keep track of issues and lessons learned. Everyone was familiar with the spreadsheet but not with database technology. There was no linkage between the software except for reference data elements (numbers of tasks and issues, for example). Ricker had not used project management software before so there was a learning curve.

While the software proved useful, the project management software was not used by line organizations or other projects so that resource allocation had to be done manually. This cost a substantial amount of time in coordination.

MARATHON MANUFACTURING

Marathon decided to extend their use of groupware to E-Business. They also had been using project management software for manufacturing projects so it was a natural step to employ it in E-Business. The groupware worked well since it not only substituted for the database, but allowed people in different locations to work on lessons learned and issues.

ABACUS ENERGY

For Abacus Energy, E-Business had a narrow scope in terms of purchasing and contracting. Initially, the E-Business leader thought that the use of the tools described in this chapter would be overkill. This turned out to be a mistake. Abacus employed two consulting firms to help with the E-Business implementation. They each had their own project plans. Coordination turned out to be a minor nightmare. Finally, they had one of the firms be the keeper of the overall project plan.

CRAWFORD BANK

Crawford had employed project management software so they immediately used this. They did not consider that they should track the issues so this was not done except through e-mail and word processing. As issues recurred, they began to consider issue tracking. However, it was basically a manual process.

E-BUSINESS LESSONS LEARNED

- **Compensate for the inexperience of an E-Business manager.**
  This inexperience tends to be reflected in two major areas. First, the manager cannot provide perspective on the status and direction of the project, since the project is new to them. Second, the manager has a difficult time sorting out which issues are important and how issues are related.

  Assist a new E-Business manager in developing the plan and setting direction. After that, monitor how the issues in the project are being addressed.
- **Look over all of your tools and methods to see how they fit or conflict.**
  Methods and tools conflict in different ways. They can require duplication of effort. They may require you to do manual work to take the results from one tool to another. Different tools may not support the same level of detail.

  In such a conflict, often one tool or method will dominate and the other will fall into disuse. Which wins? It may be the one that is easiest to use. It may be the one that is politically correct. It is not necessarily the best or most complete. This means that you have to keep a close watch on conflicts as they arise.

- **Base management directives on reality.**
  A manager may attend a seminar and become a believer in a certain tool. The manager spreads the word that the tool will be used. But if planning for integration is not performed and followup or enforcement is neglected, the tool will not be used. The manager's credibility may be jeopardized.
- **Do not add a new tool or method in the middle of the E-Business effort; this will generally slow progress.**
  If a project extends for more than a few months, it is subject to the "tool of the month" syndrome. This occurs because somebody is trying to sell the new thing. Management may feel that it may make a difference. If someone says to you, "why not try it out?", beware, there are hidden costs. You first have to divert resources to understand it. Then you have to use it. You also have to fit it in with everything else.
- **Test the method first on an E-Business subproject as a pilot.**
  Pilot projects cannot easily test both methods and tools concurrently. After the method has been tested, then people in the pilot project will have many specific ideas on tool requirements. If a pilot project attempts to test the tool and the method together or the tool alone, then the focus of the pilot is on learning the tool. Guidelines for future use of the tool will be missing, since the method was not validated.
- **Do not ignore gaps in tools.**
  This reinforces what was discussed earlier. A tool gap may occur when you have to manually load data from one tool into another. Another gap occurs when you have to perform manual work because there is no tool. A gap results in more manual effort and is more prone to failure and frustration. This increases the pressure on the team since each team and manager must cope with each and every gap. This can lead to sharp falls in productivity and accuracy of information.
- **Look for interfaces between new tools.**
  When a car is modified for a new air conditioner, it is often the case that the team does not think adequately of all of the interfaces with the engine. An example of bad design occurred with a car where the entire air conditioner had to be disassembled to service the engine. How about that—a $500 tune-up? It is the same with tool interfaces. Interfaces include data, procedures, and human interface. Data may not only have to be converted but changed to fit the next tool. People don't want to hear this. They want to test drive the shiny new tool.
- **Assign an expert to every tool.**
  Even simple tools require someone who will watch to see that the tool is being used properly. Remember that the job of the expert goes beyond answering questions. It is also to see that the tool is being employed properly and that the expected benefits of the tool are obtained.

- **Allow for the uncertainty inherent in projects rather than adhering to excessive use of formal methods and tools.**
  E-Business implementations are part science but also part art. Along with the element of uncertainty, projects involve emotions, feelings, and politics. Projects cannot be reduced to a science by quantifying them and then applying formal rules. Quantitative methods have a value, but this value is limited.
- **If someone pitches a new method or tool, only believe that it works when it works in E-Business and other projects that share resources with you.**
  A method or tool depends on the project and its environment for its success. It is working when you see it working, not when people say it is.
- **Gain proficiency in tool or method use through experience rather than through study.**
  Suppose you buy some home accounting software and set it up on your machine. After an hour you get bored. You decide that instead of sitting at the computer, you'll read the manual. That helps, but you will not understand and retain what you are reading unless you go back to the keyboard and try it out. Reading about a method or tool is not as effective as hands-on experience.
- **Look over all of your tools and methods to see how they fit or conflict.**
  Tools and methods can conflict in different ways. They can require duplication of effort; they may require you to do manual work to take the results from one tool to another. The tools may not support the same level of detail. If tools overlap, then you will end up taking data from one tool and entering it into another. An example is when a consultant uses their own version of the same tool, but theirs is customized differently.
  When two methods or tools conflict, it is not always true that the best one prevails. The victor may be the easiest to use. It may be the one that is politically correct. Keep an eye on potential areas of conflict and take an active part in resolving the conflict in the way that most benefits the project.
- **When considering a method, think about the type of person that can use the method.**
  Any method presumes that the people using the method have certain skills. This applies to basic language skills as well as to complex production systems. If the method requires a star player, and you have few stars, the method is elitist for the small group. Missing skills may mean failed methods.
- **Train close, but not too close, to the time of implementation.**
  If those trained do not use what they have learned, they will gradually forget. Six months later you will have to retrain. Conversely, if training is done right before a major use, this can cause people to feel pressure.
- **Understand how methods work together.**
  Learning one method is relatively easy, involving only one set of procedures and experts. But when you use several methods, problems occur. You have

to rely on documentation and procedures written by different people for different purposes. Be sure to fill in the linkage. Make sure people understand how to move between methods and tools.

To be effective, use methods consistently and frequently. If you use the method in different ways, you are less likely to develop proficiency and skill, since you are just adapting. House plants are frequent victims of this. People neglect them, then pay too much attention and overwater them.

- **Avoid resource leveling.**
A method that is supported in many project management systems is resource leveling—don't use it.

  Resource leveling is when the project management software attempts to solve overcommitment of resources by moving tasks around within the boundaries of slack time. This is a good idea and feature in principle but it is not practical. In many systems, you cannot undo the leveling. Watch for this feature in your software and compensate for it. Use manual resource leveling in which you move tasks and changes are reflected in a resource graph.

- **Imposing some tools may mean other subversive tools are used in the organization.**
Market methods and tools to staff and managers based on appealing to their self-interests. If upper management declares everyone will use a tool, people will pay lip service to the tool, but they may not actually apply it to basic procedures.

- **Avoid overtraining.**
Overtraining in tools can lead to inertia. You probably have seen this many times in larger organizations. Rather than no training, the organization errs on the side of too much training. People can become so bored and disinterested that any desire that they had to learn about the tool is dissipated.

- **Calibrate your tools.**
Calibration means that the parameters for using the tool and interpreting results are in place. An example of a need for calibration is when you implement a statistical software package that has three levels of difficulty. The proper calibration depends on the level of experience and knowledge available on your team.

- **Track both effort and elapsed time.**
This difference is subtle. Elapsed time is typically the duration of the task. Effort is the total number of hours that are being allocated to the task. If no resources are assigned to the task, these are the same in the software. Elapsed time is affected by the calendars and work periods that are employed.

  For example, if three people work 20 hours on a task, the effort is 60 hours. The elapsed time, assuming one shift of work per day, is $2\frac{1}{2}$ days.

However, if they work a shift and a half with overtime, then the elapsed time is less than two days. Be sensitive to the effects of changing calendars and schedules when effort and elapsed time are calculated.

WHAT TO DO NEXT

1. Here are some questions to ask about your methods and tools.
   - Do you have a standard list of methods and tools for project management in your organization?
   - How has the list of methods and tools changed over the past few years? Is there a formal method for updating and replacing specific methods and tools?
   - Does your organization employ or endorse software tools that are network-based in which information can be shared?
2. Evaluate your current methods and tools. Begin with the list given earlier in this chapter. In the first column, write each area of E-Business management. Write down the method used in each area in the second column. Write down the tool used in the third column. Next, make a list of issues and problems that you have observed with current project management methods and tools. Put these in a row in the first column of a second table. The second column of this table should contain the area of E-Business management from the list. A third column can contain the impact of each problem. The first table shows what you have; the second indicates the gaps.

Area of E-Business Management	Method	Tool

Issue	Area of E-Business Management	Impact

3. Define what tools you would like to have to use with the software your firm already owns. Again, you can use a table. In the first column, list the tool areas. In the second column, give the proposed tool. The third column is for the current tool. The fourth column can contain the benefits of transitioning to the new tools.

4. Estimate the cost and time to implement a new set of tools. Write down answers to the following questions:
   • How many PCs will have to be upgraded for the new tools?
   • Will the network have to be upgraded?
   • How many people will have to be trained in the new methods and tools?

5. In your project defined earlier, identify the methods and tools you would like to use. Compare this to what your organization employs. What advantages are offered by those you would like to use? What are the limitations of the company's unselected methods and tools?

Part II

Manage Your E-Business Implementation

Coordinate Your E-Business Activities

INTRODUCTION

In E-Business you communicate throughout the day. You will spend many hours explaining E-Business, dealing with issues, making presentations, and in general trying to keep things running smoothly through communications. You work side-by-side with team members. You talk with people from other projects. You send and respond to reports, memos, telephone calls, and electronic mail. You might be performing good work, directing people well, and showing good results, but poor communication within and outside of the team can negate all the things you are doing right. In this chapter and the next we cover communications. This chapter focuses on types of reports and presentations and provides guidelines for different media forms. The next chapter considers your communications with management on specific issues and activities. This chapter is process-oriented; the next chapter is issues-oriented.

Here is an experience and a lesson learned. A presenter was fourth on an agenda to deliver a presentation to a board of directors. Each presentation went over its allotted time. Each presentation was slick, featuring fancy graphics slides, some with animation. She sat there with her black-and-white static transparencies and wished she was at home or at the beach—anywhere but in that room.

When her turn came, she had very little time left. Some board members were starting to gather up their belongings so that they could leave. Others were nervous or bored. This was an important presentation that would determine the funding of the project. She decided to cut to the chase. She began with the problem that the project was to face—to create a product that would generate revenue. She outlined the benefits of the proposed product and discussed competition, showed an outline of the plan, and closed by asking for approval to start. This all took less than ten minutes and used only four transparencies.

How did it come out? Her proposal was the only one approved. One board member indicated that if the other presenters had spent as much time on the content of the plan as on the fancy graphics, the result might have been different for them. The lesson learned was to focus more on content than on format.

Many people take communications and presentations to extremes. They spend too much time worrying and preparing. Others just walk into a room and ad-lib. The purpose of this chapter is to help you take a balanced approach to communications. Take each contact, presentation, or telephone call seriously. Be ready to address almost any aspect of the E-Business effort at a moment's notice.

Conveying the message is very important in communications. This goes beyond getting a single message across one time. Communications involve building and maintaining communications paths with many different people, since projects involve team activities and decisions. Communications are also useful for gathering information and resolving problems more effectively. To reach the goal of a balanced approach to communications, you will define each action in the communications process, considering almost all forms of communications, formal and informal.

MILESTONES

There are many milestones. Each time you give a formal presentation, it is a milestone. Informal presentations and meetings are minor milestones as well. You can attempt to sail through the E-Business effort and not assess how you are doing. This is a mistake. You should keep evaluating yourself with each milestone. Your goal is to become more comfortable with making presentations and dealing with E-Business issues.

METHODS AND TECHNIQUES

In E-Business you should always be ready to communicate effectively. Beyond the ability to address issues and crises, this is one of the most important attributes of a good leader. If your demeanor is sour or down, then your audience may interpret this as an indication of a problem in the work. It is alright to show anger, concern, or worry if that helps in getting an issue resolved or in advancing E-Business.

ALTERNATIVE COMMUNICATIONS MEDIA

Communications have become more complex because you have to communicate with more people than people did in the past. Also, you have more choices of the medium of communications. Here is a short list of the possibilities, with specific guidelines on using each one:

- **In-person informal communications**
  This is best for discussing something or gathering information. You can get a better overall impression of what is going on if you go to a person's office rather than running into someone in the hallway. Many different topics can be explored in this casual atmosphere. You get more of the person's attention without interruptions. When you stop by, indicate why you are there, what information you need, and how much of the person's time you need.

  If someone contacts you, be ready with a smile, and look the person in the eye. Always be ready for any informal visit. You might even enter your own office as if you are a visitor and see what impression you are conveying.

  Whether you are the sender or the receiver, check facial expressions. Does the person you are talking with appear closed up by having legs or arms crossed? Do either of you appear nervous? Scan what is on a person's desk. It will tell you what the person's priorities are.

- **Formal meetings**
  This is a chance to cover topics with a larger audience in a structured format. More ground can be covered. There is an opportunity to gain consensus. Formal meetings require more preparation and thought.

- **Telephone**
  This is a good medium for following up on specific nonpolitical points if the person is remote from you. If you are on the receiving end of a call, answer with a greeting and your name. Let the caller do the talking. Just listen. Try to detect from the caller's tone whether he or she is nervous, upset, or angry. Maintain a telephone log of all calls. This will help jog your memory later. If a caller makes a specific request that impacts the project, ask for the request in writing so that it can become part of the project file, since it could affect the work or the schedule.

- **Telephone contact with an intermediary**
  Be careful here—any message you convey is subject to misinterpretation. Stick to a straightforward message that is clear and unambiguous. Organize your thoughts before you call.

  After identifying yourself on the phone, establish rapport with the person answering. Then move to the message. Imagine that you are writing down the message along with the intermediary and speak at a pace that allows this.

  If a secretary or assistant calls you on behalf of someone else, get the details, then repeat the message back to ensure that you have received it correctly. If you are asked to come to a meeting, do some research. How big is the room? Which department controls the scheduling of the room? The answers to these questions can reveal who the other audience members are and tip you off as to what may be covered.

- **Voice mail**

  Keep the message brief. Make notes before you call, writing down the subject and key points. If the call is to deliver information only and needs no response, indicate this. For your own voice mail line, keep the greeting short and avoid being cute, which may distract the caller.

- **Pagers**

  Adopt a code system for each person you will be paging frequently. For example, if the need for contact is urgent, enter 911. If the need is informational, enter 411. Returning pages promptly indicates to the sender that you treat the business seriously.

- **Facsimile**

  Try to get as much on the cover sheet as you can. Try to use electronic mail instead of faxes since it is more private. If the person being faxed is not located near the machine, call and alert the person that you are sending a fax.

  Fax the message yourself to ensure that it was sent. Someone else who doesn't really care might insert it into the machine and walk off. The fax may fail. Someone else might walk up, remove your pages and leave. Finding the pages neatly stacked, you might mistakenly assume that the fax went through successfully. Also, watch the time of day. If you fax at lunchtime, it's possible no one will be there to pick it up. If you fax at busy times and are able to get through, then your fax may end up on the back of someone else's. If you are going to send copies to several people, address each person on a separate sheet. Always hand-sign the cover sheet.

- **Electronic mail**

  If you are going to send a lengthy e-mail message, write it first in a word processor, since this is a much better editor than the e-mail text editor. Also, many e-mail systems do not have a spell-checker. Make sure the subject line is short and clear. Include any issue or topic that is the focus of the message.

  Establish group mailing lists in the e-mail system for the team. This will save you from having to type in all of the e-mail addresses each time.

- **The Web and Internet**

  The intranets, the Internet, and the World Wide Web have so much useful information for projects that being selective is the best skill to acquire. Don't flood the receivers with too much information. In one company, the leader thought it would be a good idea to establish a web page for the E-Business project and to keep people informed. It started out OK, but it quickly became a time-consuming activity to keep the pages updated. The leader eventually dropped it.

  If you are going to post documents or information on web pages, then concentrate on content. Don't spend a lot of time on making it cute by customizing HTML code. Cute stuff can backfire since the audience may assume that you have nothing better to do. If you are going to establish a web site, maintain the site with up-to-date information or go back to e-mail. Remember that a key duty will be maintaining any and all Web information you establish.

- **Groupware**
  Some people employ groupware like electronic mail. However, group-ware has the advantage of allowing several people to comment or to build documents together. In using groupware, stick to the basic features. If you use exotic features, other people may not be able to participate fully.
- **Videoconferencing**
  E-Business issues tend to be complex. At Abacus, for example, they had to deal with a number of suppliers. Face-to-face meetings would have been prohibitively expensive so they used videoconferencing at a copy center. It worked quite effectively. This approach forced them to be orga-nized before they went to the copy center. It also made them aware of costs so that the meetings were more effective.
- **Memoranda and letters**
  Keep written memoranda and letters short and to the point. Avoid E-Business jargon. Adopt a simple writing style. Avoid long sentences and complex terms. Think about what follow-up measures you will take to ensure that the message got through.
- **Reports**
  When writing the report, keep in mind who the audience is and keep the focus narrowed to this. Print on one side of a piece of paper. Although this consumes more paper, the document will be easier to follow. Number and date each page with the title so that it can be reassembled if separated. Always assume that any written communication will be copied and dis-tributed.

MESSAGE FAILURE AND SUCCESS

What constitutes success in communications? The message not only got through to the receiver, but you also received action or a response.

What constitutes failure in project communications? The message was misin-terpreted or ignored. The failure is always the fault of the sender, who is responsi-ble for all actions in preparing, sending, and following up on the communication.

SIX ACTIONS IN COMMUNICATIONS

The following six actions have been standard practice in many industries. Follow these actions in communications to ensure success.

Action 1: Define the Purpose and Audience

Whom do you wish to reach? Think about the person or people you are trying to reach. What do the people think of you and the project? What is their attitude? What is their knowledge of E-Business? What can you assume they know so that the communication can be shorter? What are they likely to do after they receive the message? To whom will they pass the communication? Answering these questions will help you to determine the degree of detail and background required, set the tone of the communication, and determine what medium is most appropriate.

Why do you wish to communicate? What would happen if you did not communicate now? With the overload of information in many organizations, treat any of your communications as if they cost great money and effort. If you are in doubt and the reasons for the communication are unclear, then wait. Is the reason for communicating complex? That is, do you need to address a number of issues? Consider breaking down the communication to address one person at a time or address smaller groups.

Action 2: Form the Message

The message is not the communication. The message is contained in the communication. Based on your skill, the receiver may or may not be able to decipher the message from the communication. To avoid confusion, first construct an outline of what you want to say. In general, your outline should include the following:

- An introduction that identifies the problem or situation
- The detailed steps of the message (who, what, when, where, how)
- The desired action of the recipient
- Expected feedback from the message

Example: Marathon Manufacturing

One of the leaders at the manufacturing firm had to request a detailed blueprint of the offices in a remote building in order to lay out the network and estimate the costs of implementing support for E-Business. However, a blueprint can mean different things to different people. What if some vague diagram were provided? It would be worthless and the information request would have to be repeated. The communications outline first listed the request and reasons behind it. This was followed by the date required and what was to be done with the information. The last item was a sample blueprint of the headquarters building as an example. This was appropriate and provided the necessary example along with the information on the request.

Action 3: Determine the Medium and Timing

Confine all discussion of issues to in-person contact or direct telephone contact. You want to have direct interaction with the person so that any questions can be answered. Use electronic mail or groupware for routine messages. Avoid facsimiles because of the many possibilities for missed communications. Keep communications informal. Use formal meetings and settings as a backup for escalation and for general impressions.

After you select the medium for the message, think about how the receiver will respond and what media will be used. Assume that the messages will fly back and forth. Timing is important if you want to get someone's attention. When should you send the message? The answer, as you saw in the discussion of various media forms, depends on the medium, the objective, the audience, and the message.

Action 4: Formulate the Communication

In this action you now package the message inside the communication. Whether you are dealing with verbal or written media, if it is important, expand your outline and build the communications. If the communication is verbal, create a series of bullet items. If the communication is written, prepare the document. Write with words of 10 letters or less whenever possible. Write in simple sentences, usually no longer than 10 words, and form short, succinct paragraphs. Avoid jargon—especially project management jargon, such as *critical path, PERT, GANTT,* and *critical resources.*

Action 5: Deliver the Communication

If the delivery of your communication brings many questions from the recipient, suggest that you go over the message with the person in a face-to-face situation. If complex questions arise during direct contact, set another meeting to resolve all the issues raised.

Action 6: Follow Up on the Communication

If you send messages and you fail to follow up, people may think that the message was not important. First, make a note in a log as to what you sent and when. Track whether you receive any feedback or response. Plan ahead for follow-up on whether the message was received and what actions are flowing from it. In most cases involving politically sensitive topics, the only evident response may be acknowledgment of receipt of the message, since the recipient will need time to think about a response.

No.: _____ Date: _____

Type: _____

Title: _____

Audience: _____

Purpose: _____

Message: _____

_____

_____

_____

_____

Media Selected: _____

Expected Action: _____

Expected Time of Action: _____

Action Taken: _____

Actual Time of Action: _____

Lessons Learned: _____

Note that type refers to subject area. Filing these by date allows you to track your progress. Also, consider filing a copy by subject so that you can compare how you do with different subjects.

Figure 7-1:   Sample Form For Communications Planning

Obviously, to do this for many messages is absurd and impossible. This is another reason for not sending out many messages. If you have to send more messages in total than you can pursue, identify the critical messages and follow up on them. Place messages on issues, budget, schedule, and important resource topics in this category. Figure 7-1 gives elements to use to track and improve communications skills. This form can be a useful planning tool to make you think more formally about communications. Place these forms in a binder and review them now and then.

EFFECTIVE REPORTS AND PRESENTATIONS

When you think about project presentations and reports, your mind will often turn to technical details and in-depth discussions of issues. Most people want to plunge in and make a list of details and then formulate a report or a presentation. This is unwise. Here are six topics that must be considered in creating an effective report or presentation.

* *Medium or format.* What is the medium of the message?
* *Length.* How long will the communication be?
* *Organization.* Where will you start your presentation? Where will it end? How will you get from the start to the end (order of presentation)?
* *Method of argument.* Will you use E-Business data, your authority or experience, or history? What will be the basis for your support?
* *Attitude toward audience.* What is the attitude you wish to convey toward your audience (friendly, hostile, polite, informal, etc.)?
* *Impression.* After your message is heard or read, what do you want the audience to think of you?

With this as your strategy, you can begin to assemble information, tables, graphs, plans, etc. This is the evidence for your presentation.

Presentation Style

Next, choose one of three presentation styles:

* *Descriptive Report and Presentation.* An issue, situation, or opportunity can be described to an audience. You begin with an introduction to the subject. Next, establish your credibility. Why are you qualified to talk about this? Here you might cite experience. Third, give an overview of the topic. This is followed by the details on the subject. Finally, bring the audience back to the initial topic so that they can relate the overview and detail to the topic.

   This style works for a traveling show or for some academic presentations but has limited effectiveness in management. In projects you are often trying to gain support or approval. Description often is too general, leaving too many loose ends.
* *Analytical Report and Presentation.* Here you might be reporting on an E-Business issue. You start by identifying what you are analyzing. First provide your credentials. The question addressed next is "What is the current state of affairs with the issue?" You can move from general to specific and back to general, as in the descriptive presentation. Now identify the methods and tools employed in the analysis. You end the presentation with conclusions and recommendations. This style is good for milestone assessment and other evaluation type work, but is not well-suited to the major presentations.
* *Persuasive Report and Presentation.* Concentrate your effort and practice in this presentation style. As with the other two styles, you begin with an introduction and qualifications. Next, what is the need? What are you trying to address? Avoid the solution or benefits. After answering these questions, answer the question, "What will happen if the need is not addressed?" Point out grim and unwelcome consequences. Then change the tone to one of optimism and talk about what will happen if the need is addressed. What benefits will accrue?

You have warmed up your audience and prepared them well. Now move to the solution.

While you use reports to inform people on topics related to E-Business, most of your limited time and energy has to go into persuasive reports where you are attempting to line up support to resolve issues, take actions, etc. Given how much there is to do, you should consider focusing on persuasive type reports.

MEETINGS

Some general suggestions regarding meetings are as follows:

- *Do a great deal of preparation for meetings.* Collect agenda items for meetings in advance.
- *Actively run the meeting.* Keep meetings focused on an agenda.
- *Minimize meetings due to the effort and the impact of lost time on the project.*
- *Meet to discuss lessons learned rather than to discuss status.*

Here are some specific comments on two types of project meetings:

- *Project Kickoff Meeting.* You are starting the project. The meeting will introduce members of the team to each other and set the stage for the work. Have people introduce themselves and explain what experience and expertise they bring to the table. This is especially important since you are establishing the tone for the first time.

    Prepare for the meeting by developing the E-Business plan from the template, but leave out the lowest level of detail. Delegate that task to the team members. Set down the ground rules for communications, reporting, work, and issues. Make this as structured as possible. If you start out vague, then you have damaged the project at the onset. To build the group into a team, develop the initial list of issues and detailed tasks as a team.
- *Milestone Meeting.* This is a meeting where a milestone or end product is presented and reviewed. As the meeting begins, provide your audience with checklists of questions and guidelines for evaluation. Let the people know what you expect to get out of the meeting. What actions are possible? As you go through the review of the end product, make notes on an easel or board as to what issues and questions are raised. At the end of the review, start going through the list on the board and either get closure or assign topics out for analysis.
- *Issues Meeting.* Identify the two or three issues to be addressed and who should attend for each issue. Set strict time parameters for each issue and invite only those needed to each issue discussion. Identify action items for each issue and decide how to follow up on these.

- *Lessons Learned Meeting.* Lessons learned are absolutely critical in E-Business since E-Business is a cumulative process. Lessons learned meetings can be based on achieving a specific milestone. You would ask what people learned in doing the tasks that led to the milestone. Another option for this kind of meeting is to establish a time period and ask for lessons learned during that period. In either case, start with a general discussion. Then identify the following elements and record them so that others can benefit:
  —How the lesson learned can be generalized
  —How someone would use the lesson learned in practice
  —The benefits of the lesson learned
  —Who to contact if a person has questions about the lesson learned
  —How to add further detail later to the lesson learned
  —How to measure the results of the lesson learned

E-BUSINESS EXAMPLES

RICKER CATALOGS

The leaders at Ricker followed a mixture of formal and informal meetings. The style of the company was geared toward formal meetings. Thus, the E-Business leaders began with mainly formal meetings. This worked in providing the basic information on E-Business and in giving status. Later, it was found more effective to use informal meetings to handle issues.

MARATHON MANUFACTURING

Even though Marathon is a large company, management decided that formal meetings would be too intimidating for E-Business. Upper-level management mandated informal meetings for the most part. Thus, while there were formal materials presented, the atmosphere was informal. This encouraged employees to contribute ideas for E-Business.

ABACUS ENERGY

Abacus started with formal meetings with suppliers. This was helpful in that it set the stage for implementing business to business e-commerce transactions. However, once these initial meetings were over, the work shifted to lower-level managers and staff. Thus, the attention shifted to informal meetings through videoconferencing.

Abacus attempted to use fax and electronic mail. Quickly, they found that things go out of sync. One fax might mention three subjects. A return fax might address two of the subjects and bring up two more. There was no effective way to track the topics. These faxes were mixed in with standard daily work. Faxes were lost. In terms of e-mail the project leaders were hit by many messages. They found that it took hours just to respond to these. Most were not meaningful. They slowed down their response time to dampen the e-mail volume.

CRAWFORD BANK

Crawford Bank followed a more formal approach than the other firms. The E-Business project had to follow established procedures and formats for presentations. While this worked in the main bank, the approach in the new organization was decidedly informal.

E-BUSINESS LESSONS LEARNED

- **Think of the self-interest of the audience when you supply information.**
  Remember that the importance of E-Business lies in the eyes of the beholder.
- **Avoid secondhand communications.**
  Secondhand communications means going through intermediaries. You know from the elementary school game of "telephone" how messages get changed as they pass from person to person. Also, it is highly unlikely that the intermediary will convey the passion, interest, or other emotion that accompanied the message. This lowers the likelihood of the message leading to success.
- **Democracy in a project has its place, but so does autocracy.**
  In a collaborative environment you seek to encourage greater communications about issues, lessons learned, and status. However, also maintain order in the work and stomp out any rumor mills. The challenge is to balance between democracy and authority for the leader.
- **Detect indirect resistance by observation.**
  When people communicate with or respond to you, they convey their feelings and attitudes. You should be able to detect resistance on specific topics. Maintain frequent one-on-one contact to detect changes or nuances in demeanor.
- **Manage small leaks of information while they are small.**
  Most project leaders can cope with leaks of information about the work to people outside of the team. The basic problem is that what might start out as an annoyance in the team becomes a major crisis through the retelling of the information again and again by different people. Coping with substantial disinformation is time-consuming. If possible, determine the source of the leaks and discuss the issue with that person.

- **Be consistent in what you relate to each of the members of the team.**
  Assume that everything you tell someone on the team is known to the entire team in less than one hour.
- **Operate on the assumption that you might create an enemy in each meeting.**
  Enemies (or friends) are made during the process of communication. Once you have made an enemy, it will be difficult, if not impossible, to undo. Be considerate and avoid unnecessary criticism of others throughout the communication process.
- **Keep the volume of written memos among members as low as possible.**
  The volume of memos is usually inversely related to progress. Experience indicates that memoranda volume increases when the project is under stress. People naturally want to cover themselves and appear busy. If people are working productively on the tasks, they have little time for memos.
- **Confine your meeting time to issues.**
  Issues are often more interesting than project status. People tend to want to get involved and put their fingerprint on issues. People are bored by status.
- **Use simple language and avoid arcane jargon.**
  Using unfamiliar or arcane words was encouraged at one time as a demonstration of intelligence. Now it is viewed negatively because people miss the meaning of what you are saying. The communications path to a person consists of first understanding the language, then understanding the words, and then deciphering the meaning of what is said. If people can't understand you, your communications are not going to be effective.
- **Share information.**
  Sharing information builds trust. People often hold information close to the vest. They think that if it gets disclosed, their position will weaken. It is always better to share information on the work. You don't have to share the political perspective or details about issues in progress, but be open about status and activities.
- **In order to raise morale, look at the worst that can happen.**
  In communications, when you encounter a difficult issue or crisis, take the time to examine the worst case scenario. Often, this is not as bad as people may have thought.
- **Have people leave their present agendas and schemes outside before a meeting.**
  As a leader, you will have to address these agendas directly at the beginning of the meeting. It is better to tell people to leave their "guns" outside and see you privately at a later time.
- **Keep meetings to no longer than an hour.**
  Meetings that last more than an hour tend to generate more heat than light. Extended meetings tend to disrupt other work. People may get too worked

up about an issue during the meeting and productivity will then drop for some time after the meeting.

- **Provide a forum to encourage the sharing of lessons learned.**
  If you do not, you will suffer the penalty of repeating the lessons. Having the team members share their experiences provides reinforcement and support. Otherwise, a team member will have to go through the same processes as other team members without the benefit of the experiences and lessons learned by the others.
- **Vary meeting dates and times to increase the level of awareness.**
  Periodic meetings are often preferred by people who like routine. But holding periodic project meetings will lull a project team into complacency. Also, issues do not conveniently mature and become ready for resolution on the same schedule. Drop the periodic meetings. Make the next meeting "to be announced" and notify people several days in advance.
- **Stick to simple visual aids and have handouts in case these fail.**
  The more you depend on extensive audio-visual aids, the more likely they will break. Exotic visual aids include electronic CRT screen projectors, nonstandard slide projectors, and overhead projectors without substantial fans. Do not trade content for slickness. Do not rely on equipment that has no spares or on-site support.
- **Evaluate yourself after a presentation.**
  After a presentation there is a tendency to want to forget everything and go on to something you like to do. But first, sit down and be your own worst critic. Did you achieve the results you were after? What did the audience do in the meeting? How did they react to you? How did they react to other speakers?
- **Consider chart appearance.**
  Charts can be confusing, even if the information is valuable and correct. The choice of colors, shadings, format, lettering, fonts for letters, and wording are all important. Create your presentation and set it aside for some time. Then go back and shuffle the presentation order. Pick up a chart at random and see if you can understand it. In a presentation, discuss the impact of the chart—not the detailed meaning of the chart.
- **Hand out all materials at the start of the presentation to make life easier for the audience.**
  The old argument was that people would read ahead of your presentation and would lose interest. However, people get more from the information if they have the materials in front of them. Also, handing out materials at the beginning of the presentation minimizes surprises.
- **Hold informal meetings more often than formal ones.**
  The more formal meetings you have, the more people will become involved in the issue. With more heat and attention, many people are likely to defer action. It is best if possible to resolve issues and get decisions informally and with a low profile. The decision can later be announced formally. Also,

informal meetings often convey more information than formal meetings. Formal meetings tend to have a rigid agenda with less time for questions. The presentation tends to be more rigid in terms of overheads, slides, and handouts. In informal meetings you can get questions and issues out more easily since there is less structure to the meeting. One good strategy is to have an informal pre-meeting to solicit issues and questions to be covered later at a formal meeting.

WHAT TO DO NEXT

1. Here are some questions to answer for your project communications.
   - What is the level of your awareness of being able to differentiate between the message and the overall communication?
   - Think through the communication process you use today. How often do you have to clarify messages that were not properly received?
   - How much project time is spent on determining status? How much is spent on issues?
   - Do you have any standard guidelines for presentations to management? Do these fit all of the situations that you will encounter?
2. Go into your files and grab several memos or copies of electronic mail that you generated. Review these by asking the following questions:
   - Does the communication fit the audience?
   - Can you discern the message through the communication?
   - What was the result of the communication? When did it happen?
3. Start keeping a log of your communications. Note the date and time of contact, the person contacted, the nature of contact, the response, the date and time of response, and the action that resulted.
4. Develop an approach for modifying your method of communicating. Start with one media form at a time. Work on electronic mail and faxes, since these are relatively short and focused.

Chapter 8

Communicate with Management

INTRODUCTION

While you can recover multiple times from problems and failure within the team, you get very few chances with management for E-Business. If you are successful in your first major presentations and contacts, the favorable impression you create will last a long time. However, the margin for error is small. If you don't pay attention to management communications and their nuances, you could undo all of your other good work.

EXAMPLE: CONSUMER PRODUCTS FIRM

The project leader of a consumer products team almost destroyed the project during his first presentation. He indicated to management that E-Business would replace many middle managers. Several managers winced and became confused. They were not aware of what E-Business was. As a result, the plan sounded drastic. The meeting ended without approval. A misimpression was created that E-Business was too revolutionary. It took two months of behind-the-scenes marketing to correct this before the E-Business idea could be presented again.

MILESTONES

This chapter focuses on key events in your management contacts during the life cycle of an E-Business effort. The purpose is to help you win support from management. This chapter provides practical advice as well as tips on how to avoid failure.

The scope of this chapter begins with getting the project idea approved and moves through the completion or termination of the E-Business effort. Both formal and informal communications with management are included.

METHODS AND TECHNIQUES

The traditional method in project management is that as you approach a major event or milestone in a project, you put together a formal presentation to management. The presentation then may or may not occur. If it does, some follow-up may be required, but the attention returns to the work. The contact with management is a temporary event, perhaps viewed as an interruption in the process. This concept of "communications with management" is fundamentally wrong for E-Business projects. Consider management communications as an integral part of overall communications. Informing and working with management on a continuous basis are major roles for the E-Business leader that are just as important as obtaining status and addressing issues.

The discussion of management communications is divided into informal and formal communications. The most effective strategy for E-Business is to use informal methods as a basis for communications, and smoothly and continuously build up to formal presentations. In that way, both forms of communications are mutually supportive. The formal presentations will then be followed up on by more informal communications.

ABOUT THE AUDIENCE

The old school of thought was that keeping your manager informed would be sufficient. However, managers come and go. Also, the elapsed time of E-Business may be such that the manager may move to another position. A suggested alternative is to identify and keep informed a set of three to four managers in different parts of the organization. These people will be your direct audience for both informal and formal communications. Keeping in touch with several managers gives you the effect of an informal high-level steering committee. You are then not dependent upon one person for support.

With which managers should you develop rapport? Choose a combination of general, high-level managers and line managers who are interested in the outcome of E-Business, or who are supplying people to the work. Alternatively, they may be the ones whose power is increased after E-Business is implemented. Make a list of several managers of each type to call on if you need backup.

This method has several benefits. First, you have a plan in place for backup if one manager leaves. You also have continuity, since the existing managers can assist in updating the new manager as well. A third benefit is that you have a wider audience to give you feedback before formal presentations.

INFORMAL COMMUNICATIONS

Benefits of Informal Communications

Here are some benefits of informal communications:

- The managers can give you their reactions to a presentation informally prior to formal presentation. People tend to be more open in a one-on-one situation.
- You provide others with information on issues. They can then take the information and work the issue for you behind the scenes. It is often best to solve politically sensitive issues "off-line."
- Status information can arm others to answer any questions or concerns about the project. This prevents both defensiveness when someone questions the project and the need to call you to clarify a point.

What do these benefits add up to? You become more proactive. You are getting information out to people. When formal presentations occur, they are almost anticlimactic, since several members of the audience already know what you are going to say. This also creates less chance of a surprise.

How to Make Contact Informally

Here are some pointers on informal contacts with management.

- *How to contact managers.* Plan on casually running into several managers each week. Planning and "casual" contact appear contradictory, but they are not. Plan how you can informally contact managers in the hallway, copier room, or their offices. Study their work patterns. Usually, the best time to run into people or stop by their office is early in the morning. An alternative approach exists if they smoke. Then you can meet with them while they are smoking.
- *Extent of contact.* Plan on no more than five minutes of total contact, unless the manager indicates that he or she wants to spend more time with you.
- *What to cover in the contact.* Always start with status. Let the manager know some good news first. This is a positive way to start the day. If you want to discuss or present an issue, gradually lead into it. Starting with the issue is too negative. Steer clear of "techie" stuff.
- *Prior to presentation.* If you desire feedback on the major points of a formal presentation, reveal some of the key parts of the presentation for reaction. You get not only the manager's reaction but also the manager's understanding.

This typically means that the manager can provide assistance during the presentation.

- *A manager's concerns and comments.* The previous point stressed the transfer of information from you to the manager. It works both ways. The manager may hear something that impacts your project. The informal contact allows the manager a chance to inform you without a record in writing.
- *A manager's ideas.* Incorporate the ideas suggested by the managers and then provide them with feedback by showing how the presentation or report changed after their input.

With this amount of contact, E-Business becomes visible to certain managers in a friendly way. However, to others you are unknown until there is a formal presentation. This is desirable. If you receive a great deal of management attention openly, people will become jealous and may take shots at E-Business and you. To keep a low profile, we favor a structure with extensive informal contacts and little obvious visibility.

FORMAL PRESENTATIONS

Before the Presentation

Whether it be a report or an oral presentation, try these guidelines:

- Keep all materials in a draft form. Label them as a draft. This will give people the impression that they can have input prior to the final form, as well as providing you with the ability to improve and make changes. The more people are involved, the more feedback you will get and the more buy-in you will receive.
- For verbal presentations, ask line managers of the team members to be present along with team members. Plan to spread the credit around.
- Use successive dry runs to keep improving the material.

During the Presentation

Here are some tips to consider in making the presentation:

- Minimize the number of charts. Too many can be confusing.
- Hand out all charts at the beginning. This allows the audience to see the entire presentation, and surprises are avoided.
- All charts should express complete thoughts and sentences. If you use lists without additional information, people can misunderstand what is going on.
- Encourage feedback and questions. Follow up on each item either in the meeting or shortly afterward.
- Make sure you have dangling items so that you have the opportunity to follow up afterwards for more marketing.
- Walk around as you give the presentation. Be animated.

After the Presentation

Follow up after the presentation with managers who were in the audience and further explain any points that were unclear. Asking what they thought is too direct and shows a lack of confidence. If a manager has an opinion, he will express it.

Immediately after the presentation, grade yourself by using the following checklist:

PRESENTATION EVALUATION

- Material
  - — How well was it organized?
  - — Was the material relevant to the theme of the presentation?
  - — Were people able to understand it easily? Did they ask what terms meant?
  - — Was there too much material?
  - — Did you find that you lacked material to respond to specific issues?
- Presentation style
  - — Were you too formal?
  - — Did you receive many questions or comments?
  - — How did you respond to comments?
  - — Did you read from the charts?
- Audience
  - — Who attended the presentation?
  - — Were the key players there?
  - — Was the audience attentive? Were there any interruptions?

After a presentation, take the time to write down the answers to the above questions and file this evaluation for reference. If needed, refine the presentation to the way it should have been.

MARKETING

Critical Marketing Milestones

Almost all projects, even the smallest, have key milestones and end products. Here are the ones to be considered in detail.

- Marketing the E-Business concept
- Marketing the E-Business plan
- Communicating E-Business status to management
- Presenting and addressing an issue or opportunity
- Obtaining management decisions
- Coping with poor management decisions

- Taking action after a decision
- Changing the direction of E-Business
- Terminating or ending the work

For each of these let's examine the background, purpose, approach, tactical suggestions and hints, and how to assess yourself after the presentation.

Market the E-Business Concept

- **Background**
  Ideas don't just surface on their own. Someone has the idea and either that person or somebody else follows up by becoming the champion for the E-Business concept. The fate of the idea is closely linked with the person who is pushing for approval of the idea.
- **Purpose**
  The aim is to gain approval from a manager to develop an E-Business plan and determine its initial feasibility. This is positive, since it gives management an inexpensive way to assess the will of the person who is pushing for E-Business.
- **Approach**
  The favored approach is to build support for E-Business gradually. Sell individual managers one-on-one. Show how the project concept fits in with their own interests. Avoid a pitch based on vague terms and concepts.

  To generate enthusiasm as well as gain approval, show the benefits of your plan. A leader in one of the examples did this for her network by pointing to how issues could be resolved through a network. This was much more effective than trying to sell dry network concepts.
- **Suggestions and hints**
  Try to have managers adopt the E-Business concept as their own and then act as apostles to market it to other managers you cannot reach yourself. Your plan is to build a set of cadres to support and sponsor the concept. Keep the concept verbal so that it is flexible. Once you put it in writing, you will tend to become locked in.
- **Measuring your performance**
  The obvious measure is the answer to the question, "Was the concept approved for planning?" But this is not enough. Also assess the degree of enthusiasm and excitement for E-Business. Another test is to ask managers what their impression of the concept is.

Market the E-Business Plan

- **Background**
  It is not enough to gain approval of the project plan; you must obtain resources as well, garnering political support to get the necessary funding.

- **Purpose**
  You should obtain the following after initial approval of the E-Business plan: support for providing resources for the first stage of work, interest in the project for continued contact, and management input on the plan.
- **Approach**
  One technique is to reveal the overall, high-level plan to managers. Show the major task areas, general dates, and dependencies. Then refine the plan and come back with more detail, as well as resources needed. It is too much to expect people to grasp all of the detail the first time. Presell E-Business top down and bottom up at the same time. Focus on the people who will benefit from the successful completion of E-Business work.
- **Suggestions and hints**
  Incremental marketing is the key. This gives you a further opportunity for management contact and contact with the future beneficiaries of E-Business. Make it appear in form if not in reality that the development of the plan is a team effort. Make sure that you give people credit for their input.
- **Measuring your performance**
  — Did you obtain approval?
  — Do people have a clear idea of the project and are they supportive?
  — Did you obtain resources to get started?

Communicate E-Business Status to Management

- **Background**
  Conveying status information is not just walking up and saying the E-Business effort is going along well or writing a memo to that effect. Strive to continue to build rapport and strengthen support. Treat the supplying of status information as a continuous process rather than a periodic activity you do once a week or once a month.
- **Purpose**
  The basic purpose is to enlist and build support for E-Business. A more immediate purpose is to convey an understanding of status. Another purpose is to pave the way for the resolution of issues.
- **Approach**
  Provide status in informal one-on-one meetings. Start with the overall state of the work and then zoom in on a detailed issue or specific milestone. Then relate an interesting "war story" or experience. Alert managers to a looming issue so that they can prepare for it.
- **Suggestions and hints**
  Develop a vision of the status of the work and what you want to say each morning. Rehearse this informally with a member of the team. Then set out on your mission to relate the status to one or two managers. Do this several

times a week. Managers you contact will become involved and more interested. They will look forward to your contacts.

- **Measuring your performance**
  — How many people have you contacted this week?
  — How has your relationship grown with them since you started?
  — Are they more interested in E-Business now?

Present an E-Business Issue

- **Background**
  Present the issue or opportunity along with alternative actions, and get a decision. This way, you are presenting solutions as well as bringing up problems.
- **Purpose**
  The purpose of the presentation of an issue is for management to understand the impact of the issue, why action is necessary now, and the suggested decision, actions, and anticipated results. Avoid getting bogged down in the details of the issue.
- **Approach**
  The first stage is to alert managers through informal communications that an issue is coming. This will mitigate any feelings of surprise. Next, follow the actions for issues (suggested in Chapter 15). When you have the materials ready, present a complete picture.
- **Suggestions and hints**
  Don't cry wolf over an issue. You can alert management and indicate that you are tracking the issue. Let it mature. Carefully plan the sequence of issues and opportunities that will be presented to management. Insert positive opportunities in between issues to avoid leaving a lingering negative impression.
- **Measuring your performance**
  — The bottom line is whether or not you receive approval for the decision and actions you proposed.
  — More than that, however, did you establish a positive pattern of managing issues?

Obtain Management Decisions

- **Background**
  Many immediate management decisions after a presentation will be negative. To deal with this, during the presentation indicate what you will do after the presentation. In that way, you can continue the work. The managers will know that work is still going on and will feel less pressure to make a decision.

- **Purpose**

  The purpose is to obtain a decision, but as important as a decision is, your ultimate goal is support.

- **Approach**

  Presell the decision through the informal contacts. Informal approval is easier to obtain than formal. Avoid a formal memo of the decision if you can. The formal presentation can stress the actions that flow from the decision, rather than the decision itself.

- **Suggestions and hints**

  A basic suggestion is to indicate that a decision will be needed way in advance. Then show that this decision does not bear any significant risk for management. Instead, focus on the benefits that will flow from the actions. This turns the spotlight away from the decision. As you approach the decision, move the attention to actions—again moving the focus away from the decision. This will make the decision more natural.

- **Measuring your performance**

  Did you get the decision you wanted when you required it? How much goodwill did the decision cost? How hard did you have to sell the decision?

Cope with Poor Management Decisions

- **Background**

  You wanted a management decision and you got the wrong one. They did not approve the requested resources or the budget. What do you do?

- **Purpose**

  The purpose is not to go back in and reverse the decision. What you seek to do, rather, is to mitigate the effects of the decision on E-Business. It is most important to keep up progress and momentum for E-Business. Do not let a cloud of doom hang over the work.

- **Approach**

  First, analyze why the undesirable decision was made. What is the difference between your perception of the situation and management's perception? Next, look at the impact of the management decision—immediate and long-term. How can you counter the effects of the decision in order to protect the work and keep going?

- **Suggestions and hints**

  Expect that poor decisions will be made. This often happens through a misunderstanding. Once key managers have taken public stances that cannot be reversed, figure out how to work informally behind the scenes to counteract the negative effects of the decision.

- **Measuring your performance**
  — Were you able to control the damage from the decision?
  — Have you determined how to go back to management with pieces of information that may persuade change in the decision?

Take Action After the Management Decision

- **Background**
  Actions flow from a decision. If no actions follow a decision, the decision is likely to have little meaning. If the gap between the decision and the subsequent actions is too big, people will not be able to understand and relate to the actions.
- **Purpose**
  The goal is to implement actions immediately after decisions are made.
- **Approach**
  Include the actions in your presentation. Link the actions to the situation by explaining what benefits will likely follow. Then you can move back into the decision.
- **Suggestions and hints**
  Make sure that you have a complete list of actions ready to go. Actions can be policies and procedures, as well as resource actions.
- **Measuring your performance**
  — Were the actions implemented?
  — Do people clearly see the connection between the decisions and the actions?

Change the Direction of the E-Business Effort

- **Background**
  On many E-Business efforts lasting six months or more, you will be faced with selling directional change to management. Such directional change occurs naturally for several reasons. For example, change external to the work may affect the project. Also, knowledge gained by the team can be employed to change the direction.
- **Purpose**
  The goal is to accomplish the change in the effort while maintaining the confidence of management in E-Business.
- **Approach**
  Bundle all possible changes into the marketing of the change. If you make too many changes, management will lose confidence in you and the effort. Managers might think that things are out of control. Indicate why the change is needed by explaining what will happen if things continue as they are. Then move to the benefits of the change.

- **Suggestions and hints**
  Point out at the start of the work that the E-Business direction could change due to events. Keep alerting people to this possibility. Then, as you approach the change, give attention to some of the different problems that could be solved by change. Indicate that you are packaging the solutions into a major change and that after this, E-Business direction will move into a period of stability.
- **Measuring your performance**
  More important than getting the change approved, do you still have management's support and confidence?

Terminate an E-Business Effort

- **Background**

  This is unpleasant but necessary. The E-Business leaders should be the champions of termination. Don't protect E-Business if it should be killed off.
- **Purpose**
  The purpose is to reach a decision on termination, or at least initiate a major overhaul.
- **Approach**
  Start by building up the history of the work from an overall perspective. Emphasize what has changed since the original E-Business proposal was approved. This will help to ensure that no one places blame for the termination. Then point to the effects of termination. Don't focus on the sunk costs. They are gone. Press for approval of the termination actions.
- **Suggestions and hints**
  Always consider termination as an option for any project. If nothing else, it forces you to validate the need for and benefit of the project.
- **Measuring your performance**
  Did you achieve the right outcome? Was termination successful without any placing of blame?

POTENTIAL PROBLEMS IN A PRESENTATION

Here are some potential problems that you may run into and what you might do in response.

- **You are not given a chance to present.**
  This is often due to scheduling or to other logistics problems. Don't personalize it. Try to get temporary approval so that the project can continue. Then present it next time. It is often better not to present than to be forced to present with insufficient time remaining.

- **The key managers did not attend the meeting.**
  If you know in advance of the meeting that this will happen, consider removing yourself from the agenda. If the audience is not right, then you may waste the impact of the presentation. On the other hand, if an enemy E-Business is going to be out of town, you might want to move up the presentation.

  If you show up and the key managers do not, make the presentation. After the presentation, go to each manager's office and offer to provide an informal, short presentation. This is your chance for follow-up.
- **You failed to respond adequately to questions and comments.**
  When people ask questions, listen carefully. Let them fully explain their ideas. Don't interrupt. Break up the points they raise in a sequence of numbers. Then address each point directly.

E-BUSINESS EXAMPLES

RICKER CATALOGS

The CEO was heavily involved in launching E-Business. This was natural given what was at stake in terms of the firm. However, this meant that the leaders had to spend a great deal of effort with the manager regarding relatively minor issues. This was never really resolved during the work. One way that the situation was mitigated was to have the manager feed the CEO with issues that required time to analyze and think about. This reduced the leaders' time in coordination.

MARATHON MANUFACTURING

The E-Business leaders had to cope with authority while the E-Business effort was centralized and driven from the top. Academically, this might appear to pose no problems due to the existence of top management support. However, the subprojects were hampered by the lack of support from the divisions and groups. The leaders succeeded with management only by showing the benefits of the subprojects to their own organizations. The lesson learned is that you must appeal to self-interest of management to gain their understanding, involvement, and support.

ABACUS ENERGY

Abacus management delegated the project to the leaders. There was limited management involvement until specific suppliers had to be brought onboard E-Business. Then management contacts were useful.

CRAWFORD BANK

Management communications was complex for Crawford. Since the E-Business effort was separate, coordination within the separate e-bank was relatively easy. Where it became complex was in communicating with line managers within the mainstream bank. This was sensitive because managers felt that the e-bank was a threat—even after they had been told repeatedly that it was not.

E-BUSINESS LESSONS LEARNED

- **Positive management exposure leads to success in getting resources.**
  Only in theory do projects compete for resources alone. In the real world they also compete for management attention. Work on getting management attention in order to get resources.
- **Telling management too early that E-Business is a success can lead to its failure.**
  Treat success as expected. Always caution that more milestones remain to be achieved. Exude an impression of cautious optimism. If people think that the project is a success, they let down their guard. When a problem later arises, it is a surprise and you find reduced support.
- **Align a project to management's self-interest.**
  Always show how the project supports the self-interest of the organization and the managers. To do this, indicate the benefits that will accrue. Prepare tables of benefits and show how the project is aligned with the needs of management and of the organization.
- **Look at the worst that can happen and then minimize its likelihood.**
  What is the worst that can happen in the work? Make a list of the top five items. These can range from lost resources to the disappearance of management support. Think about how you would respond if any of these occurred. This is not just contingency planning; it is also a way for you to practice problem-solving before you are in the heat of battle.
- **Keep the managers of team members informed of the status of E-Business.**
  Try a dry run of all of your presentations on the team. This will solicit the input of team members, inform them of the "party line," and allow them to help in marketing the E-Business effort.
- **Keep information you present to a minimum.**
  Be very careful about the level of detail and amount of information you present. Do not present detail unless it addresses a specific issue. Avoid cumulative project statistics in general except for budget vs. actual and plan vs. schedule. Concentrate on short-term issues and status in routine meetings.

- **Always plan to present in a period of five to ten minutes.**
  In a project presentation, if you are told you have 20 minutes, assume that you will actually have 5–10 minutes to present. This will force you in planning to give attention to issues and decisions you need to have the audience consider. If you plan for 20 minutes, you may find yourself filling time with status information.
- **Include alternatives and implementation in a discussion of issues.**
  At the end of many advertisements is often some action for the consumer to perform, such as a making a telephone call. It is the same in project management. If you discuss an issue in a meeting without getting into alternatives or actions, it seems theoretical. People are not pressed to take action.
- **Be self-assured in presenting issues.**
  An E-Business project's external appearance reveals a great deal about the past and present issues within E-Business.
- **Maintain a low profile.**
  Lack of E-Business visibility does not equate to insignificance. A low profile has advantages, as discussed earlier in this chapter.
- **Read between the lines and determine what is going on through impressions, appearances, and symptoms.**
  Do not wait for a neon sign with a message from management. Figure out what is needed and initiate action.
- **Give team members due credit.**
  A person who takes all of the credit is eventually a one-person team. If you take too much credit, managers will become doubtful of other things you say or write. The team effectiveness will diminish.
- **If you want to use humor, make jokes about yourself.**
  This shows that you have the ability to laugh at yourself. Making too many jokes at the expense of other projects can make your project a laughing stock.
- **Portray yourself as confident and knowledgeable about E-Business.**
  A leader's demeanor tells the management team far more than many project charts and graphs. If a leader appears beaten down or nervous, this will have a negative impact on managers. Also avoid saying "I don't know; I will follow up on that."
- **Keep content as a priority over presentation.**
  Concentrating on the format and style of the presentation while neglecting the content will lead to trouble. People who see the presentation may immediately become suspicious about the project. If problems exist, keep them out in the open. Note also that if you make a slick presentation with no problems, the same level of presentation will be expected in the future. Don't present and do work that you would not do on a regular basis.

- **Be ready to answer questions during a presentation—don't wait until the end.**
  Encourage questions at the start. When asked a question, repeat it in your own words to the audience. Then answer it. If you do not have an answer, write it down in front of the audience and get back to the audience and questioner.
- **Try to be placed in the middle of the agenda.**
  Being first on an agenda is not always an advantage. Yes, you get the audience when they are fresh. You also know you will have your assigned time. However, being in the middle or last has more significant advantages. You can compress your presentation. The audience will be more likely to remember your presentation, since it came later. However, if you are at the end, you do risk being bumped.
- **Remember your goal—to get approval.**
  People try to make a management presentation at a very high level. They want to make it appear strategic. But in fact, management sees many presentations, most of them probably poor. Many managers would rather be doing something else. So get to the point. Take a marketing-oriented approach. Your goal is to obtain approval, not applause.
- **Always be prepared to present the status or discuss an issue with management.**
  Some people attempt to isolate project management from other duties, but this is impossible. At any time you may run into an upper-level manager who asks about the status or a specific issue. If you say that you will look into it, you convey the impression that you are not on top of the issue.
- **Always end presentations with the default actions that will be taken.**
  You make a presentation and the managers say they will think about it. This is basically your fault because you did not end the meeting with closure. You left too many loose ends. Waiting for management approval is a common excuse for inaction. Instead, offer actions to be taken as you wrap up your presentation.
- **Debrief the team after a presentation—or someone else will.**
  After a project presentation, hold an informal meeting with the team. If you do not, word will filter back from other participants. Then you may spend much more time correcting false impressions. Schedule a team meeting within 15 minutes after you get back from the first meeting.

WHAT TO DO NEXT

1. Answer the following questions related to management communications.
   - How do you prepare for presentations now? How do you prepare documents? What preliminary reviews do you receive?

- Do you make the same mistakes repeatedly in presentations?
- Do you take the time to evaluate yourself after a presentation?
- Do you combine marketing and sales with providing information for understanding of the project?

2. Identify three or four key managers who are critical to E-Business in terms of their approval of major milestones. Develop a plan for how you could contact them informally at the start of the day.

3. Prepare yourself for the informal management contacts by making sure that you are aware of status and issues. Begin to update one of the managers. After doing this once a week for several weeks, expand your contacts to another manager. Every few weeks, add another manager.

4. Review your last formal presentation. What preparation in terms of contacts did you make? What efforts did you make to practice the presentation? What surprises arose during the presentation? How did the audience participate in the presentation?

Chapter 9

Track Your E-Business Efforts

INTRODUCTION

E-Business draws a great deal of attention as well as resources. People want status reports. They see competitor web pages and hear glowing industry reports. What are you doing? Is E-Business on schedule? There can also be pressure from investors. All of these comments point to the importance of tracking the E-Business work effectively. Here, the key word is "effectively." Coping with issues and crises may seem to be separate from the tasks of daily routine management, but these jobs are actually inseparable. The managers who are often best able to cope with crises are those who have their fingers on the pulse of the project and know the work.

Let's consider some problems that can arise. A project manager can become caught up in reporting to management. He or she may feel that it is great to get management exposure—like a moth drawn to a candle. However, there are only so many hours in the day and each hour presenting means one less hour collecting data on the work, addressing issues, or performing analysis. At Marathon, the three E-Business leaders got caught up in this management trap for awhile.

Another problem occurs when the manager beats on the team for constant status reports. The team members realize the person just wants status and does not seem interested in the work. The result is that the team is turned off and may just tell the manager what they want to hear until there is a disaster. This occurred with the first manager of E-Business at Ricker Catalogs.

MILESTONES

The purpose of this chapter is to help you be more effective and efficient as an E-Business manager in the day-to-day direction of the work. Good daily habits and an efficient work pattern are not intuitive; most managers have to learn them. The goal here is to teach you how to set up work patterns that will help you stay on top of the work. You should be able to administrate the effort and still have sufficient time to address issues and opportunities and to communicate with management and staff. You will learn ways to be proactive, rather than merely reacting to events. The scope of this chapter covers the day-to-day management activities that you face. Specifically excluded are addressing issues, dealing with crises, and measuring the progress of E-Business—these topics are so significant that separate chapters are devoted to each one.

METHODS AND TECHNIQUES

Here is a list of tasks on which you will spend your time as an E-Business leader.

- Group I—Administrative Tasks
  - Determining the status of the work
  - Tracking the progress of the work
  - Updating and maintaining the E-Business plan and budget
  - Carrying out administrative tasks (e.g., performance reviews, hiring, terminating)
- Group II—E-Business Work Tasks
  - Doing actual work
  - Motivating the staff
  - Analyzing the work
  - Meeting with and reporting to management
  - Evaluating the quality of the work and milestones

The tasks in Group I concern overhead and administrative work. The activities in Group II tend to be proactive—you plunge in and do the specific tasks or take on the issue. Spend most of your time on the tasks in Group II, as these move E-Business ahead. In contrast, reactive tasks in managing E-Business occur when you fail to track the project adequately. Then a problem occurs and you must react. By the time you have addressed that problem, another surfaces. You are always behind.

The more proactive work you do, the more you tend to be aware of what is going on in the work. The more reactive work you do, the less you are in control of E-Business and the more events control you. Assume some manager greeted you in the hallway and asked, "How is the work going?" Can you respond with detailed information? If not, concentrate more on the tasks in Group II to work towards better control of the work. Note that project control, as people commonly define it, includes some items from both groups.

To track where you are spending your time, at the end of each day write down the rough percentage of time you spent in both groups of activities. After you have done this for several weeks, determine whether any patterns exist based on the day of the week or the time of the month. Work toward increasing your time in Group II activities.

PERFORMING ADMINISTRATIVE TASKS EFFICIENTLY

Determine the Status of the Work

The basic objectives are to know what is going on in the work and to know where E-Business is going. Tracking the work allows you to resolve issues early and to take advantage of opportunities. E-Business can be tracked from different perspectives:

- *E-Business team.* The levels of morale and work satisfaction color the perspectives of team members.
- *End users of E-Business.* This perspective looks at the products that result from the E-Business effort.
- *General management.* The priorities are costs and schedules.
- *Line management.* Line management is concerned with the use of their resources in E-Business.

In collaborative management, the team members track progress and alert the project manager of any problems or issues arising in their tasks. This is much more effective than the traditional approach, in which the managers were left to ferret out the problems and status alone. To ascertain status, go to each team member and ask how the work is going. This will yield status information. If you ask directly for a status report, you may get a rosy, unrealistic view as the team member tells you what he or she thinks you want to hear.

Track the Progress of the Work

The first goal in tracking is to understand what is going on. Once you understand a situation, you can think about decisions and actions. When you are trying to understand what is going on, you often stumble upon targets of opportunity. This occurs when a team member mentions an idea for a small change or improvement. This often costs nothing and does not involve any high-level management action. When this occurs, take action and implement it right away.

Here are several approaches to tracking work:

- *Approach 1*: Track all work and tasks in E-Business with the same level of detail and effort. This appears fair and makes some sense when you first consider it. However, it is not a very intelligent use of your time given that it does not take into account the stages of various issues or the timing and duration of tasks.
- *Approach 2*: Track work based on the mathematical critical path. This is a traditional approach focusing mainly on the critical path tasks. These are tasks that happen mathematically to fall on the longest path. The problem with this approach is that it is not sensitive to risk and uncertainty. Also, it is not sensitive to time. Logically, you should spend more time on tasks that are in the near future.
- *Approach 3*: Track work based on the managerial critical path. A managerial critical path is a path in the E-Business plan that contains tasks that have substantial risk. How do you know which tasks these are? Look at the existence of issues and problems associated with tasks, as well as the uncertainty inherent in the tasks. Using this approach, start with the tasks that are happening now that have risk and expand to those that will have risk in the next two months. Then extend your examination to all of the tasks on the mathematical critical path that carry risk.

The third approach is favored since it is most reasonable in terms of the resources available and it is centered on minimizing risk—critical factors in E-Business success.

How should you track routine tasks? In collaborative scheduling, you want the team members to participate and let you know what is going on one-on-one. Also, randomly check on some routine tasks.

The first action in tracking work is to collect the following information:

- *Collecting information from team members.* You want to track what is going on with each team member, individually. Drop by each team member's office. Why not have them come to your office? You don't interfere with their work as much by visiting them. Also, when you visit others, you can see what they are working on. This is useful in tracking people who are part of the core team.

  During the visit, encourage team members to talk about their tasks in their own words. Take notes yourself and don't use forms. Don't use checklists or task lists. These approaches are too formal and may lead to answers of "okay" or "so-so" that aren't helpful. Prepare for these meetings by reviewing the tasks and issues each team member is working on. After the meeting, return to your office and prepare the team member's part of the status report.

- *Collecting information by observation.* Observe what is going on in the work firsthand. This is very important, since you can use your observations to update the tasks that are active. Observation does not help in updating the estimates for future tasks, but it can tell you what is going on now.
- *Collecting information from meetings.* You attend many meetings on the work and with management. At the end of each meeting, ask yourself if there was anything discussed in the meeting that has bearing on your schedule. Did you learn anything that will have an impact on resources? Do you foresee changes in methods and tools?

When should work be tracked? Today, the response is "continuously." In the past, if status or progress reports were due monthly, people would collect data on status and do tracking just before the end of the month. After the presentation of status, tracking would become a low priority until the end of the next month. A better approach is to be aware of what is going on all of the time, since the situation in E-Business can change rapidly. Continuous tracking will allow you to understand what is going on at all times.

Along with continuous tracking, update your schedule and plan as you get the information, at least twice a week. A daily update is not necessary, as this requires too much effort for what it gives you.

Here are four problems that can arise during the course of a project that relate to tracking.

1. *Management wants frequent and detailed reports.* This may occur because of problems within E-Business. It can also be due to a faulty reporting and control process. Control should be sensitive to the size, type, risk, and importance of the subproject. It is also dependent on the stage or phase of the subproject.

   How do you cope with this? Start by increasing informal contacts to let management know what is going on. This will provide management with more information. Next, propose a summary reporting process that can replace the existing detailed reports. Prepare the information yourself. Don't shift the burden to others on the team, since this can lower productivity and morale.

2. *You inherit a poorly run E-Business effort.* It has been assumed until now that you have been the leader from the beginning. What if you are taking over an E-Business effort in trouble? What should you do first? The reason for discussing this topic now is that your initial actions upon takeover are going to lie in tracking. Here is a sequence of actions in your takeover:
   - *Action 1*: Determine the status of E-Business and assess the team. Don't ask for more resources or money yet. Find out what is going on in the work. In finding out the status, you can assess the team members in terms of their productivity.

- *Action 2*: Conduct analysis to determine what could be done to improve project performance and results. Follow the actions for analysis given in this chapter.
- *Action 3*: Assess the current open issues and see if you can make some quick progress on some of these.
- *Action 4*: Develop a new E-Business plan and approach, and present it informally to management. Indicate what can be done with limited incremental resources.
- *Action 5*: Implement changes as soon as approval is given. Implement a more formal project reporting process. Management is giving you more resources. Reciprocate by giving management additional information on their investment.

3. *You have to deal with false information.* False information on E-Business can originate inside or outside the team. The damage it causes can be extensive. Your time may be consumed dealing with problems that are perceived but not real. This reduces both productivity and morale. Management may get the wrong impression about the work and institute countermeasures without asking you. This can be a major issue in that a new layer of management may be created.

    How do you head this off? First, keep your ear to the ground and determine what is being said about the project. Second, draw in the team to do the same and to support you. Third, stay in informal contact with managers you can trust to get early warning signs of problems.

4. *You lack technical knowledge.* You are managing an E-Business which has major technical components, but you lack technical knowledge. What do you do? You will obviously make an attempt at trying to learn the technical words and concepts. However, you will still lack detailed hands-on experience. Identify several informal technical advisors who can help you in reviewing plans, assessing milestones, and determining how methods and tools are being employed.

Update and Maintain the E-Business Plan and Budget

Let's assume that you are using a standard project management software package. Here are the actions in updating the plan and budget:

- *Action 1:* Update the current schedule bottom up. That is, go to the most detailed level of tasks and update these. Mark the relevant tasks that are complete; change the duration, resources, dependencies, and dates where necessary. If you are doing collaborative scheduling in which the team accesses the schedule, then set a deadline for the update. Review the update.

- *Action 2:* Move into the future and enter new task detail in the schedule. You may actually change the structure of the schedule based on your knowledge now.
- *Action 3:* After making changes to the detail, set the actual schedule. This will recompute the critical path and overall schedule.
- *Action 4:* Go to the databases that you have established for issues and action items. Update these as well, based on status.

At this point you are prepared to analyze the schedule. Note that the approach we have suggested focuses on doing routine work and no analysis. Give attention to the detailed tasks in updating. Keep analysis separate from updating. These require different types of thinking.

Carry Out Administrative Tasks

A project manager performs many mundane but significant tasks. These include performance evaluations for team members, recruiting and interviewing potential new team members, dealing with personnel problems on the team, checking up on the timekeeping and human resources of the team, and monitoring vacation time and sick time. Administrative duties also include maintaining E-Business files, determining training needs, and reviewing what other projects are doing. These are important duties. However, control the amount of time spent on them. Plan when you will do administrative work and group these duties into one portion of the workday. For example, try devoting the early morning hours several days a week to these duties and see if this is enough time to handle the work involved.

Perform E-Business Work Tasks Effectively

Do Actual Work in E-Business

It was once thought that when you became a manager, you were removed from the actual work. In cases where specific skills are required, or danger is involved, this is still true. However, hands-on work in E-Business is one of the best ways to see what is going on and to judge the impact of issues and opportunities on the project. This is especially true in E-Business where you want to gain knowledge through hands-on work so that you can respond to questions.

What tasks can you take on? You can scan web sites of competitors. You can participate in design reviews. You can work on test planning. As you choose tasks for yourself, keep in mind two priorities:

1. *Assign yourself some routine tasks.* These could involve documentation, testing, preparation, or analysis.
2. *Look for tasks that you can perform with other people.* If you work alone, you still assist the project, but you are not in touch with the team. Work with the staff one-on-one on a rotating basis. Do the job with the team members. Have them train you on how to do the work, if needed.

Your work on tasks may seem to slow things down at first, but the benefits include the following:

- E-Business benefits from additional resources working on the tasks.
- You gain an awareness of the work and potential ideas that could improve the work and results within the team.
- You maintain open communication with the team by working with them.
- You improve your ability to assess the effect of specific issues, opportunities, and crises related to E-Business and relay these assessments to management.
- Assessment of the status of the work is easier, faster, and more accurate.

How much time should you spend doing actual work? Obviously, it depends on the type of E-Business work you are doing. In general, 20 to 25 percent is a reasonable amount. If it is much higher, you will be too involved in the work and will neglect management tasks. If it is much lower, then you will waste time setting up and shutting down for work.

How should effort be split between the direct work and working with others on the team? A split of about 30 percent individual work and 70 percent working with others is reasonable. This provides you with more team contact. When you work with others on the team, don't assert authority as a manager. Let them lead you through the task, and you follow.

For resources that are shared among subprojects, work with the subproject leaders on a weekly basis to set priorities for each person during the coming week. This will ensure that each person obtains a consistent story from all leaders.

Motivate the Staff

Some leaders either downplay this or pay it lip service. They assume that getting a paycheck is sufficient motivation. Or, they may get people together and give a motivational talk. Here are some better ideas on motivation:

- When gathering status on the project from team members, show not only a sincere interest in their work, but also try to see what you can do to help them.
- Group motivation should be done through addressing issues and paying the team overall compliments. Group motivation has its drawbacks. First, if you

do it often, it loses impact. Second, diligent workers may feel slighted when you compliment a group of people in which some members slacked off.
- Follow up on suggestions by the team members concerning improvements or problems. Give them credit for their suggestions.
- Compliment people who raise many problems—the more problems the better. Hiding problems or not taking action is a recipe for disaster.

Analyze the E-Business Effort

Divide the analysis into discrete actions. A guideline here is to divide the update and the analysis. Do the update and the analysis at different times, because they require different skills.

- **Action 1: Validate the schedule**
  Review the milestones, dates, and summary tasks of the schedule to see if they make sense. If events suddenly shift, check to see if you left out a dependency or missed some tasks. Use the project management software to determine completeness of the tasks and the impact of change.
- **Action 2: Assess the mathematical and managerial critical paths**
  You want to determine how these paths have changed. If a task has become critical, why did this happen? If the path is longer due to greater detailed task durations, this indicates slippage in the work. Is the path length due to more information on the work that increased the number of detailed tasks? This is a common occurrence and not unexpected.

  You might lower or raise the risk when you update the task, depending on the issues. Lower the risk for the task if the issue has abated or been addressed. Raise the risk if the task has grown in importance, if there are new issues and if the assumptions made about the task are no longer valid.
- **Action 3: Compare the planned and actual schedules**
  Use tables and GANTT charts that compare the actual and planned schedules. To analyze them, go back to the start of the work and proceed forward in time. Consider where the schedule first began to slip. Then move ahead to note areas where slippage increases. Start with a high-level outline form of the work and then step down into more detail. Figure 9.1 gives an actual vs. planned GANTT chart.
- **Action 4: Do actual vs. planned cost analysis**
  Create a spreadsheet using project management software. You can produce a table in most project management software packages that gives the planned or actual work performed by resource (rows) over time (columns). This table can be exported to the spreadsheet. With both the planned and actual work exported, you can compare the results in terms of hours.

Actual vs. Planned GANTT Chart

ID	Task Name	Duration	January			February				March	
			1/16	1/23	1/30	2/6	2/13	2/20	2/27	3/5	3/12
1	**Task 1**	**26d**									
2	Task 1.1	6d									
3	Task 1.2	20d									
4	Milestone 1	0d						2/22			
5	**Task 2**	**15d**									
6	Task 2.1	5d									
7	Task 2.2	10d									
8	Task 2.3	5d									
9	Milestone 2	0d									3/14

Legend:

Task Progress Milestone Summary Rolled Up Task Rolled Up Milestone Rolled Up Progress Baseline

Project
Date: 2/18/00

Page 1

Figure 9-1

To do cost analysis, use the spreadsheet to convert work into money considering regular pay, overtime, and other cost factors. Figure 9.2 gives a cumulative actual vs. budget analysis. Note that in this example the actual cumulative expense lagged behind the planned expense for some time. At the current time this project is now over budget in terms of cumulative costs.

- **Action 5: Analyze variations**
  If you have found variations, why did they occur? The obvious reason is that the task dates and durations slipped. A second reason is that more information is reflected in changes in schedules and dependencies. Third, you may have added more tasks and detail that can impact the overall schedule through a rollup to summary tasks. Fourth, you may have restructured the tasks in the schedule.
- **Action 6: Perform "What if . . .?" analysis**
  At the end of the actual analysis, analyze the impact of shifting resources, adding resources, changing the schedule structure, or deleting resources. See what happens if you shake things up. This can lead you to some interesting ideas for change.

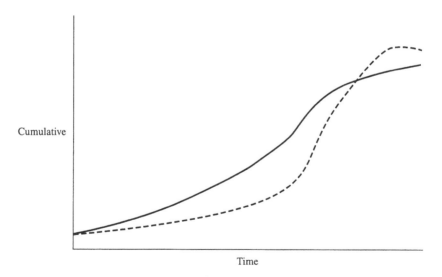

In this figure the actual cumulative expenses are shown in a dashed line while the planned budget is shown in a solid line. As you can see, spending starts more slowly for the actual than the planned and then accelerates and overtakes the budget–to speed up the project.

Figure 9-2: Cumulative Budget vs. Actual Expenses

Perform Financial Analysis

You will want to review the actual expenditures by area. Set aside time to do this analysis on a regular basis. Take the reports you are provided by accounting and review these in light of the plan. Here are questions you can answer:

- Have part-time people working on the team been charging too many hours to the project? Relate the part-time people to the tasks that they are performing to formulate your answer.
- Are the facilities use and equipment charges valid? Go back to purchase orders and the plan for your information.
- Is the overhead and burden assigned to E-Business excessive?

If possible, maintain your own spreadsheet for budget items. If you hold yourself accountable to maintain numbers, you are more likely to have the discipline to analyze the data as well.

Common Analysis Problems

The above analysis actions are inductive in that they proceed from validation to consideration of variations. Analysis can also be inductive when it is based on an issue.

- *Problem 1*: The schedule is standing still, but you know that the work and progress are going well. What is going on? Tasks are probably missing from the schedule. When these are added to the schedule, the schedule will likely show slippage. Yet, when you post actual results, this should be fixed.
- *Problem 2*: The work is showing limited progress, but the schedule shows even less progress. The schedule probably does not reflect dependencies or work correctly.
- *Problem 3*: The number of issues is growing. Not all the issues are getting addressed. However, the schedule remains unchanged. You have not reflected the issues in the dates of future tasks. Allow for these additional issues and recognize that, when these are factored in, the future tasks will slip, causing the overall schedule to slip.

Report to Management

A major guideline is to informally meet often with management to keep them up-to-date and to garner support. These meetings should be short so that the overall percentage of time spent with management is actually small. Most of the contact should be in informal meetings, rather than in formal presentations. More formal presentations indicate either that E-Business is becoming more exciting or the project is in more trouble.

Create Effective Status Reports

Here are three ways to provide status to management:

- *Status report based on work and progress.* This tends to be a reporting method that focuses on accomplishments. The detailed work and milestones accomplished are enumerated.
- *Status report based on issues.* This report identifies the various issues still open and their priorities. It also highlights the issues that were resolved.
- *Combined status report based on both work and issues.*

To ensure consistency across E-Business subprojects, adopt a standard reporting method, preferably the combined approach.

You will want to provide both quantitative and qualitative information to management at the same time. The form in Figure 9.3 provides a reasonable summary sheet for E-Business. The sections of the report are as follows:

- *Title, identification, and purpose.* This provides some basic information to identify the work.
- *Summary GANTT chart.* This is a summary high-level GANTT chart that provides status.
- *Cumulative budget vs. actual chart.* See Figure 9.2.
- *Summary of issues.* This area provides highlights of active issues.
- *Milestones and accomplishments.* This section addresses achievements.
- *Anticipated activity in the next period.* This section describes what is likely to occur in the next period.

Evaluate the Quality of the Work and Milestones

What is quality? What is acceptable quality? Answering these questions will require effort and definition for each milestone. Checking out the quality of dozens of milestones is not practical, requiring time and resources. Here are some alternatives for evaluating milestones.

- *Level 0:* Do no review.
- *Level 1:* Determine if there is evidence of a milestone. This is verification of presence, not content.
- *Level 2:* Perform a quick check by evaluating only a few items related to the milestone or work.
- *Level 3:* Conduct a full milestone or work review.

When work is routine and you trust the people involved, impose level 0. Many key milestones will deserve at least a level 2. Few will justify a level 3 review. You can escalate a review from one level to a higher level if you sense problems.

E-Business Status Summary Report

Project Name: _____   Date:_____

Project Managers:_____

Purpose of Project: _____

Scope of Project: _____

Summary GANTT Chart	Cumulative Budget vs. Actual

In this figure the actual cumulative expenses are shown in a dashed line while the planned budget is shown in a solid line. As you can see, spending starts more slowly for the actual than the planned and then accelerates and overtakes the budget–to speed up the project.

Milestones Achieved in Last Period: _____

_____

Critical Unresolved Issues: _____

_____

Anticipated Milestones: _____

_____

Figure 9-3: Example of Summary Reporting Sheet for an E-Business Implementation

Remember that you will need some approach like this, because in E-Business you will be dealing with many milestones.

What is involved in a full-scale review? Three setup tasks begin the process:

1. Determine who has knowledge of E-Business, technology, and the situation to be reviewed. Involving people in a review means time lost from working on E-Business or other projects, so enter into the review process judiciously.
2. Set the time for the review and try to manage it in such a way that it causes a minimum of disruption to the work.
3. Define the scope of the review. What will be included and excluded? For example, will only quality be reviewed or will the review include the way that the methods and tools are employed?

With the setup tasks accomplished, move to the review itself. Make a checklist of items:

- Materials that will be supplied before the review
- Materials and documents during the review
- People, equipment, and facilities access required for the review

Divide the review into two parts. The first part consists of an overall assessment by the review team with feedback as to the level of detail for the review and the areas of the project milestone or work for review. The second part consists of the actual review.

After the review of a milestone or work, implement the results as soon as possible. This may mean changing the E-Business plan. It may mean resource shifting or change. It can also be a time of getting charged up again . If the results of the review are favorable, the team's efforts are reinforced. If the results are recommended changes, you can tout success based on the changes and lessons learned.

These reviews are part of your quality assurance effort. In E-Business you pay a high price if you put out E-Business software and information that are flawed in accuracy, completeness, quality, or performance. Quality assurance plays a much larger role in E-Business than in standard projects.

E-BUSINESS EXAMPLES

RICKER CATALOGS

During the initial period of the work, management reporting was informal. The project leaders spent a great deal of time working in E-Business. This was good, but they neglected to track the work. After some unpleasant surprises were encountered, one of the managers was appointed as the "tracker."

MARATHON MANUFACTURING

Marathon had established management practices for reporting as well as information sharing among the leaders. This turned out to be helpful in allowing each leader to compare where they spent their time with other, non–E-Business projects.

ABACUS ENERGY

Tracking at Abacus was performed for both internal management and a steering committee of internal managers and suppliers. The use of the status form in this chapter helped to get attention paid to specific issues in E-Business.

CRAWFORD BANK

The project leaders in Crawford Bank quickly saw that the work could not be tracked by one person. It was spread out between the internal bank and the new company. Moreover, the leaders lacked detailed knowledge of some areas of lending. More time was spent analyzing information provided by team leaders in subprojects than was planned.

E-BUSINESS LESSONS LEARNED

- **Consider what omens mean and what pattern they imply.**
  As in real life, omens can appear for projects. These omens can be problems or successes with methods and tools, people, or other resources, for example. Rather than just tactically responding to problems, look for a pattern so that you can be proactive in dealing with them.
- **Take stock of the project when you are too tired to do other kinds of work.**
  When you are tired, you may not want to deal with E-Business anymore. This is a good time to sit back and review E-Business overall.
- **Allow ample time to do analysis before a meeting**.
  Last-minute work on the plan before a meeting can result in more chaos than benefit. Use the time right before a meeting to review what you have done before and get focused on issues. Project analysis time should be open-ended and not subject to pressure.
- **Distribute E-Business knowledge throughout the team**.
  People sometimes associate control of a project with knowledge about some aspect of E-Business. For this reason, some leaders attempt to keep knowledge to themselves, believing this will allow them more control. In a modern collaborative environment, this is clearly out of place. Control and knowledge are related, but project knowledge should be distributed throughout the team.
- **To gain wisdom, sit back and look at the E-Business subprojects**.
  An E-Business leader who is constantly working on detailed administrative or issue work loses the benefits of considering the overall picture. Gaining perspective and an understanding of what is going on in the big picture are two valuable aspects of taking time to take a step back.
- **Do analysis yourself**.
  Do not depend on others to do your work in analysis. Firstly, when this person is not available, you are helpless. Second, in meetings you will be unable to respond to questions related to the analysis. Unless you do it yourself, you are remote.

- **Suspect trouble and check up on the situation if people do not inform you of the progress of particular tasks.**
  People who are achieving results are usually happy with what they are doing. They are likely to relate their success to you. On the other hand, if you hear nothing, you have a right to suspect trouble.

- **Retain history so that you are not doomed to repeat mistakes.**
  If E-Business work goes on for a year or more, similar issues and questions will crop up numerous times. Knowing how previous problems were addressed will help you now. Also, note that some issues will recur in different clothes. Recurrence may happen with someone who lost out on an issue, for example.

- **Make use of statistical analysis of data.**
  Project statistics usually abound and are there for the taking. These statistics are often boring to work with and overlooked, but they are most useful. If you do not analyze the data, you will wake up to unpleasant trends too late. With the availability of more statistical tools in spreadsheets and other software, statistics are getting easier to work with.

- **Track and compare multiple schedules for a set of tasks.**
  In many settings, several subprojects compete for the same people, supplies, facilities, or equipment. You also may want to learn from previous, similar projects. Yet if the schedules and resources are not compatible, it will be impossible to make any meaningful comparison. What a term or task means to one person may mean something different to someone else. Work out a system that allows for comparison.

- **Look for the real E-Business bottlenecks.**
  You have been taught that the project bottlenecks can be found on the critical path. It seems logical that if you can shorten or rearrange the work, the bottleneck will disappear. The reality isn't this simple. You are watching the critical path, but problems arise from a task off the critical path. This occurs because the critical path does not include risk and uncertainty; it includes only length and duration. Real project bottlenecks cannot be detected easily by looking for the red line on the GANTT chart. How can you prevent bottlenecks? Go through the schedule and label tasks according to risk. Then filter or flag these tasks. Consider how close these tasks are to the critical path. Continue to keep a close watch on those tasks with the least slack.

- **Allow for a difference between resource allocation and resource usage.**
  Resource allocation is the assignment of resources. Resource usage is the consumption of resources according to specific schedules and calendars. These may not match, for several reasons. The resources are allocated at the level of higher level tasks but are consumed at the level of more detailed tasks. Also, the overhead associated with a resource is often not factored into resource allocation. For example, you may allocate someone for six months to a project.

However, the team member is on vacation for two weeks and in training for another two weeks. Allocation and consumption would be different.

- **Add tasks related to error fixing and rework at a detailed level**.
The inability to cope with the need to rework in a project affects likelihood of eventual success. Many people just extend a task duration to reflect fixing errors or rework. Doing this does not convey what is happening and creates communications problems. Instead, add in the actual tasks that have extended the duration of the task. If you allow the task to be slipped, you lose history and accountability later.

- **Examine boundaries of the E-Business effort periodically**.
During the duration of E-Business, the nature and boundaries of the work can change. As an E-Business leader, you should examine the boundaries as part of your "What if . . .?" analysis.

- **Manage E-Business for long-term payoff**.
Patterns of work behavior, relationships between people, and experience with methods and tools often long outlive the original E-Business effort. Side effects of E-Business may outlive the short term impact. Keep the long-term view in mind throughout the life of the work.

- **When you see a problem coming, give warning**.
Do missed deadlines have penalties? For example, you deliver a milestone a month late. In many cases, the project grinds on. Maybe no one will say anything. But you lose credibility when you don't see a problem coming and take some ameliorative action.

- **Determine deadlines by need rather than playing games with deadlines**.
A middle-level manager wants to look good. This manager imposes unrealistic deadlines on the subproject. If the team can make it, this will reflect favorably on the manager. This strategy sounds fine, but it will only work once or twice, if at all. People become wise to this strategy and start to give dates more conservatively to compensate.

- **Manage tasks that have risk as well as those that are easier to handle**.
Balance your time between different E-Business management tasks. If you devote too much of your time to tasks that are comfortable, you will not be coping with the tasks that have risk.

- **Assign as many cheap solutions and resources as possible**.
Depend as much as possible on simple, cheap resources. You will be pleasantly surprised to see the benefits from the expenditure of a small sum.

WHAT TO DO NEXT

1. Answer the following questions related to tracking.
   - To what extent are you on top of the work? Are you aware of what is going on in the work today? If you had to walk over to the team mem-

bers and go to the most critical area of a subproject, where would you go?

- Where do you spend your time? How much time is spent in the interactive, more productive work in the project? Have you attempted to spend more time here? What is preventing you from spending more time in these tasks?
- Have you adequately delegated the tracking of the schedule and work to people on the team? Have you adopted a more collaborative tracking approach?
- What milestones and work have you recently reviewed? Was the right information available? Were the correct people involved in the review? What results and actions flowed from the results of the review?
- Do you find it easy to relate the issues and action items in E-Business with the schedule? Have you identified the areas of risk in the schedule?

2. Using the list of Group I and Group II activities in this chapter, list how much of an average week is spent in each activity. Make a list for several subproject managers around you, also.

3. Evaluate your technique for assessing milestones in your work or the process in the work with which you are familiar. Should you adopt a more formal process in evaluating milestones and work?

4. Review your update and analysis process for your work. How well is it organized? Have you divided updating activities from analysis? Does the analysis that you do get translated into actions and schedule changes?

Chapter 10

Manage E-Business Resources

INTRODUCTION

A major challenge facing organizations is how to manage E-Business and other projects involving multiple organizations, both internally and externally. This is often made more complex if the team members are distributed geographically and belong to a variety of different companies. A typical E-Business effort might involve over ten internal departments, three to four consulting firms, and suppliers. Traditional project management methods were not designed for this situation. Most projects were managed as centralized, traditional projects—certainly not the case for E-Business.

Some additional factors that pertain to E-Business are:

- The systems have to be able to be interfaced so that on-line E-Business transactions are supported. This has a major impact on the IT resources related to programming.
- Technology has to be enhanced and standardized—an effort that affects the support and operations side of IT.
- Organization and process changes have to be implemented across departments in a coordinated manner.
- Different consultants who may be competitors have to work to support E-Business.
- Supplier coordination to streamline the supply chain with E-Business requires extensive coordination.

The complexity, need for commitment and involvement, and scope of E-Business efforts make them candidates for collaborative work and scheduling. More specific challenges are:

- The culture and interests differ among team members and companies.

- Many individuals assigned to the project have normal, nonproject duties that they cannot give up for E-Business; dividing their time between E-Business and their other work is a major challenge.
- Different companies may employ a variety of IT methods and tools that do not easily support integration, which leads to incompatibilities.
- E-Business subprojects have hidden dependencies that are revealed only later in the work at critical times.
- The goals of E-Business may seem very general and may not be relevant to many of the team members.

At the heart of these issues is the fact that the E-Business leaders do not have total authority over members of the project team. E-Business project leaders do not generally allocate the money or the people. They are organizers, directors, and coordinators—like directors for movies.

Collaborative E-Business Management

What is a collaborative management approach? Here are some key ingredients:

- *Each person on the team is responsible for identifying detailed tasks, updating tasks, addressing issues associated with their tasks, and participating in joint project work.* An E-Business effort is so large that even several leaders cannot do all of this work following traditional methods. They would be absorbed in administration.
- *A substantial percentage of the E-Business has to be assigned to more than one person.* In some cases, 30 to 40 percent of the tasks are joint among two or three people. Joint assignments are important in E-Business because of the size of the tasks, the benefit of different perspectives, and the benefit of a backup.
- *The E-Business leaders share all information except the really political elements with the team.* This sharing gets the team more involved in E-Business.
- *E-Business leaders share information amongst themselves.* This includes schedules, issues, and lessons learned. They share the same information with line managers in departments which are the homes of team members.
- *E-Business leaders work together and with line managers in assigning people and other resources to tasks on a routine basis (typically weekly)—obviously critical in E-Business.*

What are some of the benefits of a collaborative approach?

- Greater involvement means more commitment and understanding of E-Business.
- People working together and sharing information tend to trust each other more.

- Involvement and shared knowledge produces better quality work.
- There is backup within the team and among the project leaders.
- Working on issues together helps to build skills of the people in E-Business.
- E-Business work is more likely to end successfully on time and within budget.
- A ready forum is available in which to gather lessons learned on E-Business.
- Better communication allows for earlier warning of problems.

Collaboration does involve some additional startup work to get team members up to speed.

- Project members have to be trained in some of the project management methods.
- More project leader time is spent in managing the coordination.

However, these are offset by the benefits.

MILESTONES

Resource management involves all E-Business management activities, including the following:

- Planning when resources are needed
- Putting resources together for tasks
- Setting up resources to do work
- Directing the performance of the resources
- Reviewing the work and performance of the team
- Resolving resource questions
- Planning and staging when resources are no longer needed
- Releasing the resources
- Extracting lessons learned from the previous activities

The overall goal is to help you achieve the following:

- Get the most out of the E-Business resources
- Minimize the use of resources so as not to be an excessive burden on the line organizations
- Minimize the time required by each resource for their work in E-Business

A major goal is to achieve the E-Business objectives within budget and schedule constraints using a collaborative project management approach. This definition of purpose should be expanded to include the interests of the organizations and individuals participating in E-Business. However, the roles and responsibilities of the team are broader than traditional methods, as seen in the above list of the duties of the project team members.

These objectives reflect some fundamental lessons learned from E-Business implementation. Many problems, failures, and issues in E-Business come from poor resource management. The fewer resources you use and the less time that you need these resources the better. If managers are aware of what you are doing following this principle, they will be more likely to give you good resources. On the other hand, if you have idle resources, they may detect the waste and take less care in assigning qualified individuals to E-Business. Moreover, if you work towards minimization of resources, you put pressure on yourself as a leader to manage the resources more effectively.

METHODS AND TECHNIQUES

Let's consider how the collaborative approach is carried out with the E-Business management activities identified earlier.

ACTION 1: PLANNING FOR REQUIRED RESOURCES

Assume that you have developed the E-Business plan and that it has been approved. Now you want to plan in detail for resources. Cut a deal with the various managers to get the resources. Concentrate on the resources required for the first few months of the work. Lining up resources too far in advance is a major mistake. The distant future is vague. You have shown no results yet. You are not likely to obtain commitments for the best resources without a track record. In a collaborative approach, you are trying to build a common vision of the objectives and scope of E-Business, identify all of the things that team members are doing, and explore issues in the work identified in the E-Business concept. In addition, you and your team will be defining together how the project will help each person on the team.

Review the E-Business Objectives and Scope

Go over the objectives and scope of E-Business with each team member individually. Show how the team member's self-interest is aligned to the E-Business objectives. Discussion brings fuzzy objectives down to earth. The team member can see how their career is enhanced through E-Business involvement.

Show each team member how he or she fits into E-Business. Relate their role to that of other team members, including consultants.

After you have met with each person, assemble the team. To avoid a rehash of what you did with each person individually, go into the alternative purposes and scope that were considered in the E-Business concept definition. Also, look at E-Business from several alternative perspectives. These include the following:

- *Business perspective.* Show how E-Business is contributing to the organization. This will help reinforce the feeling that each team member is making a contribution.

- *Technology perspective.* Look at E-Business from the view of the methods and tools that will be employed in the work. Show that E-Business is employing modern techniques and that these techniques are well established.
- *Management perspective.* Explore the management controls and reporting that will be done in the work.

As you are doing this, you can indicate why each person was chosen for the team and each person's role in the work.

In this first action you are also defining the benefits of E-Business to the team members. In the past, little attention was paid to individual team members and what team members would get out of the work. Yet, paying attention is extremely important when working with team members because E-Business is competing for their attention with their other work. A prime strategy is to appeal to self-interest. Here are some things to do:

- Have each team member give you a resumé when he or she joins the team.
- Have each team member identify career goals and objectives for the next five years. Get them to think about the longer term.
- Have each team member create a new resumé that they would like to have after five years assuming that they are active participants in E-Business. This closes the loop with the previous two activities.
- Based on previous collaborative actions, work with each team member to identify tangible things that they will learn and do as well as the knowledge they will obtain from E-Business.
- Identify issues and barriers to achieving these personal goals. An example is the challenge of learning new methods and tools.
- Make these issues generic and add them to the list of issues in E-Business. This shows that you are sensitive to their concerns.

Here are some concerns expressed in some of our earlier E-Business work.

- Team members are concerned about meeting the schedule. Give some examples of other firms in doing this. Cite other internal projects such as the Y2K effort or a major software installation.
- There is worry that there will be many changes in direction from management. Answer this concern with the change control method and the role of management.

Build a Plan for Each Team Member

At the team meeting, indicate that you are sensitive to the fact that most, if not all, of the team members also have line responsibilities as well as work on other things outside of E-Business. Visit each person to determine what he or she is working on and what the schedule is. Try to obtain a copy of the schedules and any plans for their other work. Give as the reason for this the fact that you must build an overall E-Business plan that reflects the realities of the availability of the team members.

It is useful to build a small plan for each person with his or her other work. Each task the person performs in a line organization will be one task in this plan. You also have the person's tasks in other projects on a summary level.

With this done, you have a plan for each team member. When you construct the schedule for E-Business, you can combine it with these other plans and then filter on each resource to see the total commitment for each person on the team. You will be able to see points in time when people are overcommitted. Then you can plan and negotiate for people's time more effectively.

Negotiate with Line Managers and Project Leaders

Work with each manager to define a set of near-term priorities for each key team member. Next, focus on the short term of two to three months. If you negotiate for work beyond that, conditions and situations may change.

Don't try to strong-arm line managers by indicating that management thinks E-Business is important and that they had better cooperate. This just leads to hostility. After all, they have heard other "management critical" statements before. Appeal to the self-interest of their department.

Besides accomplishing the setting of priorities with these other managers, this action provides two other major benefits. The first is that you are establishing a collaborative environment for sharing resources with the managers prior to any crisis or major issue. Creating this atmosphere helps to build a pattern of successful relationships. Second, you are sharing information with them. You want to build upon this relationship to share schedules and future need information far enough in the future to support planning.

Define Issues Together

The issues are particularly important here because you want to use discussions of these as tools to build a common approach for working on problems and opportunities. Here are some guidelines:

- Do homework on several issues and introduce these to the department.
- Consider as issues the following:
    - People on the team have other duties and responsibilities. How can they be effective on E-Business work with these other duties?
    - The project may be of importance to the organization overall, but it is of marginal interest to some in the team. How will this be addressed?
- As you discuss each issue, summarize how people are to work together.
    - Identify how people should report on their work.
    - Identify how people will define their own work.

You can design a template to identify what the upcoming action is in terms of defining the E-Business effort. Include detailed tasks for each team member and schedule when the team members are to report on these tasks.

ACTION 2: IMPLEMENT A COLLABORATIVE APPROACH

Build or Evaluate a Project Template

Do you have an available project template for E-Business? If not, define a straw man, candidate template for the team members to review. Recall that the template contains high-level milestones and tasks. For each task in the template, identify the team member who will responsible. Also, identify which tasks are going to have joint responsibility. It is useful to have 30 to 40 percent of the tasks jointly assigned to foster teamwork. You should also validate the template by evaluating the issues in E-Business that surfaced in the previous action. Find the summary task in the template to which each issue corresponds. You can also scan down the tasks to see if you and the team have missed any issues.

Once you have a template, meet with each person on the team and indicate that person's areas of E-Business. Get each person to think about detailed tasks and relate the issues from the previous action to the tasks that they are responsible for.

Go Through a Simulation of Building the Detailed E-Business Plan and Updating the Plan

This is an important part of E-Business management since it basically links the work on issues with the initial meeting on purpose and scope. At this meeting, take one area of the plan and act as a team member in defining the tasks in the template. Progress from defining tasks to completing the baseline schedule for the work. Next, explain how the tasks will be updated by the team member responsible for them.

Construct the Detailed Tasks for E-Business for the Next Three Months

Each team member can now define the tasks needed to accomplish work that is to be done in the next three months. It is very important that you have identified tasks that are to be jointly performed by team members. Encourage team members to work together to define these tasks in more detail.

Each template task should be broken down into tasks that are not more than two weeks in duration. If you go longer than two weeks, the task is too fuzzy. If the task is too short, the effort requiring updating will be too great.

Here are some additional guidelines in defining tasks:

- Each task should be able to be defined as a simple sentence starting with an action verb. An example is "Prepare ground for planting trees." If you find that a task has complex wording such as "Dig up ground, fertilize, and water for trees," then split up this task into three separate tasks: dig up, fertilize, and water.
- Have each team member associate issues with the detailed tasks under the relevant template task for the issue. This further helps to validate the tasks and issues.
- Each team member should identify tasks that have risk or seem risky. This will give rise to additional issues or validate the existing issues.
- Schedule meetings with team members to discuss their joint tasks together with you.
- Making task definition a distinct step, apart from schedules, dependencies, and resources, will give a more complete task list and prevents team members from getting distracted by other facets of the work.

Establish Dependencies and Assign Resources

After reviewing the tasks, have the team members put in the minimum number of simple tail-to-head dependencies. If they are in doubt about a particular dependency, leave it out. They can discuss it later. This may indicate that you are missing a task.

In this action each team member will identify critical resources of any type that are a cost to the work or that E-Business will have to compete for with other projects and normal work.

In reviewing the work in this action, start with the dependencies. Ask team members why the dependency was created. This will lead to a discussion about the surrounding tasks. The net effect of evaluation is not only to validate the tasks and dependencies, but also to get a better understanding of how the work is to be done. The same is true with assigning resources to tasks.

Define the Duration and Dates Based on Previous Actions

With the tasks, dependencies, and resources defined, each team member can now estimate the start and end dates, and duration for each task. Give some examples to team members so that they have a better awareness of the approach. Here are some guidelines to help the team members:

- Do not pad the dates for contingencies. Put in realistic estimates.
- If you cannot estimate for a specific task, break up the task until you have isolated the part that you cannot estimate. There is probably an issue here

that is the reason an estimate cannot be given. Bringing these issues to the surface now can save time and prevent problems later.

Review each person's work with him or her when you have received all input from the team members. By waiting until you have all input, you can see the schedule overall. When the team members review their estimates with the leaders, the leaders will gain insight into how comfortable they are about the work.

It is likely that the schedule will not be realistic. It will stretch too long. Don't attack the group by saying that the schedule is not acceptable. Rather, identify where the specific parts of the schedule are in trouble. Go to the people involved on an individual basis and get at the assumptions behind the estimates. If you are lucky, you will find that assumptions have been made that caused the schedule to be longer but that were not necessary.

After reviewing the schedule, you can set the baseline plan and hold a team meeting to review it. At this meeting, hand out the schedule along with a list of issues and a map between issues and tasks. The purpose of this meeting is for the team members to gain a better understanding of the work as well as to focus on near-term risky tasks as a team.

ACTION 3: BUILD COLLABORATIVE TEAMWORK THROUGH THE INITIAL TASKS

Work now begins on E-Business. Circulate a printout of the schedule for the next three months. Have the team members mark tasks that have been completed. Add new tasks that were unanticipated or that apply to the future time horizon. If a task has slipped, have the team members create a new task and link it to the current task, also giving a reason for doing so. By repeating this several times, the team members get used to the process of schedule updating. You can then have a team member do the updating online in the network.

There may be a lack of knowledge of project management software on the part of the team members. Don't wait until the people are trained on the software to begin the collaborative approach. Implement manually with paper to get the process of collaboration going. This will take more time initially, but rushing this learning phase of collaboration will be counterproductive.

Address Initial Issues

Early on, establish a pattern for addressing issues. Identify some sample issues that are relatively minor and non-political. Get people in a group and start analyzing the issues. After some discussion, show the team how decisions are made and actions are taken. You can also indicate how the plan is updated as a result of deciding the issue.

As the work gets underway, ask for the reaction of the team to the collaborative process. Have team members share their views and suggestions to make the process better. This is a bottom up approach to implement collaboration and one that has often worked. This approach establishes a pattern for dealing with issues in a friendly and non-hostile setting. You can scale up the issues to address those that are more major.

When you do this with a team, you are accomplishing several goals. First, you are showing the team members that they can solve problems on their own without management. Second, they gain confidence in their ability to get things done as a group. Third, you are paving the way for more serious issues to be handled, based upon the pattern of success.

Conduct a Detailed Review of Initial Milestones

Review the work of the team members and milestones reached, based on the criteria given in Chapter 2. Also, give attention early in the project to tasks that have slipped. You are trying to determine a pattern for the slippage. This is done not to punish a team member but to determine now whether estimates for later tasks need to be revised. Try to get team members to feel comfortable in dealing with milestone reviews of each other's work. Another goal is to position team members to review each other's work, both positively and negatively. Team members will be able to see that people make errors, without incurring punishment.

ACTION 4: MONITOR AND MANAGE THE PROJECT FROM A COLLABORATIVE VIEW

Evaluate each major resource every day. Here are three ways to learn the information you need for an evaluation:

- Work side-by-side with the people doing the work.
- Sit in on meetings.
- Volunteer to be involved in the work.

By actually doing the work with the team members, you will learn the status of the work, gain the confidence of the workers, and gain information on any problems or opportunities that arise. If you follow up on what you discover, you will be a winning project manager.

How do people react when you become involved in the work? At first, you may be met with reservations. People will wonder why you are there. When you show up repeatedly, however, they will be more open and friendly. You will be building an enthusiastic team.

When managing team members, get back to the line managers whose people you are using on a weekly basis. Give them an honest assessment of utilization and performance. When managing facilities and equipment, consider enhancing them so that when they are returned, they are in better shape than when they first entered E-Business.

Exit of a Team Member

Prepare the team to address this situation before it arises. At the project kick-off, point out that team members will come and go. Turnover is inevitable. Have the team members identify and discuss issues associated with someone leaving. Some of these are as follows:

- The departing person takes knowledge with them.
- It is difficult to capture all of the knowledge before a person leaves the team.
- The work of the departing team member falls on the shoulders of the people remaining.

The exit of a team member brings not only problems but also benefits and opportunities. First, by the time someone leaves, progress has been made in the work. Work has been started and the person may not be critical to the work anymore. When someone leaves, it gives the team a chance to find a replacement with different skills that are needed for future tasks.

Transitioning between E-Business Phases

Larger E-Business efforts are typically divided into phases. Each phase often has a formal ending prior to the start of the next phase. How can an E-Business leader take advantage of this for the work? First, the leader can gather the team members together and gather lessons learned about what went on in E-Business. It is better to do this at the end of phases than to wait until the end of the work. The knowledge will probably be lost at the end of the work due to the elapsed time. Also, identifying the knowledge and getting agreement from the team builds teamwork and consensus.

Dealing with a Major Issue in a Collaborative Way

It is likely that the team will face a major crisis or issue in the E-Business effort. For many of the most difficult situations, you have to rely on upper management for resolution and support. For other problems, have the team work together to address the crisis. The collaborative effort on the part of the team can help the project leader focus on potential actions and decisions.

Changing Project Direction

E-Business can change direction due to management action, external factors, or events in other related projects. The leaders should prepare the team for eventual changes in direction early in the effort to avoid problems later. For example, the leaders might propose several changes in direction based on detailed knowledge of E-Business work. This allows the team to work with a reasonable hypothesis of change.

ACTION 5: BRING NEW TEAM MEMBERS INTO A COLLABORATIVE ENVIRONMENT

To bring a new team member into E-Business, include the following actions in a one-on-one session:

- Walk through the purpose, scope, issues, benefits, and other elements of the E-Business concept.
- Indicate the history of the work and what changes occurred during the work and why.
- Review each team member and what their expertise is and what they do.
- Indicate how the new member will work with the existing team members.
- Review the issues with the new team member.

Next, introduce the team member to the team. First state the new member's expertise and then explain how this person fits within E-Business. Indicate areas of joint work involving this new member and others. Have the new team member give some experience and lessons learned from previous projects.

Finally, set up and monitor the new team member's initial work. It is suggested that you assign them to joint tasks initially. This strategy will make them more comfortable working in the team and provide feedback on how they are doing. Each new team member should be assigned both individual and teamwork tasks. This will allow the new team member to experience a team approach.

RESOURCE QUESTIONS

How Do You Address Morale Problems on the Team?

When you take over failing projects or suffer a reverse in E-Business, a common problem is bad morale. Why does this occur? The people often were not managed or motivated properly. They may have developed a negative attitude from ineffective leaders.

This attitude can be turned around. Get involved with individuals in the work. Build morale from the bottom up. Give people confidence in themselves by complimenting them on their work. Get them additional support where appropriate and possible. Do not plan a group pep talk in the early stages. Get the team together only when you have begun to boost the morale.

If morale is good, don't assume that everything is fine. A team can get too confident. View morale as an ongoing issue. Keep building morale up. Compare the project to your past projects and to projects in general. Never build morale by comparing E-Business with other active work and projects. If you denigrate a project, presume that the project leader will learn of it and that this will reflect negatively on you.

How Do You Handle Problems among Team Members?

For political or other reasons you inherit or take on a team member who either has a poor track record or is not suited to the work. What do you do? You cannot just discharge the person. Go back to the E-Business plan and examine what tasks are not assigned. Where could this employee do some good? Where could the employee do the least damage? Assign tasks and monitor the work, as you would do with a consultant. Ensure that this employee does not disrupt the work of other team members. Through your direct intervention you might be able to produce useful results.

If you try these suggestions and they don't work, try to persuade the person to leave the team on a voluntary basis. Don't criticize this person in front of others. If you are asked by team members what is going on, indicate that you are aware of the situation and are attempting to address it.

Here are some examples of problems with employees and how the leaders handled the situation.

- *A team member was an alcoholic.* The team member went through counseling, but the problem continued. The answer was isolation from the team until the person was removed from E-Business.
- *An employee misrepresented his skills to the previous manager.* It was obvious that the person was not qualified. A review of the entire effort was instituted. It indicated that tasks had to be reassigned. This review led to the employee's removal.
- *Another person appeared less than competent.* However, it turned out that the person was salvageable through direction and guidance.
- *An employee constantly criticized E-Business and the team.* Morale was affected. The approach here was direct confrontation when the person was caught doing it. The person was reassigned.

After you have terminated someone from the team, tell each person on the team individually and answer any questions. Then hold a team meeting to go over what happened and the lessons learned.

Try to handle personnel problems yourself. Unless necessary, do not alarm management by reporting that you have a major crisis. If there is a crisis, focus on the issues and not on the personnel. This makes it easier to set aside emotions about the team member.

How Do You Cope with the Procurement Process?

Procurement is a cumbersome process that is essential for E-Business. Procurement tends to follow some bureaucratic processes for the purpose of control. They are often not geared up for speed.

Here are some guidelines for procurement:

- Go to purchasing and get a presentation on the procurement rules. Obtain any forms and directions.
- Get a single contact person in purchasing to work with.
- Establish rapport with the contact person by going through the schedule with them.
- Fill out requests for all of the resources you will need—even for resources in the distant future.
- Review all requests with the procurement contact.
- Establish a schedule for procurement.

Look at E-Business from the perspective of procurement. Procurement staff often feel unappreciated. They get requests at the last minute. The requests are incomplete and incomprehensible. If you act in a cooperative and sympathetic manner, you will get more support from procurement. Offer to include the procurement person in team meetings that relate to the resources you will be getting.

When procurement begins, support the process. Volunteer to interview potential vendors. Visit their facilities and talk to their managers. Keep the requirements specific and direct. Indicate the importance of the part or component to the project. Indicate how you will test and evaluate what is delivered. Update purchasing as you obtain and use the resources.

How Do You Get People to Work Together?

People may enter the project who did not get along before the project even started. Don't just force them to work together. Organize the tasks so that they have limited contact. To each person involved, acknowledge that the problem exists and that you will help minimize the effect on the project. When the people involved have to work together on a task, try to be there and participate. This will help head off problems. Work to keep them focused on the technical part of the work.

How Do You Manage and Direct Technology Work?

Many managers take technology for granted. They lack technical knowledge and treat equipment as if it were a mysterious black box. This is the wrong approach. While you don't need to know the details, all technology requires management. How is the technology being used? Is it being employed effectively? Do the people using the technology have the proper skills and training? Many times you will find that the use of technology becomes more effective if you actively assess how you are using it. Encourage the gathering and sharing of lessons learned. Do not be afraid to ask any questions that come to mind; as the project manager you are not expected to come to the project with a thorough knowledge of all the technical aspects involved.

How Do You Address Nonperformance and Schedule Slippage?

When you detect signs of this in advance, pin down the cause of the slippage. Here are some potential causes of nonperformance:

- Some tasks were not in the plan.
- Quality problems indicate the need for rework.
- E-Business is not receiving the resources on schedule.
- The team is not performing the work on time.
- Time is being wasted.
- The tasks are vague or ambiguous.

Some of these situations can be prevented through front-end planning. If the problem arises, go to the team and see what can be done with current resources to address the problem. This will reveal the extent of the problem and what is going to be required in terms of management patience and support. If you have to choose between asking for more money or more time, choose time. Adding money means adding resources that could further delay the project.

As you are doing this, alert management through informal channels that an issue has come up that could affect the schedule. Let management know that you are working on the problem and will get back to them. Gradually unfold what is going on to management. Give management options as to what to do with your recommendations. You want them to buy into the decision and become supportive.

E-BUSINESS EXAMPLES

RICKER CATALOGS

Ricker embarked on a limited collaborative approach. The team shared about 20% of the tasks with at least one other person. However, they did work collaboratively on identifying issues and addressing them. There probably could have been more collaborative work with more employees. This would have led to a better web site. However, they felt that they were under time pressure and decided that more collaboration would have slowed down E-Business.

MARATHON MANUFACTURING

In Marathon's case, management involved almost all employees in the project through employee contributions to design and function, supply of information, and voting on alternative features and their implementation. Within the team much of the work was collaborative. This was favored because employees had to do their normal work as well. Having several people assigned to tasks meant that work would be done on the task even if one person was busy.

ABACUS ENERGY

Abacus had a relatively small team internally for implementing E-Business. The team expanded when they considered the suppliers who had to be involved in the work. Rather than wait until everything had been developed and then push E-Business onto the suppliers, Abacus management decided to involve the suppliers at the start of the work in a collaborative way. A steering committee of suppliers was formed and the suppliers were assigned tasks with the internal staff. A newsletter on the Internet was then employed to disseminate information to the other suppliers regarding status and issues.

What was interesting for this example is that in several cases they used a voting method to have the suppliers make decisions on the user interface, functions on the web site, decisions on the rollout and implementation, and coordination in the future. This was a very useful collaborative vehicle to gain even more involvement.

CRAWFORD BANK

At Crawford a traditional project management approach was taken for E-Business. This began to alienate the employees of the bank from the E-Business subsidiary. The leaders then decided to adopt a collaborative approach to implementing the new bank on the web. Over 50% of the significant tasks were joint between employees of the bank and employees of the subsidiary.

E-BUSINESS LESSONS LEARNED

- **As the complexity of the E-Business work grows, the benefits of collaboration grow.**
  The subprojects most unsuitable for collaboration are those that are small, short, and performed in one location. For very large subprojects there must

be a practical partitioning of the work among organizations and collaboration must occur at upper levels between groups.

- **Work with the other managers to set priorities.**
People are sometimes pulled off the team to do other work not related to E-Business. If you and other managers have jointly set goals, this problem will be less likely to occur.

- **Give rewards for work, but avoid financial awards.**
Financial awards are often counterproductive. People will start expecting them and take the money for granted. Money is probably not the right incentive. As an alternative, give time off, which has the added benefit of preventing burn out.

- **Make sure that people maintain awareness of their home organization.**
In an E-Business effort of substantial duration, some people on the team can become hangers-on and stay too long on the team. This happens when people have been on the team so long that they lose touch with the line organization that serves as their home. Encourage people to visit their friends and their line manager. If you know that the project is going to last a long time, start this policy at the inception of E-Business.

- **Use the issues meetings to allow people to clash and argue about methods, tools, and approaches.**
Clashes in the team are expected given the pressure. Carefully direct these meetings to be fair and do not allow the senior people to dominate the team meetings. Younger team members can contribute new ideas and hard work, and should not be overlooked.

- **Monitor part-time team members.**
Managing part-time people in E-Business is a challenge since their time is spread across many activities. Furthermore, you do not have full control. How do you get part-timers to continue to work on E-Business? First, follow up on what they are doing. Set the duration of their tasks and level of detail of work so that you can monitor the work more easily.

- **Always have junior, less experienced people on the team.**
These team members are often energetic, intelligent, and eager. They may lack experience, but their more recent training and knowledge may be valuable assets. The junior people are more open to change and new ideas.

- **Periodically review the roles of each team member.**
You have defined the roles of the team members earlier. However, E-Business work goes on for months and people forget or lose sight of their roles. Not knowing the roles, the team members invent them. To avoid such problems, regularly review the roles of each team member to the group. Otherwise, you risk losing control of the work.

- **Deal with conflicts in an open manner.**
External organizational conflicts will be reflected in the team. Get the people involved in the conflict together in a room and acknowledge the

conflict. Indicate that E-Business is a different entity and that they will need to work together effectively on it. Reinforce this whenever problems arise.

- **Pay particular attention to the timing of a resource change.**
  Timing of changes is important—sometimes more important than the change itself. You may want the change to occur in a critical period to shake up the work. It is not necessarily true that the best time to make changes is when everything is calm.
- **Be flexible on controlling the team members in terms of their time.**
  Managing the team by the clock will yield presence but probably not results. If people are doing project work at home and you have evidence of this, tread lightly.
- **Cultivate your power of memory.**
  When managing resources, take notes and reinforce your memory. You want to be able to relate events to each other over time.
- **Carefully consider team member substitution.**
  Substituting project staff can cause unforeseen ripples. The person who is being substituted for may have developed personal ties and may have performed work of which you are unaware. Investigate to see what the impact of substitution might be before making a decision.
- **Remove people from a large subproject to speed up the work.**
  For large subprojects that are in trouble, consider removing resources from the team. This can be carried out in conjunction with narrowing the scope of the subproject and restructuring the work.
- **Be careful when you shift resources between tasks.**
  Moving resources between tasks can slow down both tasks. People have to transfer what they know to their successors. They also have to pick up information from their predecessors. Shift resources only as part of a major project change to minimize the overall disruption.
- **Keep the overlap of people entering and leaving the E-Business effort to a minimum.**
  Overlap is good in that you can transfer knowledge. However, it is best if this is short. Otherwise, it is awkward for the person entering the task. Bad habits and misinformation can also be transferred.
- **Nurture relationships with team members for later E-Business work.**
  Try to get acquainted with the people who are performers on the project. You may be seated next to the same person on the next E-Business effort.
- **Allow people to express emotion.**
  People on the team can become emotional on a wide range of issues. This is not a problem in itself. Allow people to vent some of their frustration or happiness relating to E-Business.

WHAT TO DO NEXT

1. Answer the following questions related to collaborative work.
   - Do you have an approach for doing work in a collaborative environment? Notice that the word *work* was used and not *projects*. It is helpful to have a pattern of joint work habits.
   - How are projects managed that involve several divisions of your company? How are division-specific issues and problems addressed?
   - How are projects managed that involve outside consultants and contractors? Do the consultants have any role in defining the tasks and work? Who evaluates the milestones?
   - How are personnel issues addressed in the project? Are they largely ignored until there is a crisis?
   - What amount of time is consumed by idle resources? What is the impact of idle resources on the productivity of the team and project?
   - How many missing tasks exist in planning, in setting up, in getting ready, and in shutting down resources?
2. Identify potential opportunities for collaborative work outside of projects. On projects, try to have about 30 percent of the project tasks assigned to several people. Select a small project involving several organizations and build a collaborative team. As the project goes on, attempt to gather lessons learned to improve your techniques for the next project.
3. Conduct an assessment of how nonpersonnel resources are being managed. Determine the impact of resource problems on E-Business.
4. For personnel resources, identify the interpersonal problems that exist within the team. Has anything been done about these? What steps do you think can be taken now?
5. Return to the E-Business plan and add tasks that include procurement, setting up resources, and removing resources. What is the effect on the overall schedule? If the result has a major impact, you are missing a significant amount of work and your schedule is probably not realistic.

Chapter 11

Manage E-Business Work

INTRODUCTION

So far you have constructed the E-Business plan, started the activities, and managed the resources. All of these things are important, but the bottom line is the work in the E-Business effort—how to set up for work, perform the work, improve the work, and evaluate the results. As a leader, you want to be able to evaluate the work and improve the work wherever possible. When evaluating work, many E-Business leaders immediately consider the most routine, common work performed in E-Business. Experience shows, however, that problems are more likely to occur in areas of exceptions, rework, workarounds, and nonrecurring work. Mistakes are more likely to be made in these areas. These are the areas where people are not familiar with the tasks. In E-Business, setting up the new processes is one area of risk; another is handling changed requirements. Estimates of resources required and the schedule are likely to run into trouble here as well.

As an example of nonroutine work, consider workarounds. A workaround occurs when you have a problem with some aspect of the work, such as tools, methods, systems, facilities, or even certain people. In order to get the work performed with the available resources, you have to invent a way to get around the problem—a workaround. If you manage routine work and ignore workarounds, you are ignoring a substantial percentage of the work. Instead, spend time managing the workaround. Once you turn your attention to a particular workaround, the best tactic might be to try to eliminate the workaround by backing up and addressing the specific problems that created the need for it in the first place.

MILESTONES

The purpose of this chapter is to determine what is going on in the actual work and to consider how to improve the work. Improving the work will benefit the schedule by reducing uncertainty. The scope of what is going to be considered includes all aspects of the actual work, from setup to performance through shutdown or completion.

METHODS AND TECHNIQUES

First, we will examine which tasks to consider for analysis. We will cover how to review these tasks. Ways to improve the work are offered. Specific situations are then analyzed.

ACTION 1: CHOOSE WHICH E-BUSINESS TASKS TO ANALYZE

You don't have time to check all tasks. When choosing which to evaluate, the obvious place to start is with the ones that are in trouble. To know which ones to check after that, assess risk. Risk is examined by considering the issues underlying the risk and estimated by looking at the likelihood of slippage and the problems that will result if slippage occurs. Tasks that have moderate likelihood of slippage and exposure are often more dangerous to your project than something that has a high likelihood of slippage but low exposure, or vice versa.

Review your list of active and soon-to-be active tasks and first determine the importance of each task to the overall E-Business schedule. Take into account more than the mathematical critical path. Also consider the potential side effects on other tasks and projects—the ripple effect. This process will give you a list of the tasks with some amount of exposure.

Next, think about the people doing the work. If necessary, do a brief on-site review of the work and determine which tasks have some likelihood of slippage. Look for tasks that have exceptions, workarounds, and rework. The times for these things are less easy to predict. After evaluation, you should be able to determine which tasks have the greatest risk of slippage.

When looking at which tasks to analyze, separate out the exceptions. Look for instances where the routine work (which is likely to be the most efficient) breaks down. Another area to investigate is nonroutine or nonrecurring work. These are tasks that involve more thinking. People will tell you that these cannot be planned or worked through quickly. However, you will find that many of the subtasks and detailed work are similar to standard work.

An important area to consider is where and when work is turned over between people. This occurs between shifts, or when people are going to move on to another task. Many things can go wrong in a hand-off. Often, the time allowed is too short. Also, people may write cryptic notes and just take off from work. This then necessitates telephone calls to get status. When one worker requires information from another, both can waste time with the "telephone tag" syndrome.

ACTION 2: EVALUATE WORK RESULTS AND MILESTONES

Once you have determined which tasks to evaluate, rank these tasks according to levels of review, as follows:

- Level 0—No review
- Level 1—Evaluate for existence of the work
- Level 2—Evaluate for presence of the work
- Level 3—Assess the content of the work

Levels are helpful in evaluating work because it is difficult to evaluate all the work at Level 3. For some tasks you will take people at their word that they completed the work. Differentiate between existence and presence. Checking existence simply means checking that the work is there. Checking for presence means checking the form of the work as well as existence, but not addressing content. Level 3 reviews and analyzes the internals of the work. Decide on the level for a milestone based on risk and importance to E-Business. Many milestones must be evaluated at Level 1 due to the number of milestones and the limited time and resources available.

Once you determine the milestones for detailed review, you can identify who will participate in the review. These people should be familiar with the work; they can be other members of the team. However, if the same people are always used, the quality of the review will degrade over time.

What do you hope to accomplish in the review? First, determine if the work product is of sufficient quality so that you can continue. Second, transfer and share knowledge between the reviewers and the people who did the work. This helps build a team and can assist in providing backup later if someone on the team who did the work is no longer available.

Should reviews be planned or unannounced? Planned reviews have the advantage that materials will be available. However, in a dynamic setting, the leader and the team have to be ready for a review at any time.

How should a review be structured? It depends on the nature of the milestone. The project team members who performed the work may present the milestone without intermediaries. A sequence of steps might be as follows:

- *Step 1*: Hand out materials for review in advance of a meeting.
- *Step 2*: Set the agenda for the meeting by posing specific questions and issues about the milestone.
- *Step 3*: Conduct the review of the milestone.

- *Step 4*: At the end of the meeting, determine what is to be done and what actions are to be taken.

The project leader should orchestrate all of these steps and also act as a scribe during the meeting. The review should concentrate on the milestone. Bring up the details of the work only if there is a major problem.

Possible results of the review are as follows:

- The milestone is turned back as totally unacceptable; work stops.
- The project will continue but the team will rework the milestone.
- The milestone is acceptable, but additional work will be done later.
- The milestone is acceptable but additional tasks will need to be performed.
- The milestone is acceptable; no additional work is required.

Now expand your review to how the team members are supervised. Here are some areas to consider:

- How team members are supervised on an hourly or daily basis
- How team members are assigned work
- Preparation time allowed for the work
- Problems that team members have with coworkers
- How reported problems are handled by supervisors
- How supervisors accept and follow up on suggestions for improvement
- How work is checked and evaluated
- How supervisors respond to problems related to equipment, parts, and supplies

Working with supervisors to change priorities is difficult and may require intervention from a line manager.

Now review your spending of money. Spend money in chunks so that you can trade off among different spending candidates. If you spend money on one item at a time, people's patience and your money will run out. Give higher priority to action items that involve one-time expense rather than recurring expense.

ACTION 3: IMPROVE THE WORK

Where should you start to look for improvement? Consider all activities that don't require money, organization approval, or involvement. Ask the people who are doing the work what they would like to have happen and change. Test out simple, inexpensive, and non-political changes.

Here are some examples of such changes from past E-Business efforts:

- Relocate where the work is performed.
- Rearrange the work layout.
- Change the involvement of team members.

- Upgrade the procedures with the new versions.
- Have people share experiences.
- Obtain updated procedures.
- Train staff in policies and procedures for the new processes and the current processes.
- Make small procedural changes on an interim basis.

Your best sources of information are direct observation and the people who are doing the work. Examine how exceptions and rework are handled, since these can consume much more time. Start with the question, "If you could do things differently, what would you like to do?" This should solicit responses that match some of the items on the previous list. Next, start to implement changes. Morale will climb.

Here are some action item candidates for improvement:

- Upgrade equipment or software.
- Upgrade facilities.
- Upgrade skills.
- Add on to the support for the project.
- Add different types of people.
- Consider outsourcing or insourcing.
- Replace the people.
- Change the process around the work.
- Increase the extent of testing and quality of testing; improve quality assurance.

For each idea, determine costs associated with acquisition, installation, training, setup, adaptation, modification, usage, and management. Once you have groups of changes, you can determine the overall impact. You can change the schedule to accommodate groups of changes.

HOW TO RESOLVE WORK QUALITY ISSUES RELATED TO E-BUSINESS

Situation 1: Work Quality Is Poor

A task may have been in trouble from the beginning, but other explanations for poor quality are possible. First, the measurement of quality may have changed—this task would have passed three months ago. Second, the standard of measurement may have changed. Third, work quality itself may be acceptable, but the appearance or impression of the work is not acceptable.

Look for causes and effects. If problems are due to one of the first two situations, management changes in direction are a strong possibility as a cause. Personnel turnover, new equipment that is not calibrated, new procedures that have not been shaken down, the work being sped up, and morale problems are other possibilities. Consider combinations of events in a limited period of time that may affect E-Business.

After you have determined possible causes for the problems, answer the following questions:

- What event suddenly caused the work to be unacceptable?
- What problems have been gradually getting worse?
- What is the effect of poor quality on the subproject? Can the work continue?

Interview the staff to find the source of the problems and the interaction between the causes. After finding a likely source, run a pilot test to determine what effect improvements could have. Look at related areas. Has the problem spread? After your analysis, you can make an effort to improve the process overall.

Situation 2: The Situation Isn't What Was Planned

Surprises are part of the life of E-Business. Perhaps the purpose of E-Business changed in a meeting, causing half of all of the work to date to be superfluous. Or, the scope keeps expanding. It seems to grow like a crop of wheat. Or, you thought that the task a team member was working on was going to take two weeks. Two days into the task, the new estimate is four weeks and climbing.

Here are some steps you can take when you encounter surprises:

- **Step 1: Gain perspective.**
  A first response to situations such as these is to sit back and get an overall perspective of what is happening. When you modify the purpose, scope, or work, you will add tasks. Make an effort to do this immediately. This will test your understanding of the changed conditions as well as provide you with information for the new schedule.
- **Step 2: Determine how the situation happened.**
  The intention is not to place blame. You want to examine in retrospect why the situation occurred so that you can improve your estimation and management in the future. Could the situation have been predicted if you had watched the work more closely? This step will sharpen your monitoring skills in the future.
- **Step 3: Seize the opportunity.**
  Use this situation as an opportunity to see if the work and the work environment can be improved. Can you eliminate or combine any tasks? Can dependencies be changed? Can the quality or quantity of assigned resources be reduced? Implement changes while the situation is fresh.

Here are some guidelines for product development, software development, and technology implementation—all usually part of E-Business.

Product Development for E-Business

E-Business sometimes resembles product development. Because the products are new, each manager considers the work to be nonrecurring. Each product then tends to have a unique product management plan based on the style of the manager. Managers feel autonomous since they are each being held accountable. Managing the work across the product development projects is a challenge, because the projects are developed individually. All of these comments apply to E-Business.

How do you treat nonrecurring work? The first step is to break it into components. Once divided into units, some tasks will reassemble and become recurring. This narrows the field of nonrecurring work. For a nonrecurring task such as the product design, aspects of the design still follow a pattern. At the core of the firm's project is the standardization. Nonrecurring work can be placed into a recurring structure since it is only the content and detail that is nonrecurring. Durations, dependencies, and other tasks remain as usual.

Software Development

Software development is a fuzzy area. Only when you can test the results of programming with tangible computer code do you know what you have. You do have requirements, design, and specifications, but these exist only on paper. That is why most modern software development now employs prototyping, so that people can see and touch mockups of a system.

How do you manage the work of the developers on a project? One suggestion is to keep the project team small. Divide the project into small tasks so that milestones are defined frequently. Conduct work reviews and meetings with programmers and analysts to see what they are doing and assess the quality of their work.

Software development management gets more complex in integration. Determine how to integrate the software programs and how to repair errors that are found, all at the same time. It is a moving target—fixing, testing, and integrating. Most large software development firms have turned to the method of successive builds of the system. In this method, the software is integrated on a regular basis and then tested weekly. When the programmers are working on errors from release 23, the testers are working on release 25 and the integrators are putting together release 26. The method of successive builds of software is like a series of dress rehearsals for a play.

Technology Implementation

Deploying technology is no longer a simple task. Multiple vendors are involved. There is integration of subsystems. Testing and analysis of results must be undertaken.

Here are some things that can go wrong:

- The vendor products do not interface.
- Vendor staffs do not share information with each other.
- You are always waiting for the latest fix to the latest problem that you encountered.
- You may be the only one who has attempted to integrate these very specific products into a system.

How do you manage this work? Vendors should have their own plans. Then you can integrate the overall plans. Define dependencies between tasks so that when work on a specific task is being discussed, you will be aware of the other work and tasks that are going on concurrently.

E-BUSINESS EXAMPLES

RICKER CATALOGS

In Ricker there were no formal milestone evaluations, nor was there a formal evaluation structure. Instead, the E-Business leaders attacked each milestone as it came up. All milestones were treated equally. This is generally a mistake since people tend to focus on the milestones and work that they are most familiar with.

MARATHON MANUFACTURING

For Marathon Manufacturing, managing the work at the sites for E-Business was delegated to a manager in each area. To increase consistency, this was later augmented by having an oversight consultant go out into the field and review the work as it was being performed.

ABACUS ENERGY

Abacus used the supplier steering committee to assist in reviews of work and to indicate which areas required more in-depth reviews. On the technical side, they engaged a consultant who acted as a quality assurance person to do reviews.

CRAWFORD BANK

Managers at Crawford Bank directed the work in a hands-on mode. This was the best approach for internal work. However, many of the subprojects involved contractors and subcontractors. These had to be managed by having the managers visit the vendors. The most successful managers were those who undertook frequent site visits, some of which were unannounced.

E-BUSINESS LESSONS LEARNED

- **Be selective in deciding which areas to enter as an E-Business leader.**
  In some cases, if you interfere in the work, you can create more problems and issues than you address.
- **Formulate acceptance and rejection criteria for milestones.**
  Work is driven by milestones and end products. Without a detailed understanding of what is expected, it is difficult for team members to structure, perform, and measure the work. The project then moves out of control.
- **Know whether to close off alternatives or keep them alive.**
  In the day-to-day work of a project, hesitation can cause work on the tasks to freeze. People say that they cannot do the work without the information or a decision. Therefore, make the effort to close off alternatives to maintain momentum.
- **Concentrate on the result, not on how work was done.**
  In reviewing a milestone, it is often tempting to ask why someone did something the way it was done. This leads to probing into how the work was performed. The problem here is that this detracts from the milestone itself.
- **Periodically examine some of the irrelevant but interesting tasks.**
  People often ignore these tasks, thinking them too mundane. However, if you could improve the work and schedule of these tasks, you could devote more time and resources to the more risky tasks.
- **When measuring success, count on your own opinion.**
  Work success can be measured in terms of schedule, cost, and quality. But these are sometimes difficult to measure. Some managers rely on the assessment of team members. This is dangerous since it can be misleading. Also, you are depending on others for their assessment. Measure work by what *you* did or by what effect *your* work had on the organization. Do not depend on the organization implementing and using the results immediately. Actual use may be a separate subproject.
- **Focus on achievement rather than work.**
  Work is not the same as achievement. If people tell you they worked hard, what comes into your mind? Do you assume that because they worked hard, they accomplished a lot? If so, you might be mistaken. Ask what they accomplished. Achievement means that people organized the tasks, performed the tasks, and got the desired results. Doing work means only that they performed the tasks.

- **In most cases, work problems are best turned around without new, massive amounts of resources.**
  Adding resources can demoralize the current resources. Compounding this problem is the additional time required to bring the new resources up to speed.
- **Get work from each person on a regular basis.**
  Review samples of what people are doing. This shows that you, as a manager, care. It shows that you are interested in the project all the time, not only when there is a crisis or problem.
- **Change purpose and scope if the schedule is stretched out.**
  If a schedule slips several times and no one takes any action or attempts to adjust resources, people will stop taking the work schedule seriously. Work within routine tasks may slip. The project slowly moves toward failure.
- **Monitor tasks people are working on to make sure that the more difficult tasks are not being avoided.**
  Some people work on easy tasks to build volume, while the risk and importance lie in more difficult work. It is human nature to perform many simple tasks first, to show that something is being accomplished. This can provide psychological momentum to tackle a difficult task. However, this method can be misused to avoid the difficult work.
- **Consider the degree of uncertainty in estimates of work.**
  Slack in a task is the time that you have before the task begins to affect the overall schedule. Slack is a matter of interpretation. If you start with slack of five days on a five-day task and after one day the slack slips down to three days, you are encountering uncertainty about the work. The amount of slack in a task depends on the degree of uncertainty. When you review the work in a task, try to get an understanding of how a person determines whether he or she is definite about estimates of work.
- **Look for fuzzy tasks.**
  A fuzzy task can usually be identified by its wording and weak assignment of responsibility and resources. Hidden behind a fuzzy task is typically a set of undefined, yet-to-be-determined, detailed tasks. Make the poorly defined tasks more specific by adding detail.
- **Hold one person accountable, even if several are involved in a task.**
  Separate who is doing the work from who is accountable for the work. Have single-point accountability for each task.

WHAT TO DO NEXT

1. Answer the following questions related to project work.
   - How do you measure your own work in a project? What quality standards do you attempt to meet?

- To what extent is an effort in place to define tasks with risk and tasks to which project management attention is directed? Or, alternatively, is each project manager left to his or her own devices to figure out how to review the work?
- How is the management of nonrecurring, exception, workaround, and re-work effort managed? Is it handled differently from routine tasks?
2. Practice analyzing work. Take a specific task that you or a friend perform. Divide the task into component parts, as discussed earlier. Define several alternatives for improving the work. How would you implement the changes? How would you measure the results?
3. If you are in a large organization, how are milestones reviewed? Is the process different among projects? Do you use standardized checklists? How often are end products turned down as not being acceptable?

Manage E-Business, Projects, and Regular Work

INTRODUCTION

E-Business implementation consists of a number of parallel subprojects carried out simultaneously with regular business work. Figure 12-1 gives an example for Marathon Manufacturing. More detail is given in Appendix A, which contains project templates for E-Business implementation.

There are several challenges here.

- *How do you manage and coordinate the subprojects within the E-Business effort?* This is an obvious challenge, but is worth noting since there are dependencies between these subprojects. People are shared among subprojects. Results from a subproject are predecessor milestones to tasks in other subprojects.
- *How do you manage resources between the E-Business subprojects and other projects and regular department work?* People cannot be assigned to the E-Business project full time except in special cases. Most people are shared between their normal work and E-Business.

This is not unique to E-Business. Today, you deal increasingly with multiple projects in general for the following reasons:

- People have learned to break up large projects into several smaller projects. Smaller projects are easier to manage, although coordination is required between the projects.
- Projects today potentially have many elements in common so that interfaces and coordination are a part of project management.
- Management wants to manage resources more efficiently and make decisions that apply to all projects.

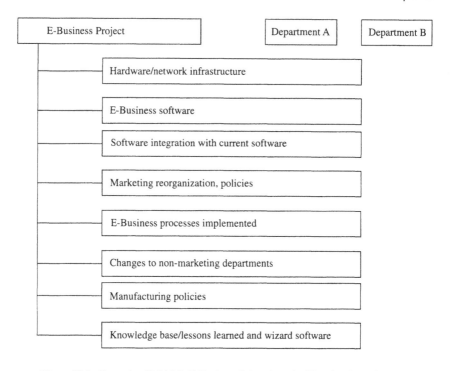

Figure 12-1: Example of Multiple E-Business Subprojects for Marathon Manufacturing

To manage multiple E-Business subprojects and other work, first consider how the projects can be interdependent. Then consider how to direct multiple projects with different sets of goals. With these steps accomplished, you can turn to discussing the specifics of management.

Many of the benefits and results from project management occur in the management of multiple projects. This aspect of management enables you to carry out trade-offs in resource use. You can gather lessons learned from one area and apply them to other subprojects. Managing multiple projects allows you to deal with issues and status across the subprojects. You can observe the impact of management style and practice on specific subprojects.

MILESTONES

The purpose of this chapter is to help you monitor and manage the E-Business subprojects at the same time as normal work. An overriding purpose is to manage the subprojects so that E-Business implementation is assisted and not harmed by project management. You can benefit from suggestions on how to exploit synergy between subprojects. You also want to ensure that future projects benefit from lessons learned in past projects.

Your detailed goals are the following:

- Ensure that there are sufficient resources on the E-Business subprojects to ensure progress and meet the overall implementation schedule.
- Minimize the disruption to departments due to managers and staff working on the E-Business subprojects.
- Ensure coordination among the subprojects so that a subproject is not delayed by waiting for a milestone in another subproject.

The scope of the effort includes all active projects that you have at one time as well as those in the future. Even if the subprojects are independent, an overall understanding can aid in the progress of the individual subprojects.

METHODS AND TECHNIQUES

Fortunately, the technology is in place to support the management and coordination of E-Business. In the days of mainframe computer dominance and stand-alone PCs, coordination of multiple projects was difficult. Networking, the Internet, and client-server computing all have made managing multiple projects easier and more affordable.

When you address multiple projects, the situation changes, opening up new positive possibilities, such as the following:

- Opportunities for resource trade-offs between subprojects as well as between E-Business and regular work
- Opportunities to set priorities and define policies across multiple subprojects
- Opportunities for greater economy due to methods and tools being deployed across more projects, people, and organizations.

A negative aspect of multiple project management is the possibility that diversity will lead to misunderstandings, lack of communication, and other similar problems.

Some of the benefits of breaking up the E-Business effort into component subprojects are as follows:

- Greater parallel effort is achieved
- There is increased accountability since different managers are responsible for different subprojects
- Coordination within the project is simpler, since the individual projects are smaller and less complex
- Less bureaucracy and more attention to issues is possible
- Problems and opportunities have greater visibility because they cross organizations

Potential risks are that you will have to manage the multiple subprojects and that the potential exists for greater disparity between subprojects.

HOW E-BUSINESS SUBPROJECTS INTERRELATE

When you consider multiple projects, reflect on how they can interrelate. What do they have in common and what do they share? Efficient management of E-Business involves being able to group elements of the work.

Some factors to consider in analysis and grouping are listed below. This discussion shows you how you can generate alternative groupings of subprojects within E-Business.

- **Technology**
  The subprojects may share the same technology. This is the case with all of the examples, but may not be true in a very large E-Business effort. Such subprojects compete for people with the same technical expertise. The payoff in managing this group of subprojects efficiently is the sharing of technology-related resources and the sharing of lessons learned.
- **Resources**
  Subprojects may be similar and compete for people, equipment, or facilities. Resource allocation among competing projects is a major focus of managing multiple projects. The benefit of managing resources well among multiple projects is the more efficient deployment and allocation of resources.
- **Time**
  For subprojects occurring in the same period or in overlapping periods of time, it is possible to share resources, project templates, methods and tools, and technology.
- **Project Templates**
  Projects not only may draw upon a common resource pool, but also may fit within a common task framework using the template that was discussed in Chapter 2.
- **Methods and Tools**
  Projects can employ the same methods and tools discussed in Chapter 6. The benefit is the opportunity to capitalize on lessons learned and to share expertise in the use of the methods and tools.
- **Direct Dependencies**
  Some subprojects are directly interdependent. That is, the milestones and activities in one project are employed by other projects. This is clearly a high priority grouping when you are considering an overall schedule.
- **Organization**
  Projects can be grouped by the organizations that they affect or involve. The benefit here is to center attention on a group of projects that impact a single organization.

- **Management**
  You can group subprojects that fall under the same general manager. This is similar to, but not identical to, the organization approach above. It has appeal as a way to group subprojects because one manager at a high level can make decisions for the group.
- **Business Processes**
  Subprojects may be grouped according to which ones affect the same business processes. If these are key business processes (e.g., order entry, inventory, accounting), this grouping is very important. Otherwise, changes brought about by individual projects could disrupt the business process, affecting costs, revenues, and service.
- **Customers or Suppliers**
  Here you are grouping projects according to whether they relate to or impact the same customer or supplier segment.

Consider all of your subprojects using the above groupings, since these groupings will help you by providing alternative perspectives. Note that you can have overlap, since several projects may share more than one of the above list in common.

OBJECTIVES AND BENEFITS OF MANAGING MULTIPLE SUBPROJECTS

Here are some objectives to keep in mind as you manage multiple subprojects:
- Synergy among the subprojects
- Smooth interfaces and shared resources
- Effective and efficient use of resources
- The sharing of cumulative experience so that the lessons learned among several subprojects are passed on and employed by a future project

These are reasonable goals even if they are not easily achieved.

Assuming that you reach these objectives, experience and observation show that the following benefits will accrue:

- In subprojects that have dependencies, the flow of information and interface between the subprojects is such that there is no misunderstanding or miscommunication. The schedules of the future subprojects are more likely to be met.
- Projects that have common resources in the same time frame are able to resolve resource conflicts through collaborative decision-making at lower levels of the organization, thereby reducing project management overhead and providing a clearer direction for the subprojects.
- Projects sharing the same methods and tools benefit from the shared experience and lessons learned so that productivity in the subprojects is better than if they were separate.

- Management has greater control and direction over subprojects. Using a collaborative management approach, the E-Business leaders work with established frameworks and structure to achieve results. This extends to resolving conflicts, using the E-Business template, gathering lessons learned, and resolving issues.

BARRIERS TO EFFECTIVE MANAGEMENT

It is evident that many benefits derive from actively managing and directing multiple subprojects as opposed to treating them as separate, individual projects. Why don't all organizations with several projects do this?

Observation has shown the following major constraints and barriers to multiple-project management:

- *Corporate culture.* In some companies the focus is on achieving short-term goals. Gathering lessons learned and taking the time to coordinate can fall by the wayside. This is very difficult to overcome. New projects have to be implemented outside of the standard corporate culture in order to have any chance of success.
- *Project manager style.* Management may have encouraged an "explorer" image and style for project managers. They are treated as explorer Sir Francis Drake was—they are told to go out into the world with their project, to sink or swim. Using a collaborative approach on multiple projects undermines the autonomy of the individual project manager.
- *Nature of the work and geography.* The projects in the organization may truly be very different from each other. Moreover, they may be performed in different parts of the globe. In that case, you have to ask what they share, independent of tactical work and geography.
- *Lack of controls over project management.* While many companies endorse tools and methods and require some basic reporting structure for projects, there is often a general lack of controls. Few standards are enforced. Instead, people customize the methods and tools to a specific project and to what they remember from the past.

THE E-BUSINESS LEADERS

Managing multiple subprojects calls for skills and capabilities beyond those of a manager of a specific subproject. Instead of driving toward one set of objectives, the leaders of multiple subprojects or E-Business overall must balance and trade off resources to prevent conflicts among the subprojects. They must also allocate time and work at a different level of detail from a standard project manager.

How does one become a good E-Business leader? One way is to manage several projects at one time informally. This allows the manager to get a feel for how to allocate time, what the proper level of detail is, and how to manage and track issues, actions, and the project plans across multiple projects.

MULTIPLE PROJECT MANAGEMENT GUIDELINES

Several alternatives for managing multiple subprojects will be discussed and then we will focus on the one that has the greatest promise.

- **Alternative 1: Treat each subproject separately.**
  In this case, you receive little economies of scale. There is little chance of getting lessons learned since information is not shared. When faced with a resource conflict, management may be swayed by the best marketing job as opposed to the real situation. In addition, people may not even agree on the real situation, thereby confusing management more.
- **Alternative 2: Group all projects in one set and manage all of the subprojects together.**
  This is the micromanagement of all subprojects in a similar way. However, projects can differ greatly—even within a homogeneous company. Treating small projects like huge projects can swamp the smaller subprojects in administrative trivia.
- **Alternative 3: Establish several task forces (task group committees) to address subprojects at the group level.**
  Each task force is based on a grouping. Also set up an overall steering committee to address strategic issues and opportunities for all subprojects. The most important task group committee is the tactical resource group. This group deals with resource conflicts in the near term (one to two months) and with dependencies between subprojects. A second group is the E-Business management process group. This group addresses the development of E-Business templates, methods and tools, and technology. These committees meet on a regular basis and produce specific actions and results. The groups of managers and staff act to implement collaborative decision-making. The steering committee addresses overall strategy and priorities among subprojects. It endorses the use of specific methods and tools.
- **Alternative 4: Use collaborative scheduling.**
  In collaborative scheduling, the E-Business team shares, updates, and accesses the same E-Business work information. E-Business leaders can even work with a common schedule. For multiple subprojects, information is available to leaders of all of the subprojects. That is, leader A can read B's plan and schedule.

Additional alternatives would be, for example, employing just the steering committee. This is a poor choice because too many issues and questions are referred to upper management. The task forces or task group committees act to buffer upper management, provide consistency, and allow for more detailed issues.

COLLABORATIVE SCHEDULING AND DECISION-MAKING

Across several projects, collaborative scheduling allows each project manager to do "What if . . .?" analysis to determine trade-offs. With suitable project management software, a manager could, for example, extract five different schedules and combine them with a copy of his or her own schedule. Dates, durations, and resource allocation can be changed to see how to resolve a conflict. This is just the tip of the iceberg, since project leaders and key staff could view each other's action items, issues, and other project information, but each could change only their own data.

Once people are sharing the same information, they tend to arrive at a common view of reality with respect to the work. No longer is everyone coveting his or her own schedule. No longer are project managers having meetings in which people argue about status using different versions of the schedule.

With such common ground, it is possible to establish decision-making. Rather than have all decisions flow up to the highest level of management, collaborative decision-making empowers the E-Business leaders and their key staff members to arrive at solutions to resource issues, conflicts, and other problems.

The benefits of this approach are substantial. First, the elapsed time to resolve conflicts is reduced. Second, because the decision was reached by group process with the same data, chances for later reversal are small. Third, through participation, managers feel that they have a stake in the action and are more willing to work toward a solution.

EIGHT ACTIONS TO MANAGING E-BUSINESS SUBPROJECTS

The following actions can be taken to put into place a collaborative process for managing multiple E-Business subprojects:

- *Action 1*: Determine subproject similarities and differences. In this step you attempt to understand all of your subprojects.
- *Action 2*: Define approaches for grouping the subprojects. Employ the groupings suggested earlier in this chapter.
- *Action 3*: Group the subprojects. This is the management decision as to what subprojects will be considered part of the same group.
- *Action 4*: Define minimal standards for subprojects. This is the definition of what constitutes a set of rules for all subprojects. It can be graded in levels to projects of various size, complexity, and risk.

- *Action 5*: Develop an analysis and reporting process across subprojects. Reporting on subprojects was explored in an earlier chapter.
- *Action 6*: Define a process for sharing lessons learned across subprojects.
- *Action 7*: Resolve resource conflicts among subprojects. Decide to what extent you will implement collaborative decision-making.
- *Action 8*: Implement a project management steering committee and the group committees.

Action 1: Determine Project Similarities and Differences

To get started, gather information on recent projects, current projects, and future projects. Classify the projects in terms of a series of attributes. Here is a table to help you:

Subproject	Importance	Size	Organization	Duration	Key Resources

To fill this in, use subjective estimates. Importance in terms of impact on the organization might be low, medium, or high. "Duration" can be treated in terms of a time frame (e.g., small—less than three months; medium—up to a year; or large—more than a year). "Organization" is the main organization benefiting from the subproject (not the organization performing the work). "Size" refers to subproject size in terms of budget (set your own intervals here). "Key resources" refers to the number of distinct types of personnel, equipment, and facilities important to the subproject.

You could add many more attributes in this table, but you should avoid getting buried in detail. This table reveals some ways in which to arrange and sort the projects. You can determine the relative number of subprojects that fall into each category. This table and others have also proven useful in indicating the mix of projects to management.

Action 2: Define Approaches for Grouping the Subprojects

The table here is intended to identify the critical subprojects from the analysis of Action 1. In both the row and the column headings, put the name or identifier of the project. In the table elements, you can place several codes as follows:

- R—subprojects share resources
- D—subprojects are interdependent

- M—subprojects are under the same general manager
- O—subprojects affect the same organization
- P—subprojects address the same business process
- T—subprojects share the same technology
- MT—subprojects share the same methods and tools
- C—subprojects address same customers
- SU—subprojects address same suppliers

You are likely to have multiple entries in each cell. Your next action is to shuffle the rows and columns so that subprojects that have much in common are in the same block of the table. The result will appear as shown in the box below where the heavy lines split the four subprojects into two groups. Begin grouping using resources as the primary criterion. Within this, group by business process. Note that the diagonal is blank since the row and column are the same and the table is symmetric. In this example, subprojects 1 and 2 share resources, business processes, and management. Subprojects 3 and 4 share a dependency and the same methods and tools.

	1	2	3	4
1	R, P, M	O	T	
2	R, P, M		C	S
3	O	C		D, MT
4	T	S	D, MT	

Action 3: Group the Subprojects

Place the groups based on an analysis of the previous two Actions. This will determine how you will manage the subprojects overall and how issues will be evaluated.

Action 4: Define Minimal Standards for All Subprojects

Recall that you have a large range of subprojects, small to large. What are the minimal standards that you want subprojects of any size to adhere to? If you impose too much, you will drive small subprojects underground. To provide flexibility, minimize the number and extent of standards that will apply across all subprojects. Minimal standards are required for the following areas:

- Management reporting
- Work and milestone review

- Methods and tools to be employed in each subproject
- Contents and structure of subproject plans

Action 5: Develop an Analysis and Reporting Process Across Subprojects

Each month do a rollup of all subprojects. To make this usable, insist on a standardized format. Let's first assume that the subproject plans for all projects are electronically stored and available on the network for access. Use the standard management report discussed in Chapter 7. Define the overall analysis approach to be employed across subprojects.

Here are some suggestions:

- Summarize the top milestones achieved in the last period.
- Indicate the top ten issues, their status, and what is expected of them.
- Present a combined plan that summarizes all of the individual subproject plans.

The combined E-Business plan can be obtained by rolling up detailed tasks into summary tasks and summarizing them, and by combining the summarized subprojects into a single E-Business plan.

Action 6: Define a Method for Sharing Lessons Learned Across Subprojects

Based on groupings in Actions 1 through 3, you can determine which subprojects can share specific lessons learned. Each experience or lesson learned can be classified as to technology, method, tool, organization, etc. Employ this information to identify the subprojects to which the lesson learned is applicable. If you employ groupware or a database as a means of storing and accessing lessons learned, then managers and staff can access the relevant items for specific issues or topics. In follow-up, evaluate whether the lesson learned can be expanded after it has been applied and make the effort to see if the benefits were achieved.

Action 7: Resolve Resource Conflicts Among Subprojects

Using collaborative scheduling and management, the approach would be to gather leaders in a room to meet regarding a group of subprojects that will have resource conflicts over the next four weeks. Have a moderator first introduce each issue and conflict. If possible, project the computer screen on the wall of the room so that everyone has a visual of the conflict. If you combine the detailed schedules of the subprojects in conflict, you can perform "What if. . .?" analysis by assigning resources to some subprojects while allowing others to slip due to lack of resources. By trying out several alternatives, the leaders will be able to arrive at an agreement on what to do. The schedules can then be changed to reflect the results of the meeting.

What are some alternatives to this approach? A traditional method is to have the leaders go to their own managers to seek priority for the resources. This entails more meetings and coordination. Higher level management must be involved. This method was used at Ricker Catalogs before collaborative scheduling. The drawback was that this method consumed too much management time. Decisions often were based on the marketing skills of the leader.

Action 8: Implement an E-Business Management Steering Committee

The steering committee is a management committee that oversees all E-Business work and other work as well. The committee reviews and approves new work as well as significant changes. It can terminate, merge, and redirect subprojects. The members of the steering committee represent a cross-section of the organization. In some organizations this is called a technology committee; in others it is called a process committee. The committee provides a company-wide perspective on all work. Disputes and issues that cannot be resolved within the subproject, E-Business, or within the conflict-resolving process are presented to management through the steering committee. The committee also reviews all new ideas.

Benefits of the steering committee approach include the following:

- Upper management does not have to be involved continuously in project issues since the committee represents a forum for them.
- Projects tend to get treated more fairly, since most of the units of the company are represented on the committee.
- The committee represents an appeals process if the deconflicting process does not work.
- Upper management tends to be more interested in and excited about the work with the committee in place.
- The committee provides a structured approach for dealing with new technology and E-Business ideas.

Both Marathon Manufacturing and Ricker Catalogs implemented the steering committee approach. In the former, the committee was expanded to include procurement of major components and systems as well as the construction projects. In the latter, the committee was expanded to include all new technology in support of product development.

What do you have when these Actions have been completed? Here is a summary list:

- A standard set of project templates that can be used as the basis for most new projects
- Minimal standards that apply to all projects, along with guidelines to be applied to projects based on risk, size, complexity, and other factors

- A process for reporting to management on all subprojects
- A summary reporting and analysis method
- A process for gathering, storing, accessing, and disseminating lessons learned
- A process for resolving conflicts between projects (deconflicting)
- A project steering committee for overseeing subprojects

MANAGE RISK

If the projects are interdependent, you can combine them into one large schedule and attempt to find the management-critical paths. Risk and exposure are to be found in areas such as technology, the process, methods, tools, organization, and management. In other words, risk tends to reside in the groupings that were developed earlier. Therefore, to assess risk, identify the group of projects affected by the area of risk. Assess risk as a group by considering slippage and problems within each subproject.

E-BUSINESS EXAMPLES

RICKER CATALOGS

Ricker divided up the E-Business effort into the following subprojects:

- Development of the web site for E-Business
- Implementation of new processes for web content
- Marketing processes and organization
- Technology infrastructure
- Software systems
- Other processes and organizations

This worked in general. However, some of the subprojects such as the last two became too unwieldy. This makes coordination more difficult. Also, the leaders did not use a standardized approach to roll data together from the subprojects.

MARATHON MANUFACTURING

Marathon used a project template similar to that in Appendix A. At any given time one of the leaders was analyzing, reporting, and addressing issues that crossed multiple subprojects full time. This job was rotated among the project leaders every month. While there were some continuity problems in transition, it did make the project more standardized and routine.

ABACUS ENERGY

Subprojects were employed at Abacus. The following division of the E-Business effort was employed.

- Hardware and system software
- Network-internal
- Network-external with suppliers
- Business processes-internal
- Business processes-external
- Organization and policies
- Marketing to suppliers
- Supplier relations and servicing

CRAWFORD BANK

Crawford divided up E-Business into three major subprojects: the subsidiary only, the parent bank only, and the interfaces between the subsidiary and the bank. The subsidiary subprojects included the marketing, software development, and infrastructure. The parent bank subproject included organization, interfaces, and policies. The interfaces dealt with specific areas of lending and other banking services.

E-BUSINESS LESSONS LEARNED

- **Put external comparisons with multiple subprojects into place early.**
  Begin to benchmark subprojects early so that you can track where you are going and how you are doing. This also helps motivate the team as they see how they are doing vis-a-vis the other subprojects.
- **At the start of a subproject, determine what controls, methods, and tools are appropriate to the subproject.**
  Treating all subprojects the same will smother small subprojects and let large subprojects creep out of control. Projects and project work are not democratic institutions.
- **Take control of the resources only when you are doing actual work.**
  Some leaders use schedules to hoard resources. This problem will surface immediately when you address resource conflicts.
- **Use different teams on successive E-Business efforts.**
  A common argument goes that if a team can succeed in one E-Business effort, the team should be moved to the next one in total. But the same team

may not be successful on this different project. Also, the team may have developed ties that are too close and that can disrupt the work of new team members. Also, keeping an existing team intact means that the next manager will inherit baggage in terms of problems, mistrust, hatreds, etc.

• **Identify subprojects in groups to support lessons learned.**
A subproject that is based on technology is often plagued by gaps created by the numerous differing technologies, methods, and tools. This can happen with several subprojects that are going on in parallel. Because of limited communications between subprojects, it can happen that each subproject solves the gap problem differently. This duplication of effort can be eliminated by the sharing of lessons learned.

WHAT TO DO NEXT

1. Address the following questions related to how your organization handles multiple projects.
   • How does your organization address multiple projects that are not related? That are related?
   • How does your organization roll up the overall projects?
   • How does the organization cope with assigning and prioritizing resources between projects?
2. Develop the table in Action 1 to determine the resources and other factors required by a set of subprojects.
3. Next, develop the table in Action 2 that supports grouping. Proceed to Action 3 and group the subprojects.
4. Now evaluate how the organization is managing the group of subprojects. Are you taking full advantage of the common elements between the subprojects?

Manage E-Business Contractors and Vendors

INTRODUCTION

E-Business implementation can be carried out successfully without outside assistance. However, it is a daunting proposition. The employees in business units are busy doing their normal work. They may lack knowledge of E-Business and skills in building new business processes and changing current processes. Moving over to the IT group you find that they are also busy with operations support, maintenance and enhancement of current systems, and other projects. They typically lack skills, knowledge, and experience in e-commerce software and process improvement.

Using internal staff for E-Business implementation requires the following:

- *Reprioritizing the workload so that some projects and normal work are deferred.* This can impact both revenue and costs.
- *Enduring a long learning curve for current employees to acquire expertise in E-Business.*
- *Overcoming resistance from employees who may not want to learn new skills.* It is not true that all people welcome learning something new. Many people are comfortable with what they are doing and what they know.
- *Being patient with respect to the implementation schedule for E-Business.* It is going to take substantially longer than desired.
- *Hiring new staff with selected skills and absorbing them into the organization and culture.* This takes time.

With an internal-only approach to E-Business you are going to incur:

- Longer elapsed time for the work—raising the level of risk.
- Enduring a learning curve that may lead to false starts and errors—more risk.

- Unpredictable costs—often leading to high costs.
- Lost sales opportunities due to a longer lead time.
- Potential damage to relations with current customers.

It should be evident by now that getting some outside help is probably a worthwhile idea to consider. Even with outside help you should probably do much of the work with internal employees. As they gain experience, you will implement faster. What can consultants bring to the table? Here is a list.

- Consultants provide specific technical expertise that you will not require after the work.
- Consultants can fill a position when you are unable to find or hire the people with the right skills.
- Consultants can provide a different perspective and act as agents of change.
- Consultants can be motivated to do work quickly with the proper reward structure.

What are the potential benefits of consultants to E-Business? Here are some of the benefits firms have cited. Note that you have to carefully manage and orchestrate the project to obtain these benefits. They don't come automatically.

- Consultants can apply their experience to speed up your E-Business implementation.
- The use of outside help can allow your current staff to do more of their normal work.
- Consultants can transfer knowledge and experience to the internal staff so that they can become more self sufficient.

However, there is a downside. Here are some factors to consider.

- Consultants can take the experience they gained on your work and go to a competitor.
- You can become overdependent on consultants and then they will never leave.
- You can lose control of the E-Business implementation to the consultants.
- Consultants may use tools and techniques that lock in the dependence.
- Costs for outside help may end up being much more than you projected.

Saying that you want to consider outside help and following up are two different things. You should have an overall approach for managing consultants and contractors as well as software package and other vendors. You will then be able to achieve the benefits without incurring the negative factors listed above.

MILESTONES

The goal is to achieve the following:

- More rapid E-Business implementation
- Overall controlled cost implementation

- Transfer of knowledge from the consultants to the staff to pave the way for greater self sufficiency
- Improved-quality web site and business processes

You want to recoup your expenses for consultants through increased sales, improved internal productivity and processes, and reduced long-term costs. You also desire to protect your investment and any competitive edge.

The scope of the consideration of using vendors includes all aspects of E-Business. This points to the need for a plan.

METHODS AND TECHNIQUES

ACTION 1: DETERMINE YOUR GENERAL NEEDS FOR OUTSIDE HELP FOR E-BUSINESS

Let's first make a list of potential areas where you might want a consultant for E-Business. Here is a list that you can add to for your own company.

- Overall implementation of E-Business-system integrator
- Project management for the implementation
- E-commerce software and installation support
- Custom development of the web site
- Setup of the catalog contents and maintenance of the content
- Software packages to replace some of the current systems
- Credit card interface
- Shipping
- Marketing strategy and support for E-Business
- Warehousing for E-Business items
- System integration of the custom software and existing software
- Business process improvement
- Network analysis and support
- Hardware and system software installation and support
- Staff training
- Benchmarking and competitive assessment

What are some of the criteria for selecting an area for consultants? Here is a list of factors.

- Your overall E-Business strategy
- Internal experience with E-Business
- Availability of internal resources to support a specific part of the implementation
- Protection of the competitive edge and position of the firm in E-Business
- General schedule

- Funds available for implementation
- Internal project management skills and available managers
- Skills, availability, and knowledge of IT staff in E-Business

Consider some examples. If you are under time pressure and money is not a problem, you might consider handing over all of the project to an overall system integrator. If you are concerned about maintaining your competitive position and ensuring that there is internal knowledge, then you might consider only setting up the web content, the network, and the hardware. In other words, you would contract for generic work.

To help determine your needs, carefully review the task lists in Appendix 1 which addresses templates for E-Business implementation. You can take the lists and use them as the first column of a table. Then you could take the criteria that are listed above and use these as columns. Your next step is to enter a score from 1–5 (1–low; 5–high potential for contracting) in each table entry.

Ricker Catalogs used a more casual approach and began by using consultants for network and hardware support and for process improvement. As they became aware that the internal staff was not available for the project and lacked expertise, they contracted out more of the implementation. This created a number of problems since the management of the E-Business implementation continued to get more complex as more firms were engaged for work.

Marathon Manufacturing determined that the best use of contract help was in the area of marketing and design. Abacus Energy contracted out for the software. The Crawford Bank E-Business subsidiary employed the same contractors that the parent bank had used for their web page work.

ACTION 2: DISCOVER WHAT FIRMS ARE AVAILABLE AND INFORMATION ABOUT THE FIRMS

Once you have identified the areas to be contracted for, you can proceed to search for firms on the web. You may be overwhelmed by the number of firms available. You can also get references from people in your organization.

ACTION 3: DEFINE MIXES OF SOFTWARE PACKAGES AND CONSULTANTS AND AN OVERALL STRUCTURE FOR THE CONTRACTORS

If you are going to employ software packages, then obviously you will narrow the list of candidate consultants to those with experience in those packages. Since you have determined which areas that you will employ contractors for, you can define an overall structure for reporting and management for these consultants.

Who reports to whom? What information generally will have to be provided to each one? How will the consultants relate to the internal organization? Which parts of the organization will be interfacing with the consultants? Get these questions answered prior to selecting consultants.

ACTION 4: PLAN AHEAD FOR THE USE OF CONTRACTORS AND CONSULTANTS

In this action you should develop a limited plan for each area to be contracted for. This should include the following:

- *Determination of how an area relates to other areas to be contracted out and those that are internal.*
- *Identification of potential risks in using a contractor for a specific area (protection of intellectual property, ability to complete the work, etc.).*
- *Support requirements for the contractor in terms of what the internal staff and other contractors will have to provide.* This is very important since if the support is not provided on a timely basis, there could be substantial problems and delays.
- *Controls over the contractor.* This includes how the contractor will be measured and managed.
- *Management of the scope of the work and dealing with expansion of scope.* This will be individual to each area being contracted out. This is important since you want to define the scope of what the contractors are to do and construct a process and policy for handling expansion of work and assigning additional tasks.
- *Preparation required for the contractor before they start work.* The more preparation that can be done, the more productive and efficient the contractor work will be.

ACTION 5: GET READY FOR THE CONSULTANTS

You will have to prepare a statement of work for each consultant as well as how you want them to work with you and other parts of the project.. The best way to do this is to follow these steps of preparation:

- Clean up any business processes yourself and measure these ahead of time.
- Document the technology configuration and all hardware, network, and software components.
- Identify specific issues that you would like a consultant in a specific area to address or at least be aware of.

- Document how the consultants will work with internal staff and make presentations to internal staff to get them ready for the consultants.

Doing these tasks will reduce the time for selection and contract negotiation as well as the startup time after the contract has been signed.

ACTION 6: OBTAIN PROPOSALS FROM POTENTIAL CONTRACTORS AND CONSULTANTS

You should prepare a Request for Proposal for potential contractors. Your purchasing department will have standard formats for this. However, you can cut down the time by developing the following items.

- Statement of work describing the services and products that you expect the contractor or consultant to provide. This includes a list of deliverable items, a description of tasks, attachments related to your E-Business effort, technology architecture documents, and other papers related to business processes.
- Any additional tasks that you might contract for, but that are not within this initial scope of work.
- How the proposals will be evaluated and the winning consultant selected.
- Pricing of goods and services to be provided.
- A standard proposal format so as to make it easier and possible to evaluate proposals from different vendors.
- Contract terms.
- How disputes and problems will be handled.
- How the contractor work will be managed and measured.
- Critical dates and deadlines.

For some of the larger items, you will follow up the issuance of the Request for Proposal with a bidder's conference. This is an opportunity for you to present the overall structure of the E-Business work. It is also a time for the potential contractors to ask questions. Write down all questions and send out written answers to each question to all bidders.

ACTION 7: EVALUATE AND SELECT CONTRACTORS AND CONSULTANTS

Your company probably has a standard evaluation method for proposals. Nevertheless, here are some suggestions.

- *Create a review committee to assess all proposals.* The committee should include managers from business units that the consultant will be working with.
- *Prepare a list of evaluation criteria and review this with all members of the committee.* The criteria relate specifically to the statement of work you prepared.
- *Have committee members prepare a list of questions to be asked of finalists.*

Purchasing will now receive the proposals from potential contractors. Copies of the proposals will be routed to the committee members who will use the evaluation criteria to come up with scores. Typically, the committee will then meet to review their scores and select 3–5 finalists.

Each finalist will be asked to attend a meeting with the committee. The meeting typically starts with an introduction by purchasing followed by a short presentation by the proposing firm. After this, the committee members can pose questions.

After all presentations and meetings occur, the committee meets and votes to select a winning proposal and a second place proposal. The second place is important because if contract negotiations stall with the winner, you have an alternative.

ACTION 8: PROCURE AND SET UP CONSULTANTS FOR WORK

Some specific areas to pay attention to in the contract are:

- Scope of responsibilities and services to be provided
- Project management—how they will manage their work
- Skills and abilities of employees to be provided to the E-Business project
- Availability of staff to work on the project
- Rights of the consultant to reuse and employ any intellectual property, software, knowledge with other firms
- Change control method to address any expansion of the work
- How the consultant will be measured and evaluated in terms of performance
- Penalties for performance failure
- Cancellation and termination clauses of the agreement
- How disputes will be identified and resolved
- How the consultant work will be reviewed
- What additional technology upgrades you are entitled to
- Maintenance and support of the technology, software, or other work that is performed, if appropriate

Some firms have been very careful in their E-Business efforts up to the point that the consultant staff members show up. Then they let their guard down or lose interest. Here are some specific guidelines.

- *Carefully analyze and work with the consultants when they first arrive.* Micromanage them on the first tasks. After you have established a working relationship, you can back off.
- *At the start of the work, indicate to all the employees what the role of the consultant is to be.* The employees may feel resentful and jealous of consultants. They may feel that the consultants are getting the interesting work, which may be true, since consultant work is often creative. How do you handle this situation? Tell the employees that their job is to learn from the consultants so that they can do the work in the future themselves without the consultant.

One of the first tasks from a management view is to establish management reporting to you from the various consultants. You must establish answers to the following questions.

- How often will the consultant report progress?
- What will be the format and structure of the progress or status report?
- What is the structure of their tasks in their plan? Here you should integrate all of the consultant plans into that of your overall E-Business plan. This will save you a great deal of time in reconciliation later.
- How will issues be identified and tracked? There should be a common issues database with all of the contractors.
- How will issues be resolved? An overall method for issues resolution should be employed.

ACTION 9: MANAGE THE WORK OF CONSULTANTS

You should have regular meetings with each consulting firm manager assigned to your firm. In your meeting you can use the following agenda.

- Progress on work to date
- Costs incurred for the work performed
- Staffing provided by the consultant
- Outstanding and new issues that are relevant to the consultant
- Future actions and steps to resolve issues

If the contractor's work has problems, schedule more frequent meetings.
Here are some potential problems with consultants.

- The consulting firm may try to take over the work.
- The consulting firm may use your E-Business work as a stepping stone to obtain other work.

- The consulting firm may try to keep adding people to your effort.
- The consulting firm may substitute less qualified people on E-Business to increase profits, sending in the "A team" first and then gradually sending in the "B team" or "C team."

Some of the worst cases of abuse come from large E-Business efforts when the consultant firm puts in 20 or more people, which is too many at one time. Or, the consultant firm says it will supply certain people and then, when you need them, they are working on other projects.

How do you prevent these events? Recognize that these events can occur. Carefully think about what you require. Insist that you obtain certain individuals. If this is not possible, specify people with defined skills.

In E-Business we have generally found that it is a good idea to have the specific members of the consulting firm as active team members. You want them to feel like a part of the effort and be committed to E-Business.

Another idea is to schedule regular meetings to gather lessons learned and share experience. This must be done on an organized basis. If it is done too casually, then there will probably be no opportunity to share the experiences.

Here are some lessons learned about managing consultants.

- *Play to the self-interest of the consultants.* That is, indicate that you will provide a good reference and that you will try to help them with additional opportunities if they perform well. Don't go so far as to promise them anything that you may not be able to deliver, however.
- *Don't wait until there is a crisis if a vendor is performing poorly.* Contact the manager of the consulting firm with the details of the problem and the potential impact if it is not solved. Show that it is in the consultants' interest to solve the problem.
- *Do not be defensive if the consulting firm tries to run the work.* They may start by volunteering to help in planning. To deal with this, get material from them and incorporate it in the plan yourself.
- *Go directly to management and find out what is going on if the consultants go behind your back to management.* Before they come on board the project, indicate to management that this may happen and explain how you are going to manage the consultants. Ask managers to come to you right away if they have any concerns.
- *If a consultant is called in by a manager to audit or review the E-Business effort, carefully pin down the scope of the review and the objectives.* Verify this with management. Provide information to management within the objectives and scope only. Don't whine about what impact this has on the schedule. Don't appear defensive. Inform the team that management thinks that the project is important or has concerns and wants the review. If you show limited cooperation, the potential damage will be limited. Use your

knowledge and your understanding of the political structure to your advantage when you talk with management.

- *Have very clear guidelines on when the work is to stop.* Otherwise, the vendor may try to have the consultants on hand all of the time to run up the billings. Implement strong guidelines on vendor performance and enforce them.

Another idea is to implement a consultant score card. Here you evaluate the consultant performance on a regular basis and then share the information with the consulting firm. Criteria to use in the vendor score card are:

- Number of staff assigned
- Turnover of staff
- Quality of work
- Timeliness of work
- Number of open issues remaining that are the responsibility of the contractor
- Cost or number of hours of effort
- Transfer of information and knowledge to internal employees

Using this score card forces you into measurement.

Managing Multiple Consultants

In E-Business you will be likely managing several consultants. One consultant may try to place blame on another if they cannot meet their deadlines. Here are some guidelines for managing multiple consultants.

- *Play one consultant against the others with regard to issues.* Each consultant will act from his or her self-interest and perspective. This will yield better solutions to problems.
- *When addressing an issue involving multiple consultants, get all of them in a room with the staff, if possible, and sort out what can be done.*
- *Establish in the meetings exact tasks that each vendor will perform.* Establish a coordination process.
- *If one vendor criticizes another vendor, get them together and state the concern.* Don't show favorites. If you know that you have a poorly performing consultant, use the other consultants to provide data to justify terminating the first consultant.

ACTION 10: TERMINATE THE CONSULTANTS

You should have an exit plan for each consultant. Here are some tasks to perform.

- Develop a final list of deliverable items that you want the consultant to produce. Set a schedule for this.
- Determine the staffing for the work and how people will leave the effort.

- Develop a checklist with internal employees and other consultants regarding what they need to know from the departing consultants.
- Establish formal sessions for the transfer of knowledge.
- Set up review procedures for the assessment of the consultants' work.

E-BUSINESS EXAMPLES

RICKER CATALOGS

Ricker tended to manage the consultants individually. They did not have an overall plan and coordination among the consultants. The responsibility for coordination among the consultants fell to the consultants themselves. While this worked, it did raise issues when invoices were submitted that indicated coordination time. Different project leaders at Ricker managed their consultants differently. This led to inconsistent reporting.

MARATHON MANUFACTURING

Marathon was probably the most organized and methodical of the example companies. They established formal meetings with all consultants as well as with individual consultants. They also set up subprojects for coordination among consultants. Marathon also enforced strong procedures concerning the transfer of knowledge from consultants to the internal employees. In addition, they quizzed the employees to see if they were picking up the knowledge.

ABACUS ENERGY

Abacus Energy employed only a few consultants. However, their suppliers ended up having to be managed as consultants in some cases. Abacus project managers found that unless Abacus people managed the supplier work and even visited and coordinated some of the supplier efforts and testing, there was a lack of progress.

CRAWFORD BANK

Crawford Bank followed a formal project management approach with the templates and issues. The leaders in the subsidiary managed the consultants through the line organizations in the parent bank where the consultants did most of their work. This worked, but it took more time, made communication more complex, and resulted in slightly higher cost.

E-BUSINESS LESSONS LEARNED

- **When evaluating consultants, don't just ask about skills and experience.**
  Pose situations to them to which they have to respond. Test their creativity
  and common sense through this approach.
- **Ensure that the consultants transfer the knowledge and lessons learned
  to the regular staff.** Insist on meetings in which they reveal what they
  learned. Work on the assumption that they will take what they learned and
  try to sell it to your toughest competitor. Exercise caution when using consultants, and debrief them often.
- **Once they are established, make the consultants feel like part of the team.**
  Don't differentiate between consultants and employees unless you have to
  for personnel reasons. You want to establish rapport and a relationship with
  the individual consultants. You want them to have a stake in the work.
- **Don't wait until there is a crisis if a vendor is performing poorly.**
  Contact the manager of the consulting firm with the details of the problem
  and the potential impact if it is not solved. Show that it is in the consultants'
  interest to solve the problem.

ACTION ITEMS

1. Answer the following questions related to contracting and contractors.
   - Do you make efforts to ensure that there is transfer of knowledge from
     consultants? Is there any validation?
   - What is the turnover rate for consultants?
   - Does your firm track issues and open problems with contractors?
2. What detailed work is required to prepare for consultants? Here is a list in
   the first column. Place the departments that are affected in the column
   headings. Rate the items on a scale of 1–5 in terms of level of effort required. This table will give you a comparative means to assess the preparation effort.

Departments			
Activity			
Training of staff			
Prepare formal procedures			
Define a measurement process			
Streamline the current process			
Construct/modify interfaces			
Cleanup information and data			
Change the staffing levels			

Chapter 14

Measure the Effectiveness of Your E-Business Effort

INTRODUCTION

This chapter is concerned with measuring the work in the E-Business effort. Measurement is taken in its broadest sense. That is, you are interested not only in understanding what is going on, but also why and how it is happening, so that you can make informed decisions in your future E-Business activities. Measurement is an area that receives little attention. The traditional measurement approach concentrates on milestones. Measurement of the effort is left to budget vs. actual and earned value analysis. We will examine the modern-day versions of these.

Why is measurement important? It makes marketing and selling possible. It requires you to be knowledgeable about issues and E-Business activities because you must actively do something with what you see and hear. If you passively look over E-Business, it is unlikely that you will absorb as much information. When you measure the work in E-Business, you will define what information to collect, gather the information, and analyze it. Through this process, you will understand what is going on.

Effective measurement has many benefits. First, you are credible to management and staff because people will respect your analytical skills. Second, if you are the person doing the measurement, you gain some political clout. Also, measuring will assist you in evaluating different E-Business subprojects. It may clarify which ones are winners and which should be redirected or terminated.

MILESTONES

The objectives of this chapter are to address the following questions for each major activity within the project life cycle:

- What are specific measurement goals?
- What is to be measured?
- How is the data to be collected and analyzed?
- How are the results to be interpreted and what are alternative decisions?

The scope of this chapter goes from the initial E-Business concept to the completed E-Business work, since you will want to measure everything in between.

METHODS AND TECHNIQUES

Here are the major items and milestones in the E-Business effort that you should address during measurement:

- *The E-Business concept.* Is the concept sound and feasible?
- *The initial E-Business plan.* Is the plan complete and accurate?
- *An updated E-Business plan.* Does the plan reflect reality?
- *Money, work, and resources consumed by E-Business.* Are you on target?
- *The end products of E-Business.* Will you get what you paid for?
- *The process for managing the work.* Do you have an effective way to manage the E-Business effort?
- *The E-Business leaders.* How effective are the leaders?

ASSESS THE E-BUSINESS CONCEPT

Goals of Measurement

An E-Business project concept begins with an idea about E-Business for your firm. The concept includes the purpose, scope, major milestones, and some idea of relative costs and benefits. How do you measure something this fuzzy? One goal is to assess if E-Business fits with the business goals and major thrusts of the company. For example, an E-Business idea might be to centralize accounting and create invoicing electronically with suppliers. At the same time, management prefers to decentralize departments to make them more accountable. Because of lack of analysis and measurement, the E-Business might go on for six months before it is killed. The scope and purpose were not aligned with the goals of the company. Had the scope included more transactions being performed with suppliers electronically, the work would be distributed out to suppliers—compatible with the management goal.

Another goal is to determine if the concept is feasible in your company with your resources. Does the E-Business concept require you to be experienced in technology, products, or some area in which you have little experience? This is a key question when E-Business involves a company moving into a new line of business.

A third goal is to assess the impact of the concept on other projects. If you fund E-Business, what resources will you take from other projects? Also, is this project necessary because of the requirements of other projects? For example, it is hard to implement E-Business if the company is in the midst of installing an ERP system.

How to Conduct Measurement

If the desired end products of E-Business were in place, what benefits would your organization reap? How would business processes, the organization, and other factors be different and improved? Would your competitive position change? Of course, we all want favorable answers to these questions. But if the scope or some other element of the E-Business concept is not right, then these benefits might be beyond your grasp.

If the E-Business concept passes this test, answer the following questions:

- Are the E-Business goals clear and consistent with the focus of the company?
- Is the scope of the E-Business concept compatible with the objectives?
- What things outside of the E-Business concept are going to be required to support the work?
- If this is such a good idea, why hasn't it been thought of before? What is unique about this day and time?
- Has the company carried out work on a similar scale in the past?
- Are the potential resource requirements in line with experience?
- Where is the inherent risk in the work?
- If you put together parts of the E-Business concept, is the whole greater than the sum of the individual concepts? Are there any synergies between the parts?

The ideal scenario is that all project concepts would be reviewed in a consistent way. The fact of life in many organizations is that E-Business is often started ad hoc or under the table. In some companies they attempt to grow a passive web page into E-Business. In others a group such as marketing attempts to start the effort on their own. The idea some have is to "Get it started and then after we show something, management will put money into it." This approach ensures that a lot of money is consumed in small E-Business projects that lack strategic benefit.

At the other extreme is the large project approach. Here management sets priorities and approves all E-Business ideas. While this allows some strategic E-Business efforts to start, it stifles other E-Business subprojects that have a more narrow scope. Between these two extremes is where you want to be. A management steering committee should approve all parts of the E-Business initiative.

Alternative Decisions

If you decide not to proceed with E-Business as originally planned, several alternatives exist. An E-Business concept can be shelved for a year. In most cases, this is the kiss of death for the concept. The concept can be approved for more in-depth work to generate a plan. Or E-Business can be combined with another existing or future project. Additional options are to change the purpose and scope and proceed, or fold E-Business into an existing project by expanding its scope. For example, you just attach it to the implementation of some new software package.

ASSESS THE INITIAL E-BUSINESS PLAN

Goals of Measurement

Consider how to assess multiple E-Business subprojects and other work. Let's assume that you have evaluated each plan and narrowed the field by eliminating those with low priority, high risk, and poor feasibility. What you are left with are good, viable candidates.

Your goal now is to select the mix of subprojects that can support both intermediate and longer term objectives of the company. You also want to select subprojects that work together and have synergy. Otherwise, you may end up in a situation where all of the E-Business initiatives end up disjointed.

How to Conduct Measurement

Once your initial E-Business plan is in place, answer the following questions to help you evaluate the plan.

- What is the contribution of E-Business to the company in the next year?
- What is the contribution of E-Business to the company in the long-term future?
- What risk does the E-Business bring to the organization in terms of its normal work?
- How would you rate the fit of E-Business with the organization?
- What is the availability of staff? How good are staff members' skills?
- What technology risk does the project carry? What is the degree of technical complexity of E-Business?
- Is contractor/consultant risk involved?
- What is the size of the E-Business effort? What resources are required? What is the cost?

- How much revenue will be generated?
- Does E-Business allow for competitive position enhancement?
- Does E-Business have leverage to support other projects and work?
- What is the available potential leadership for E-Business?
- What degree of interdependence with other projects does E-Business have?

Employing a formal method to evaluate E-Business forces management to be more aware and involved in E-Business itself. One method is to evaluate E-Business from the following perspectives:

- Corporate
- Business unit
- Customer/supplier
- Systems and technology
- Risk
- Project leader and team
- Relationship with other projects

A common mistake is to apply inconsistent rules for funding E-Business based on politics. E-Business is special so it deserves special rules. Another mistake is to base the allocation on fairness. When you attempt to be fair in allocation, you give many departments projects or roles in projects. This tends to spread out and dissipate resources. It is better to allocate resources to fewer projects where you will have major benefits than to pursue many small projects. The bottom line here is that if you undertake E-Business, don't be deluded into thinking that you can carry out many other big projects.

Alternative Decisions

These are basically the same options as for the E-Business concept. Since you have gotten this far and more work has been performed, political fallout must be addressed. Should you tell members of a losing organization that their project has been deferred, or do you admit that it was killed off? Don't pursue either approach. Instead, visit the department and determine what the need was based on. See how this can be addressed without a formal project. For example, maybe the work can be addressed within the line organization.

ASSESS AN UPDATED E-BUSINESS PLAN

Goals of Measurement

Don't assume that the updated plan reflects reality—even if people say that they have been updating the schedule each week. The goal here is to answer the question, "Do the current schedule and plan reflect reality?"

How to Conduct Measurement

Get a copy of the updated plan and the original approved E-Business plan. Put them side by side. What is different? Where? Does the updated plan compare actual with planned schedules?

The updated plan in many cases will change, reflecting some or all of the following:

- Additional tasks appear due to unplanned work and rework.
- The updated plan becomes more detailed to reflect actual work.
- Resource assignments change as they mirror what really happened in the work.

However, you may not see any of these things. The resources may not be different; the schedule may not be different. This can mean that the plan is not being maintained or updated.

After the review, visit the person who developed the updated schedule and pose the following questions:

- **How often do you update the schedule?**
  The ideal answer is weekly or twice a week. Less than that leaves too much inaccurate data. More often than that means too much time spent in updates.
- **How do you receive input about the schedule?**
  Answers could vary from "I place a few calls" to "I go out and see the work."
- **Do you verify what you are told? Or, do you accept what you are given?**
- **How do you fill in more detailed tasks? By yourself or with others?**
- **Who else reviews and uses the schedule? Is there any separate validation?**
  Go out into the project and see where the work really is. Match the tasks you see being performed to the tasks on the GANTT chart printout. This will provide a healthy dose of reality. It may cause you to get rid of the existing plan.

Verify everything before going into budget vs. actual or projected work quality. If the people who are doing the scheduling see you doing this, they will be more careful at the next update.

Alternative Decisions

What do you do if the updated plan is not based on reality? You don't have the time or luxury to go back to the start of the work and re-create history. Begin with the tasks that are active and build a new set of detailed tasks. Next, go to the people doing the work and have them provide you with detailed tasks for the next month. Third, go back and review future estimates based on the plan and the first two steps. You now have a decent starting point for the actual results.

Before turning to the E-Business work, let's consider costs and measurement. Costs are based on work or hours and effort. Any analysis that you do for costs should first be based on work, as that is a more tangible item to measure than hours and effort.

ASSESS THE MONEY AND RESOURCES CONSUMED BY E-BUSINESS

Earned Value Analysis

Earned value is based on the original estimate of the schedule and the progress to date, and is used to determine if you are on budget. Let's take one task and work through a simple example.

The task characteristics are as follows:

- Planned or baseline duration—10 days
- Planned start date—May 1
- Planned end date—May 12
- Resources assigned: Person 1—$20/hour; Person 2—$10/hour
- Calendar—five days a week, eight hours per day

The total planned cost of the task is $2,400 (80 hours × ($20 + $10)). The actual start date is May 1. At the end of one week (May 5), the project is only 40 percent complete. Both resources have worked for the entire week. The actual cost incurred so far is $1,200. However, since you still have 60 percent of the work to go, your new estimate of completion is May 17, assuming that they are working along at the same rate and there is no new slippage. This is a slip of five calendar days and $3^1/_2$ working days, producing an overrun of $600. The new total estimated cost is $3,000.

Let's use this simple example to examine some of the concepts associated with earned value. Note that if you assigned no resources to a task, you have no work and no costs or earned value—another reason to assign resources to tasks.

- *Budgeted Cost of Work Scheduled (BCWS) is the earned value of the task based on the plan.* The planned percentage complete on May 5 is 50 percent. Multiply this percentage by the planned cost ($2,400) and you get $1,200 as the BCWS.
- *Budgeted Cost of Work Performed (BCWP) is computed by multiplying the percentage complete (40 percent) by the planned or baseline cost ($2,400).* The BCWP for this simple example is $960.
- To find the Scheduled Variance (SV), subtract the BCWP from the BCWS. Using the above figures, the SV is $240. If this were negative, you would be

doing well since you would be beating your plan. Here you are not. You are in the hole.

- Actual Cost of Work Performed (ACWP) is the sum of all actual costs incurred to date. This includes any fixed costs incurred for the task. For you, this is $1,200. If you were to have the people work overtime, the costs would be higher.
- Earned Value Cost Variance is the difference between what was planned (BCWS) and what occurred (ACWP). This tells you if the task is on target with reference to costs. In the example the number is zero so you are on target.
- Total projected cost for the task is $3,000. This is also called the Forecast at Completion.
- The Cost Variance is the difference between the baseline or planned cost and the actual cost. The variance is $600 and positive—you are going to overrun. If this were negative, you would underrun.

People like to use earned value to measure the budget or planned vs. actual, since this reflects cost as well as budget.

Activity-Based Costing

In activity-based costing, divide the project and organization into activities. With each activity, associate an average cost. The total cost of the project or product is the total of all average costs associated with all of the activities. Based on experience you can update the average cost of future activities. You can also compare actual average costs with planned average costs. Idle time is reflected in the difference between resource use and resource spending. This method is often used for scheduling and planning. The limitation of this approach is that it assumes stability in the activities. Activities and tasks can change.

Value Engineering and Kaizen Costing

In value engineering you want to reduce costs associated with work. This is target costing—you examine how to reduce the cost of each task. "Kaizen costing" is the continuous effort to reduce and control costs. In both of these you will focus on costs. These are equivalent to considering the same approaches relative to task structure and how the work is to be performed. One problem with this approach is that attempting to reduce costs in the middle of the project can actually drive costs up, due to the disturbance you cause. If you use this method, focus on tasks in the near future to minimize disruption.

Here are some guidelines:

- *First, consider if the work is complete.* If it is not complete, assessing quality is not meaningful. Have some of the tasks been pushed off to another part of the project in order to meet deadlines?

- *In analyzing quality of work, consider the extreme areas.* Look at the results of work for the most complex tasks. Then look at the results of the work done on simple tasks.

ASSESS THE END PRODUCTS OF E-BUSINESS

Goals of Measurement

When looking across multiple subprojects, the objective is to determine whether the limited attention and resources that can be directed toward reviewing milestones are pointed in the right direction. Ten active E-Business subprojects, each with ten milestones over a period of a year, would require you to review two milestones every week. This is too much for management attention.

After you decide that you are considering the right milestones, the next issue is to develop a consistent approach for all milestones to reduce overhead and to ensure consistency. Strive to be both efficient and effective, given the limited time.

A third goal is to ensure that the effects of the review are fed back to the team and appropriate managers and staff in an unfiltered and accurate way. Much disinformation may crop up after a review. Related to this is follow up on what is done after the review.

How to Conduct Measurement

Don't get bogged down with detail. Begin at a high level and determine the major milestones associated with each project. Create a project plan that contains each of the major milestones of the projects and summary tasks. You can now begin to pick and choose among the milestones. You can also assess when the reviews should occur. At the same time, you will be defining a milestone review process to be applied consistently across all subprojects.

The review process will identify the following:

- What documents, narrative, presentation, or proof will be offered for the milestone
- How the review will be conducted
- Who will conduct the review
- What the potential decisions regarding the milestone can be
- How follow-up and the decision on the milestone will be undertaken after the review

Experience shows that the more this review can be planned and orchestrated in advance, the better the efficiency and flexibility in coping with schedule changes. The review must be conducted consistently across all subprojects. Keep in mind the politics of the projects. Don't stretch out a review. Apply whatever resources are required once it starts. Once a review is completed, issue the decision as soon as possible. Don't let the project team and others hang in the wind. That costs money and effectiveness. After a decision is announced, a follow-up method should be put into place immediately to ensure that the steps will be taken.

Alternative Decisions

You can accept the milestone as it is. You can reject it totally, although this is un-likely, since it is assumed that you have been involved in the process up to this point and had the opportunity to head off serious trouble. You can request rework and changes. These may hold up some of the project tasks. Finally, you may in-sist on changes subject to work being performed later. If you select the last alter-native, ensure that you actively pursue these changes later. If you let it drop, you lose your credibility.

EVALUATE THE E-BUSINESS MANAGEMENT PROCESS

Goals of Measurement

Here you want to evaluate the entire E-Business management process. You want to answer fundamental questions such as: "Should I continue with this approach to management?" "Can I improve how we manage E-Business?" These questions deal with the fundamental issue of whether or not the approach toward E-Business man-agement is worth the cost.

How to Conduct Measurement

Here are some questions you typically ask about E-Business management:

- What is the quality of the E-Business leaders? How do they work together? Are they getting better over time?
- Are you getting good ideas and concepts for the work and E-Business in gen-eral?
- Did the approved subprojects work out? If not, why not? If so, why?
- Should you have selected different subprojects at the start?
- What surprises occurred that you could have predicted, in hindsight?
- Which E-Business subprojects that were approved should have been placed on hold? Why?
- Are people learning from the work and improving their skills and techniques in E-Business?
- What was the greatest failure? What was the greatest success? Why?
- Are lessons learned, gathered, interpreted, and folded back into the work?

Create a table of how you are doing concerning the management process. Here is an example. The first column contains the phases of the E-Business effort. The second contains your rating on a scale of 1–5 (1 is low; 5 is high). The third column indicates what you learned in this phase.

Phase	Score	Lessons Learned
E-Business concept		
E-Business plan		
E-Business approval		
Updating the schedule		
Cost and work analysis		
Issue management		
End products		
E-Business leaders		

This table serves as a scorecard that clearly sets forth both positive and negative results. It is a key to showing management how the management process can be improved.

Alternative Decisions

You can continue the approach as is. This is unlikely, given that improvements are always possible. One common remedy for problems is to improve specific rows in the table. Another is to begin to treat subprojects with different characteristics differently. You can make the process more formal and bureaucratic. Alternatively, you can lighten up on part of the process. You can mix formal and informal methods. Make the approval of the plan and milestones more formal. This puts the spotlight on them. Other parts can be treated less formally.

ASSESS THE E-BUSINESS LEADERS

Goals of Measurement

You are reviewing all of the E-Business leaders down to the level of the subprojects. You will find some good ones and some that require improvement. You can employ the comments and ideas about the E-Business leaders mentioned earlier. Your goal is not to eliminate the lesser leaders but to improve their work.

How to Conduct Measurement

Begin by writing down the subprojects and work managed by each person over the past two years. Then assess each manager individually in terms of growth and improvement. Is the manager getting better at dealing with issues? How is the manager's ability to estimate and control resources?

Next, move up to E-Business leaders as a group. Rank their abilities in terms of problem-solving abilities, motivation and human resources skills, ability to control and direct the project, ability to cope with crises, etc. These topics could be columns in another table. The rows would be the names of the project managers. Rate each manager on each attribute.

Alternative Decisions

Ask the best E-Business leaders that you identified to share their lessons learned and techniques with the other ones. Consider a mentoring program in which the best leaders spend time with the others and guide them through issues. Try to salvage and improve poor leaders rather than removing them.

E-BUSINESS EXAMPLES

RICKER CATALOGS

Ricker Catalogs opted to minimize the extent of measurement for E-Business. Recall that they were under tremendous pressure to get the web site out there and have it be competitive. This is understandable. What did they lose by not doing the measurement? They did not really understand where things went well and where things could have been better. Because they did not do the measurement, they also missed out on the lessons learned.

MARATHON MANUFACTURING

Marathon mandated that every step be reviewed through the steering committee. The purpose of management was to ensure that ongoing efforts would be better than past efforts. They employed measurements such as the following:

- Number and quality of lessons learned at each stage
- Specific changes that would be made for the next E-Business effort
- Conversion of issues that arose in specific activities into lessons learned
- Refinement of the E-Business template

ABACUS ENERGY

E-Business at Abacus was rather narrowly focused, so there was no real effort to gather general lessons learned or do measurements. The exception was in supplier relations where lessons learned were gathered and a database of experience was established for each major supplier to Abacus.

CRAWFORD BANK

Crawford Bank management insisted on measurements of the subsidiary as well as the contribution of the regular bank departments to E-Business. A regular measurement scorecard was used with a "traffic light" system. If a department was not supporting the E-Business effort, they received a red dot. If they were supporting it, the color was green. If there was only limited involvement, the color was yellow. Activities where there was no involvement needed were blank. This was an effective way to put pressure on departments to get more involved in E-Business.

E-BUSINESS LESSONS LEARNED

- **Match up the milestones in the plan with the original goals of E-Business.**
  Projects with unrealistic goals are often reflected in unreal milestones. Milestones seldom deliver more than the objectives; it is not uncommon for the milestones to deliver less.
- **If management asks for frequent reviews, target small tasks that can be done in a day.**
  Measurement and review of a subproject can be excessive if a project is receiving too much management attention. Some projects seem to be in a state of almost continuous audit. Management wants daily reports. Target small tasks that can be done in a day to show progress.
- **Enforce policies or they will have no meaning.**
  Policies are rules that the project manager and team are supposed to follow. Put teeth in the policies in terms of review and enforcement so that people pay attention to the policy. A caveat here—if you enforce the rules, then you have to be flexible in interpreting the policies for each subproject. A policy that fits a large project can swamp a small subproject with overhead.
- **For good E-Business quality, focus on good integration of project parts.**
  Quality of individual parts is relatively easy to determine. Quality of an integrated subsystem is more difficult to assess. Look for integration problems and then trace these back to components in the work.

- **Provide interpretation of the goals from different perspectives—management, the project, line organizations, the company as a whole, etc.**
  Whether or not a goal is achievable or has been achieved depends on point of view. The E-Business concept and plan define specific goals and targets. Even if clearly stated, there is room for interpretation based on the audience. It is best and safest to look at the issue from different points of view.
- **Use measurement to keep credibility for the plan.**
  Lack of measurement of E-Business can result in lost credibility for the plan. Without measurement you really don't know what state the work is in. You will likely be surprised when a major milestone slips or is unacceptable. Then it may be too late to recover.
- **Conduct post-implementation reviews after major milestones to capture lessons learned.**
  Gather lessons learned as you work on E-Business. However, you are also under the constraint of time. Often, the best time to define lessons learned is after a major phase of the work and at the end of the effort. The experience is still fresh in your mind, yet it was not absorbed in daily work.
- **Make external comparisons with other projects.**
  Comparisons with other projects are often useful if put into place early. Putting a standard comparison method in place at the start of projects makes life easier. People will then expect and anticipate the comparison. They will understand how they are being measured and respond positively.

WHAT TO DO NEXT

1. Answer the following questions related to measurement.
   - Do you have a formal process for moving from a project concept to the project plan, or do plans just get created? How many of the plans created actually get started?
   - In retrospect, of the plan ideas that were shelved, which would have been winners and should have been approved? Go back and review why they were killed.
   - To what extent are plans reviewed in terms of accurately reflecting the status of the project? Are costs and analysis developed based on the assumption of accuracy? How often have cost and work problems surfaced that were later proven to be false when people checked the actual state of the project?

2. First assess how your project is doing, using the measurement methods of this chapter. Then you can expand this method to multiple subprojects.
3. Define to what extent your organization addresses each of the management areas on a formal or informal basis. What changes would you suggest? What benefits would accrue from your changes?

Part III

E-Business Issue Management

Chapter 15

Address E-Business Management Issues

INTRODUCTION

As you have noted, E-Business is complex. Political, technical, organizational, competitive, management, and process issues arise throughout E-Business implementation and operation. An issue can be a problem or an opportunity. Managing issues is a key ingredient (or critical success factor) to E-Business success. If a critical issue or set of issues are not addressed, E-Business progress may slow or stop. How and when issues are handled impacts the schedule and the plan. Moreover, if not addressed, an issue can blossom into a full-fledged crisis. In this chapter we will discuss how to address E-Business issues. How to address 100 specific E-Business management issues is covered in the next chapter.

When you began the E-Business effort, you defined initial issues as part of the E-Business concept. Recall that you did not want to rush out and solve these then. Elapsed time is necessary for analysis, additional information, and a deeper understanding of the issues. As the work goes on, more issues surface. Some of these are the same as some of the previous issues, but dressed in different clothing. They are different symptoms of the same issue.

At any time, active issues may or may not be interdependent. Almost all problems and slippage can be traced to specific E-Business issues. Issue management tests the range of the E-Business managers' capabilities far more than project control or project administration. Required skills include identifying an issue, collecting data, performing analysis, developing alternatives for resolution, obtaining concurrence on the solution and getting a decision, selling the solution, and implementing the actions to support the decisions. We think that this is probably the most important skill for E-Business management. It is definitely the one skill that has distinguished good leaders from mediocre or poor leaders in E-Business implementation.

MILESTONES

The purpose of this chapter is to help you manage and direct the outcome of single and multiple issues. You will be provided with guidance on identification, analysis, decision-making, and implementation of solutions. The scope includes all of these activities across all of E-Business.

Why devote time to this? Why not just shoot down issues as they come up? That chaotic approach can lead to big problems in E-Business. A systematic approach is more efficient in addressing issues. Through analysis of multiple issues, you will be able to address families or sets of issues. By tracking issues you will add to your lessons learned. Your ideal dream here is that most issues can eventually be handled by lessons learned.

METHODS AND TECHNIQUES

Let's examine a list of issues that you might encounter in E-Business. The list below has been drawn from recent E-Business work in different organizations. The potential impact of each issue is indicated.

Sample List of Issues

Issues	Potential Problems and Impacts
Project restructuring	Parallel effort and reduced project time
Loss of a key person from the project	Slowing of the schedule
Team morale drops	Reduced productivity
Line manager opposition to E-Business	Road blocks to decisions
Falling behind schedule	Milestones slippage
Expanding scope	Schedule slippage and missed deadlines
Competition for money and resources	Slowing of the schedule due to lack of resources
Conflict over work assignments	Lost productivity and low morale

Because issue management is so important to E-Business, you want to follow a step-by-step approach for identifying, analyzing, and resolving issues.

HOW TO SPOT POTENTIAL ISSUES

Listed below are questions that you should answer when you feel that something is a potential problem or opportunity. For each question, rate an issue on a positive or negative scale from −4 to +4, where positive numbers indicate benefits and negative numbers are disadvantages. The rating 0 means no impact. When finished, you can generate a bar chart such as that in Figure 15-1. Two examples for Marathon Manufacturing are given in Figures 15-2 and 15-3. In Figure 15-2 an issue arose related to controlling the work of the vendor. The issue had the strongest potential negative impact with the work, technology, management, and the business processes. In Figure 15-3 the issue is replacing the network servers for E-Business. As you can see, the only negative potential impact is on the project schedule with potential delays.

- What is the urgency of the issue to E-Business?
- What is the potential impact of the issue on the schedule for the E-Business subprojects?
- What is the impact of the issue on resources available to the E-Business subprojects?
- Which business processes are impacted by the issue? To what extent?
- How does the issue relate to the systems and technology in place?
- Does the issue have any impact on the company overall?

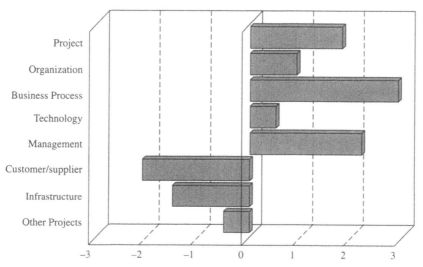

Figure 15-1:   Sample Rating of an Issue

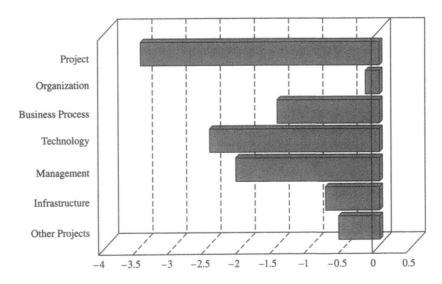

Figure 15-2: Marathon Manufacturing—Control of Vendor Work

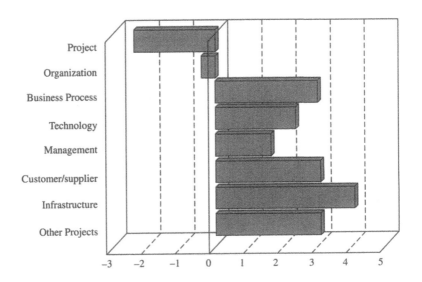

Figure 15-3: Marathon Manufacturing—Faster Network Services

- Are there potential side effects if a decision is made regarding the issue?
- What is the effect of the issue on other projects?

You can now assign a priority to each issue based on an overall weighted assessment of the ratings. Determine to leave the low-priority issues alone unless they are grouped with a high-priority issue. At the manufacturing firm, it was decided that work would be performed only on issues with ratings of –2 to –4, and +3 to +4. These are the most severe problems and best opportunities. Other issues can be put on hold until they become clearer.

How Rushing to Solve Issues Can Make Things Worse

When an issue surfaces, you are faced with several choices. If you adopt the wrong approach, you could make the issue worse. Just calling attention to the issue can be harmful. For example, suppose that you notice that the E-Business work is falling behind schedule. You could react by telling everyone that "We must all do more work to catch up." This may instill panic. People on the team may react by slowing down. Another reaction is to recruit a number of new team members. They have to be brought up to speed. This takes people away from productive work. Coordination and decision-making are slowed down. The lesson learned—issues that were acted upon incorrectly can provoke a crisis.

The Issues Database

Seek an organized approach when tracking issues. A database is useful and requires minimal effort. This database provides the information for graphs and tables. In the chapters on methods and tools, database management systems and groupware are discussed. Both can support an issues database. Another alternative is to use paper. However, generating the reports and doing analysis will require more intensive manual work. With many subprojects, all four of the modern examples saw the wisdom of establishing a standardized available system on a network.

Having each manager spend time developing databases that are not compatible with other managers' work is not the best use of time and effort.

Here is a list of data elements to employ:

- *Identifier of the issue.* Use a separate code for each issue.
- *Status of the issue.* Based on where the issue is in the life cycle, sample codes might include the following:
  - I—identified
  - A—assigned and being analyzed

- AD—awaiting decision and resolution after analysis
- R—resolved
- F—followed up on
- RE—replaced by another issue
- T— terminated or eliminated
- *Type of issue.* There are technical, management, vendor, organization, process, etc. issues.
- *Priority level of the issue.* Define several levels of priority:
  - A—extremely important in that the project is impacted within days if not resolved
  - B—the project will be impacted in weeks if not resolved
  - C—impact is marginal on the organization and project
- *Organizations impacted.* This is the major organization affected by the issue.
- *Date the issue was created.* This is the date the issue formally begins to be tracked.
- *Description.* This is a summary description of the issue in business terms.
- *Impact.* This field identifies the effects of not addressing the issue.
- *Related projects and tasks.* These are the tasks (by number) in the subprojects that are impacted by the issue.
- *Related issues.* This includes how the listed issues are related.
- *Person assigned to the issue.* This is who the issue is assigned to for analysis.
- *Date of expected resolution.* This is the date by which you can expect the issue to be taken care of.
- *Resolution code.* Examples are:
  - R—replaced by another issue
  - D—decided
  - S—shelved indefinitely
  - T—terminated
- *Decision on the issue.* This is a statement of the decision made.
- *Actions.* These are the actions that flowed from the decisions made.
- *Comments.* This field is for free-form comments on the issue.

Typically, each issue is associated with a series of events or actions. An event log would have the following elements:

- Identifier of the issue
- Event number—A unique number assigned to the event
- Event date
- Person recording the event—May be different from the person responsible
- Type of event—Meeting, telephone call, fax, and e-mail
- Result of the event

- Impact on the issue
- Comments

The event log links to the issues database using the identifier of the issue. The index to ensure uniqueness is a combination of the identifier and the event number. How would you use these files? Set these up as databases on a file server. The information can be accessed by all of the team members and other project managers. Access to update the log could be controlled.

Begin with the issues in this and the next chapter. This gives you over 100 issues to start with. Make sure all of the team members (IT, business, and consultants) use the same issues database.

Use the database to summarize issues for E-Business. A sample rating is in Figure 15-4. Across multiple subprojects you can integrate information by the following criteria:

- *Priority of the issue.* This can isolate all high-priority issues so that management can address the entire set of issues on an organized basis.
- *Organization.* This can indicate the extent to which issues are impacting specific organizations.
- *Families of issues.* By clustering by families of related issues, you can attempt to deal with groups of issues as opposed to single issues.

You can also analyze the issues by doing aging analysis. You can construct the following graphs:

- *Total number of issues by date discovered.* Figure 15-5 shows both desired and undesirable graphs. In the undesirable situation you are still finding more issues at the end of the E-Business implementation—not good.
- *Total number of open issues by date discovered.* Figure 15-6 contains two graphs for desired and undesirable situations. In the undesirable case there are major unresolved issues that have been known, but not resolved for months.

Priority—High

Issue Type	Date Opened	Issue ID	Issue	Status	Date	Resolution
Work	6/1/00	012	Ability to track work of other departments	Open		
Technology	5/12/00	007	Upgrade network servers	Closed	6/3/00	Upgrade to multi-processor servers

This report is first sorted by priority and then open issues are presented.

Figure 15-4: Example of Issues Report for the E-Business Implementation

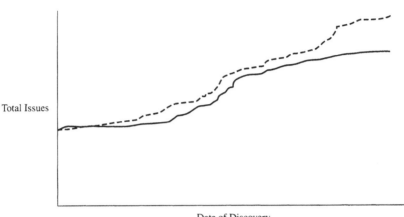

Total Issues

Date of Discovery

The solid line shows a desirable trend where there are not many new issues found at the end of the project. The dashed line shows a less desirable pattern where a number of implementation issues surface toward the end.

Figure 15-5: Total Issues by Date of Discovery

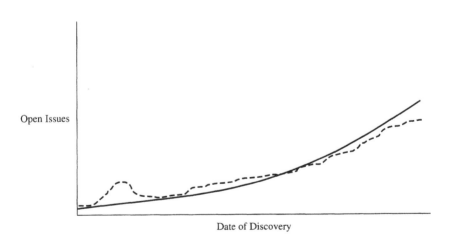

Open Issues

Date of Discovery

The solid line shows a desirable pattern where there are few old, outstanding issues. The dashed line reveals that there are some old, major outstanding issues remaining late in the project. In both cases, issues just discovered are not resolved.

Figure 15-6: Open Issues by Date of Discovery

- **Average elapsed time to resolve an issue by date discovered.** You want this to decline over time as this would reflect that you and the team are getting better at resolving issues faster. Figure 15-7 shows both the desired and undesirable curves.

You can then take each of these graphs and add the qualifier of type of issue or priority. An example is shown in Figure 15-8 where technical, organizational, and process issues by date of discovery are shown. In this chart at the start of E-Business there are a number of technical and process issues. These gradually taper off as you resolve them and fewer new issues of these types are found. However, consider the organizational curve—it increases toward the end. This happens in E-Business because the E-Business leader and others may underestimate the issues that they will face. They then finally surface as implementation is completed.

COMMON MISTAKES MADE IN ADDRESSING ISSUES

In E-Business, we have identified eight recurring problems or failures in addressing issues. Let's discuss each of these in terms of how it can happen and the impact:

- **Failure 1: Being unaware of the issue**
  If you keep too narrow a focus, you will find that you are missing details. You will be missing signs and symptoms of problems. Instead, be constantly on the lookout for more issues.

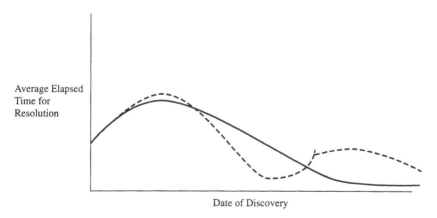

The solid line indicates that after an initial period the elapsed time to resolve issues is decreasing. The dashed line shows that the project is having trouble getting issues resolved toward the end of the project.

Figure 15-7: Average Elapsed Time to Resolve Issues

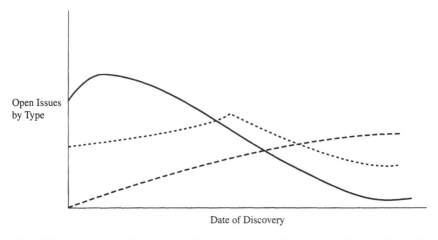

The solid line is the technical issues. Most of these are known early and few are discovered later. The dotted line is for the process issues and shows that these surface in the middle of the project. The third category is organizational and indicates that in this E-Business project a number of organizational issues surface at the end of the project.

Figure 15-8:   Issues by Type by Date of Discovery

- **Failure 2: Misdiagnosing the issue**
  Once you have identified the issue, a common error is to plunge in and attempt to address the issue without analysis. Misdiagnosis of the issue is likely. Then you either make the issue worse or lose credibility as a manager.
- **Failure 3: Not selling the decision to management**
  After the issue is identified and the analysis performed, a decision is made and seems logical. If the E-Business manager jumps in to act on the decision without selling it to management, problems may occur. Actions taken as a result of the decision can affect resources, costs, and the schedule. If management wasn't consulted, the bill for these extra costs may be a shock. Failure to market the decision to management opens the door to attacks on the decision as well.
- **Failure 4: Making decisions without planned action**
  A decision is announced. Everyone who hears it asks, "What does it mean?" The answer is "nothing," unless the decision is followed by action. Some people seem to think that they can announce a decision and then wait for weeks to take action. As time passes, the credibility of the decision is questioned. When the action finally comes, the situation may have changed, making the decision inappropriate.

- **Failure 5: Acting without the framework of a decision**
  Another problem occurs with E-Business leaders who are action oriented. They move from their assessment of the problem to immediate action. This is fine in a true emergency. However, this can be deadly. First, the actions will appear chaotic without the framework of a decision. Second, the actions will probably be incomplete, requiring additional actions. These additional actions may contradict or overlap the previous actions.
- **Failure 6: Failing to act when you should**
  Some people cannot decide when to act. While many favor a conservative approach, action must be taken immediately after the decision is announced.
- **Failure 7: Acting when you should wait**
  This is a common mistake with new managers and in E-Business where there is tremendous pressure to act. They make decisions and take action on the spot.
- **Failure 8: Taking actions that are inconsistent with decisions made**
  This occurs because people do not think through whether the actions support the decisions.

SEVEN ACTIONS IN MANAGING E-BUSINESS ISSUES

Action 1: Recognize the Issue

Trouble can often start with a question or offhand comment. "What's happening with Harry?" is a question leading to a personnel issue. "I heard you won't need that piece of equipment by the first of the month after all." This can imply that the project is behind schedule. A verbal message may be the first symptom of an issue. Respond by answering the following questions:

- *Does the symptom relate to a current active issue?* Is it just another symptom of a known problem? If so, employ this information to gain a better understanding of the current issue with which it is associated.
- *Can the symptom be grouped with anything else going on?* You can group by organization, technology, management, customer, and supplier. If you see no such connection, wait to raise the issue.
- *What are the characteristics of the issue?* At this point, define the issue. Use the database of issues and fill in the elements. A form is included in Figure 15-9.
- *What priority should be assigned to the issue?* Set priorities by urgency of the project. Do not use other criteria, such as benefits to the organization or management, since mixing criteria complicates decisions on priority.
- *What should be done with the issue initially?* Discuss it with the team to collect ideas and to see who has the most interest in the issue. Assign the issue

Issue Management Form

ID:_____ Name: _____ Priority: _____

Title: _____

Type: _____

Description: _____

_____

_____

_____

Impact, if Not Addressed: _____

_____

_____

Assigned to: _____ Date Assigned: _____

Issue Activity:

Status	Date	Entered by	Action/Result

Date Resolved: _____ How Resolved: _____

Comments: _____

Figure 15-9:   Sample Issues Form

to someone who cares about it. Giving an issue to someone who dislikes the subject will result in the issue getting little attention.

Action 2: Analyze the Issue

Use a combination of direct observation, interviews, review of documents, and meetings to collect the information for the analysis. In collecting the information, don't draw attention to the issue. Instead, talk about symptoms and impact. If you zero in on the issue, people may expect too much in terms of resolution. Also, by tagging the issue too early, everyone accepts the preliminary definition, which may be in error.

Start with the person who proposed the improvement and collect as much information as you can. Find out how the project team and the work can be affected, as well as the end products of E-Business.

Categorize the issue for the database, using the topics and information earlier in this chapter. Next, draw up the following table. This table allows for different interpretations of the issue (from conservative or minimal to radical). Obtain different views from the various members of the team and others. For each interpretation, list the symptoms of the issue in one column, the impact of the issue in another column, and the principal dimensions of the issue, based on the interpretation, in the last column. An example is shown in Figure 15-10 for Marathon Manufacturing.

Now focus on the effects and benefits of the issue on E-Business itself. Construct another bar chart, using the following categories. An example is given in Figure 15-11 for Marathon Manufacturing. The issue here is whether or not to distribute the work across organizations within the company. The benefits are better work quality and an improved team as well as better E-Business management. The potential negatives are on the schedule and other projects.

- E-Business team
- Tasks and work performed
- Methods and tools employed in E-Business
- Project management and control
- Schedule of the implementation or expansion
- Costs and resources required
- Quality and nature of end products and milestones
- Interfacing projects and subprojects

Action 3: Define Alternatives

As you perform analysis, also define alternatives for decisions. Consider the following suggestions or actions and estimate the effects that will accrue to E-Business, the organization, or the team.

Interpretation	Symptoms	Impact	Dimensions
Lack of control over vendors	Miscommunications	Cost overruns; schedule slippage	Work and financial controls
Weak project management	Lack of direction to vendor	Loss of control	Project management
Invoicing	Billing for extra work	Decentralized structure	Management

Figure 15-10: Example of Categorization of Issues for Marathon Manufacturing

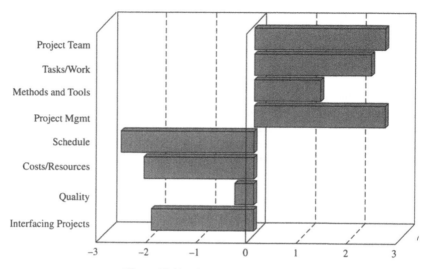

Figure 15–11:   Marathon Manufacturing

- **Alternative 1: Do nothing.**
  This is the alternative to adopt most often. Wait and let the issue mature. As it does, the impact of the issue will become more evident. Note that even if you do not take action, you continue to track the issue; you still treat the issue as valid.
- **Alternative 2: Restructure the work with no new resources.**
  This alternative helps you see what you can do with the resources you have. It forces creative thinking in organizing the work.
- **Alternative 3: Apply resources to the issue without regard to cost.**
  If you consider applying resources to the issue in virtually unlimited amounts, you can see the limits of what can be bought. This is an important alternative because it reveals the true limitations of resources. When you apply additional resources, you actually slow the work, since there is more coordination involved in the handling of the resources (bringing people on board and setting up equipment, for example). Always be ready to answer the question, "What could you do with additional resources?"
- **Alternative 4: Reassign resources within the E-Business team.**
  This alternative is often useful for personnel problems and conflicts within the team. Consider setting up subproject teams of different people to see if that works. This alternative tests your knowledge of the team and also defines the limits of their flexibility. A shake-up of resources is especially good for E-Business efforts with long elapsed times.

- **Alternative 5: Remove resources from the E-Business effort.**
  This could be applied to personnel issues. It could also be considered after a major phase of work in the project is finished, when you are trying to downsize. Removing people makes management easier and increases the focus.
- **Alternative 6: Expand the scope and/or purpose of the E-Business effort.**
  The issue may be very important to E-Business. However, taking the issue on in the subprojects will lead to the scope or objectives of E-Business being expanded. If this is a possibility, consider an overall strategic change in the project to address more than the one issue. If you let the scope expand naturally to handle the issue, you are likely to run into schedule problems and resource shortages as you scramble to address the expanded scope or purpose.
- **Alternative 7: Reduce the scope and/or purpose of E-Business.**
  This is the flipside of the previous alternative. If you encounter a major obstacle, you may wish to avoid direct confrontation with the cause. Instead, you might consider downsizing the project and avoiding the problem. This is not cowardly, since with success you can often later return and expand the scope. This is a good alternative when there has been "scope creep" and you have to meet a deadline.
- **Alternative 8: Treat the issue outside of E-Business.**
  Under this alternative, you are attempting to insulate E-Business from the issue. You will attempt to address it away from the project. This may be useful for political issues that transcend E-Business.
- **Alternative 9: Change the mix of methods and tools being used.**
  Look for a better way to do the work, using better or different methods and tools. The trade-off against the potential benefit is that there is a learning curve for the new approaches. This alternative is feasible, but risky due to the effort to make the changes required.

Action 4: Make Decisions

After considering alternatives, think through each in terms of defining the potential actions that will flow in support of the decision. Employ the following table to analyze the situation further before making a decision.

1. Issues Addressed	2. Alternative Decisions	3. Actions	4. Effects	5. Risks

Select different issues to address (column 1). For each, identify several alternative decisions (column 2). For each decision, identify actions that will implement the decisions (column 3). What would be the likely effects of the actions on the issues? This is column 4. These effects are not guaranteed, which leads to column 5, in which risk is identified. This approach will allow you to resolve incidents of conflict in resources.

For E-Business we prefer to have people argue about actions that will be taken. These are more precise than decisions. When you compound fuzzy decisions with vague concepts and understanding of E-Business, you may be in big trouble and get no decision. Therefore, start with actions and when these are defined, back into a decision that fits the actions. The decision then validates the actions.

The actions typically involve politics, changes in the plan, and resource actions. After you select the decision and identify the actions, inform management of the issue and the recommended approach.

Action 5: Announce the Decision and Actions

Announce the decisions and the actions at the same time. Complete paperwork on the actions prior to the announcement. This strategy will let people know that you are serious. Also, benefits will begin earlier and people will be more likely to be supportive.

Action 6: Take Action

Take all actions at the same time—if possible, right after the announcement. Change the team, resources, plan, and scope all at once. If you attempt to do it sequentially, you will end up having a mixture of old and new for some period of time—leading to confusion. You want to establish an entirely new mindset. This is another reason for considering bundles or groups of issues at one time.

Action 7: Follow Up

The results of the actions and decisions should be seen quickly after implementation for most issues. In the followup to the actions, answer these questions:

- Did the issue get addressed or were only symptoms treated?
- Are side effects of the actions and decisions creating new issues?
- Do additional areas exist in which one can apply the same actions and decisions to handle even more issues with little added effort?
- What lessons were learned for the future?

MANAGING SETS OF ISSUES

Typically, in E-Business you have to address many issues. They are in different stages of being identified and addressed. How can you more effectively manage sets of issues?

Here are some guidelines.

- View all of the open issues at one time and compare the mix of issues now with the issues of several months ago. Do you see some lingering issues? Has the number of important issues increased? Has the average time to resolve an issue increased?
- If you devoted a solid day to working on issues, what could you accomplish? What things get in the way of resolving the issues?
- Do you know the status of the issues? How effective is your tracking?

DEALING WITH E-BUSINESS CRISES

A crisis arises in E-Business when several issues remain unresolved for some time and impact the project. One tends to think of being powerless in a crisis. Don't feel this way. Adopt the following strategy. You can affect and impact how a crisis is handled and resolved. Therefore, be proactive. A crisis can be employed as a tool to carry out fundamental change in the organization and processes.

What can you do about a crisis? You can understand and solve it. You can also guide and orchestrate it. You can play a role in defining the timing and presentation of a crisis, affecting the media surrounding the issue. That is, a crisis is open to interpretation.

A significant point to keep in mind is the difference between a perceived and an actual crisis. In a project it is important to act upon perceived crises as well as actual crises. Otherwise, if people perceive a major problem and you do nothing as an E-Business manager, you and E-Business lose. You can use the perception of a crisis to achieve a breakthrough in the project in terms of resources or other factors.

If you announce that some situation or issue is a crisis, you have to back up your statement. If, on the other hand, you begin to point out that the impact of an issue is getting bigger, and risk and danger are growing, people get the impression of urgency without hearing the word *crisis*. That is the preferred strategy. Save the term *crisis* for true emergencies.

When people see a crisis, it is usually because they perceive an impact on their organization, E-Business, the team, or some other resource. This perception can stem from internal as well as external factors. Thus, you must consider how these perceptions arise, how to determine if the crisis is real, what to do about it, and how to implement decisions.

E-Business efforts tend to have more crises than traditional IT or business projects for several reasons. First, E-Business projects have political issues. Second, the processes that are changed or created by E-Business challenge the status quo. Third, E-Business projects tend to be large in scope. They cross organizations that may not get along with each other. Your E-Business is subject to change brought about by industry or competitive factors—uncontrollable within the team.

Here are some common symptoms of crisis:

- Being overwhelmed by new issues
- A lack of decision-making, or only partial decisions are made
- Attempts by workers to leave the project team
- Overrunning the budget
- A lack of team enthusiasm for work in E-Business
- Unresolved important issues remaining for long periods of time
- Excessive calm as people try to ignore the crisis (like the eye of a hurricane)
- Excessive excitement as people address the crisis ("panic in the streets")

Here are some guidelines for making a prediction about an E-Business crisis:

- Take a broad perspective over time. This allows you to see what has been accomplished in E-Business work, the rate of progress, and trends in E-Business.
- Look at how long important issues have remained unresolved.
- Observe how the managers and the team have dealt with previous situations.
- Think of other projects in the past that are similar to E-Business in terms of issues.

Here are two steps to take that lead to implementing a decision to resolve a crisis.

1. Determine whether the crisis is actual or perceived. Ask yourself, "What has changed to make this situation a crisis?" Another test is to ask, "If nothing is done, what will happen? How will things worsen?" If your answers to these questions are that nothing has changed and the situation will not likely deteriorate, you have a perceived crisis.
2. If the crisis is actual, determine the scope of the situation and how much time you have left to make a decision and implement it.

If the crisis is perceived, not actual, decide what is behind the perception. Why do people feel that a crisis exists? Don't take action until you can answer this. Also, ask who benefits if there is a perceived crisis. The perceived crisis may be a result of a misunderstanding. The analysis should reveal some interesting communications paths of the project. Take this opportunity to learn more about informal communications in the project. Determine the action that is appropriate. If you attempt to deny that a crisis exists, you will not be credible. Instead, think about what you want to say and the scope of your response. This is especially pertinent if you wish to use this opportunity to advance the project politically or gain resources.

For example, go to management and indicate that the situation is bad but not hopeless. Identify what should be done before a crisis does erupt. You are not crying wolf. You are warning management before the crisis arises that the possibility exists.

We have emphasized the benefits of a collaborative approach to managing E-Business. Here are some benefits from this collaborative approach as it relates to a crisis.

- *The team members work together to head off the crisis, thereby building and reinforcing the strength of the team, as well as solving the problem.*
- *A crisis tends to be identified earlier and addressed earlier.* Therefore, it is less likely to turn into a serious crisis.
- *The factors in one subproject that are creating havoc are often present in other subprojects.* With the shared information the issue can be addressed systematically and not ad hoc on each individual subproject.
- *Team members who have worked on other subprojects may have experienced similar problems and can give good advice.*

Hone your skills prior to an actual crisis. One of the hardest but most important skills to develop is the ability to have perspective and patience when confronted with a set of symptoms.

Here are some suggestions to help you accomplish this:

- *Examine your list of outstanding issues.* Ask if these are complete. Add to the list any politically sensitive issues.
- *With the complete list, note the age and importance of the issues.* Sort the issues by order of importance. Within a group of issues of the same importance, sort by age.
- *Take the top five issues in importance and age and assess what the trend has been for each.* Has the issue deteriorated, remained the same, or improved?
- *For each issue, develop a scenario for the reasonable worst case.* That is, how could each issue turn into a crisis? What would be the symptoms of a crisis? What would cause the issue to worsen to this extent?
- *Determine how you would detect deterioration in each issue.*
- *With an assumed crisis, attempt to develop countermeasures you could take.*

Following these suggestions will help to prepare you for a crisis. Get in the habit of evaluating issues each month to raise your level of awareness of the possibility of a real crisis.

E-BUSINESS EXAMPLES

RICKER CATALOGS

Ricker faced several crises during the E-Business implementation. The first one was to deal with the scope of the project and approach. Recall from earlier chapters that Ricker had to modify its E-Business strategy from overlay to integration. This caused an upheaval in the project. The second crisis occurred when they realized toward the end of the software development that their web site was not really competitive with other similar sites. Rather than stopping implementation, they decided to roll out their E-Business as version 1 and then immediately start another project to generate version 2.

MARATHON MANUFACTURING

Marathon faced a number of major issues, including organizing the marketing and sales organization, dealing with manufacturing priorities, and trying to draw the line on the wizard and lessons learned databases for customers. Marathon employed an issues database on the network to increase awareness of issues. They also produced issue graphs on a regular basis.

ABACUS ENERGY

Abacus never really had a crisis in their E-Business implementation with suppliers. However, they did face technology issues in terms of relating and interfacing to suppliers. They also had management issues in getting and encouraging suppliers to use E-Business. They resorted to faster payments if suppliers participated in E-Business with them.

CRAWFORD BANK

The project leaders thought that they could handle issues as they arose. This worked for the first issues. Then things became more complex. The elapsed time to resolve an issue dragged out and more issues were active at the same time. People would call with status reports on issues. The names and titles of the issues were very similar since they all involved the network. This created more confusion and return calls. To compound the situation, management wanted to have information on specific topics. Reviews of these requests indicated that they were tied to the issues.

After the issues database and formal approach to issues management were implemented, the situation improved somewhat. However, the E-Business leader was the only one doing the entry and tracking. The problem was that the issues management function was not made into a collaborative effort with the field leaders.

E-BUSINESS LESSONS LEARNED

- **Deal with political problems in E-Business to avoid paralysis or collapse.**
  Political issues in E-Business can undermine morale. If several political issues are allowed to fester and multiply, the situations will feed off of each other and get worse.
- **Consider large and small issues together.**
  Patience in E-Business includes not jumping on the easy issues. It is a real temptation to resolve simpler issues quickly. Everyone feels good that something is getting accomplished. This is a false sense of security. If the bigger issues require resolution that undoes what you just announced, your credibility is lost and you have to start over. This is another reason to consider issues in sets. Also, when you do resolve the big issue, you can undo what actions you took on the smaller issues.
- **Determine the relationship between issues.**
  A few underlying causes can generate many seemingly independent issues and many more symptoms. What can happen is that several issues or causes of issues "join hands" and begin to impact across E-Business. More symptoms are generated. Group issues by areas of the subprojects such as the resources used, the organization involved, or the method being used. Take action on a group of issues at once, if possible.
- **Reward people (including yourself) for identifying issues.**
  This motivates you and others on the team to be on the watch for new issues. It can be overdone if people just complain. However, if the focus is on finding issues or suggesting improvements, the complaints have a positive effect.
- **Know which issues are constraints.**
  A constraint is something that you cannot change. What issues do you accept as constraints and which do you address? This is a key decision, since it determines how the issue is interpreted. Look at a stand-alone issue as a constraint. A stand-alone issue is rare and exists in a vacuum—no other issues are involved. Whatever action is taken will impact only that issue.
- **Decide whether an issue is secondary or artificial.**
  For every real issue in E-Business you can generate five to ten artificial issues. When symptoms of problems appear, you may fix a symptom only to see another appear if you failed to pinpoint the real issue. Before you treat

symptoms, decide if the issue represented is artificial or secondary. This is important in E-Business where you tend to have multiple related symptoms of the same issue appearing.

- **Analyze the underlying source and concern behind the E-Business issue.** What is behind the issue is almost more important than the issue itself. The issue may be just one manifestation of an underlying problem. Understanding the cause of the issue can lead you to discover whether additional issues stem from the same cause.
- **Know when something is out of scope to keep E-Business on schedule.** Many issues relate to parts of E-Business that are not within the original scope of the E-Business concept. When one of these comes up, the team and leader cannot deal with it quickly since it is beyond what was originally in the concept. Test the scope with each issue.
- **Delegate the task of researching issues and follow up in tracking.** It is impossible for you to follow up on every issue. You must delegate. To be successful, track how the followup is going and how the issue has changed or has been transformed through further analysis.
- **With issues involving outside vendors, try to prevent one vendor from criticizing another.** This is not an unusual practice. Be aware that it can happen and point this out to each vendor prior to a meeting. During the meeting, if a vendor is not present, try to mitigate any criticism of the vendor and turn the conversation into action steps regarding the issue. If one vendor has a complaint, have them focus on the technical or business work and not on the other E-Business vendor.
- **Address basic E-Business issues to prevent the team from working on less important, though visible, work.** During the E-Business effort, management issues can emerge. Usually no emergency exists for most issues. However, if the elapsed time without resolution continues to grow, the team may get the impression that management does not care or is not interested in the project. The team may think that the issue is not important. This can lead to a lack of confidence among team members. The team members may work on tasks that are not impacted by the issue. If the issue is important, the tasks related to the issue are usually important.
- **Test the degree of flexibility in an E-Business plan gradually rather than precipitously.** Changes in E-Business implementation and expansion occur over time. Change tests flexibility. Change is often generated by the solution and resolution of issues, so change depends on how issues are sorted out. Each time you resolve an issue, you may change the plan, testing the flexibility.

- **Accompany changes in E-Business leaders with other changes in the E-Business project concept.**
  When you make the major change of replacing one of the E-Business leaders, consider other changes at the same time, including project scope, roles, and purposes.
- **Take time to gain an overall perspective after setbacks on issues.**
  Winning on an E-Business issue means getting feasible decisions and actions so that the issues disappear. You cannot expect to win on every issue. What do you do when you lose? Take an overall perspective on what just happened. You will gain a more general view of the situation and gather lessons learned for the future. Lick your wounds and get ready for the next round.
- **Don't jump to conclusions on either symptoms or causes of issues.**
  Unless a true emergency exists, do not take any precipitate action. Instead, show that you are working on the issue and continue to do analysis and collect data.
- **Ask yourself if there is benefit in forcing a crisis in E-Business.**
  When faced with a crisis, you have a trump card to play—the timing and posturing of the crisis. You can position the crisis and select the timing of unveiling the crisis and potential solution. If you have been unable to get attention, but you retain management support, consider the cost and benefits of forcing the crisis.
- **Work out a strategy for change in an E-Business crisis situation.**
  During E-Business implementation and expansion, you must introduce changes to the subprojects gradually so as to avoid major disruption and impact on other subprojects. These changes can be very smooth at first. However, as time goes on and the number of changes increases, team members experience increasing anxiety and uncertainty. In a revolutionary change to an E-Business effort, a major change is made. This is followed by relative calm as the changes settle in. Decide in a crisis whether to take an evolutionary or revolutionary approach. We favor the revolutionary approach because change leads to calm.
- **Ask yourself who benefits from how an important issue is resolved.**
  E-Business issues can be addressed, shelved, or made to disappear. They can disappear if you change the assumptions, purpose, or scope underlying a project. Once an issue is resolved, winners and losers emerge. This is especially true for political issues. Analysis of this outcome can assist you in seeing what is behind the issue and what positions people are taking with respect to the issue.
- **Be cautious when confronted with a critical issue in E-Business.**
  With a critical issue, the tendency is to plunge in and address the issue. However, first review how the issue surfaced and evolved into being critical.

What were the main events along the way? This is important because it helps to frame the issue and give perspective.

- **Draw analogies in E-Business situations to calm temporary crises.**
  One value of having experienced people in E-Business is that they can provide perspective and experience when dealing with an issue or a crisis. They can recall a similar event in a previous project. Use these stories to calm people during a crisis.
- **Look for different interpretations of a crisis in E-Business.**
  When people present you with an issue, they sometimes disguise it by emphasizing the action they desire. Alternatively, they may offer only one view of the crisis. As you have seen, many interpretations are possible. Dig deeper when someone hands you a situation.
- **In working on E-Business, learn to enjoy dealing with the unexpected.**
  One reason that people enjoy E-Business is that this work deals with the complex and encounters the unexpected. E-Business tends to involve change. Change typically involves issues. Issues lead to the unexpected. If you don't enjoy E-Business, it may be because of having to deal with the unexpected. Learn to enjoy this aspect of management, rather than dreading it.
- **Play out or simulate what would happen if an immediate crisis were resolved. Ask what new crisis might take its place.**
  E-Business efforts tend to experience some crises. Do you have the right interpretation of the crisis? Would the solutions you are considering fit? To help answer these questions, jump ahead mentally and assume that the crisis has been handled. What do you think is the next issue that will become critical and, perhaps, a crisis? Does a link exist between the two issues?
- **Follow up on decisions with actions to maintain management credibility.**
  Managers should consider both decisions and actions together. Through understanding and seeing the actions, you can better evaluate the decisions.
- **Correlate actions with decisions.**
  To evaluate this, make a table with the rows being the decisions and the columns being the actions. In the table write a paragraph on how the action supports the decision. An action may support many decisions, and many actions may apply to a given decision. Keep this on hand throughout the E-Business effort.
- **Compromise on E-Business issues to bring later rewards.**
  When considering decisions, maintain an attitude of conciliation and compromise. When you move to actions, you have less flexibility. Decisions have many shades of gray; actions tend to be more black-and-white. When considering decisions, you can also trade off with opponents on the decisions vs. the actions. If you have to concede points on the actions, you can eventually recover if the actions prove to be inadequate.

- **If you fail to obtain a decision or if you disagree with a decision, pause and let the situation alone.**
  Let things cool off. Take time to gain new perspective. Later, you can resurrect parts of issues. E-Business issues tend to generate a great deal of heat.
- **Focus on achieving success rather than beating off failure.**
  In many companies an E-Business was implemented and it worked minimally. Is this a success? Forget it. It doesn't generate money. Customers are unhappy. Morale is in the dumps. It would have been better, in retrospect, to terminate the effort and start over. The lesson learned here is that overcoming failure is not the same as achieving success. When you overcome failure, you naturally feel that you have accomplished something. In fact, you may have only depleted your energy dealing with a problem project.
- **When you stop an E-Business subproject, give a viable explanation for your actions.**
  Stopping a subproject without explanation fuels rumors. While you don't have to go into detail, explain the major reasons for the decision. Stress the changes that have occurred since the subproject was started that necessitated your decision. Early project decisions are sometimes made in haste and based on external pressures—only to be reversed later.
- **Delay a decision in an E-Business subproject to provide time for assessment.**
  This strategy is beneficial for several reasons. The first is that, if the time is not right for a management decision, you will spend energy on the decision but get nowhere. Also, while the decision may be clear, the followup actions may still be undefined.
- **Be willing to place an E-Business subproject on hold to provide time for perspective.**
  When you place an E-Business subproject on hold, you can still continue work at a low level. You are no longer caught up with the events, so you have time for thinking and perspective. Also, a pause gives team members time to assess how they are doing in their work and what small changes they might make to improve performance.

WHAT TO DO NEXT

1. Assess your abilities in each of the following areas:
   - Identifying issues
   - Determining the ramifications and impact of issues
   - Deciding on the issues and timing of announcements
   - Defining the action items to be taken

2. Evaluate your organization in dealing with issues. Answer the following questions:
   - Does the organization have a standardized issue management approach?
   - Does the organization have standardized software for issue management?
   - What escalation process is employed for issue resolution?
   - Are decisions clearly separated from actions? Are actions linked to decisions?
3. Evaluate how well your organization tracks issues by answering the following questions:
   - Do you know how many issues are open and closed in a specific project?
   - Do you know which issues have the highest priority?
   - What is the age of the oldest outstanding issue?
4. For a project that you are working on, identify several issues (both open and closed). Determine the step that each is currently in. Next, assess how effectively each issue was addressed in previous steps.
5. Try applying the alternative decisions that were identified in the issues in Question 1. What did you learn about the issues after doing this that you did not know before?
6. Look back at several attempts to address issues. Were the benefits and effects as anticipated?

Chapter 16

101 Specific E-Business Issues

INTRODUCTION

Success in E-Business means that you can address issues that arise in the implementation while at the same time working proactively to achieve results. Over the past decade in EDI, E-Business, and supplier/customer projects, we have encountered a wide variety of issues. One hundred and one of the most frequent and pressing of these issues are discussed here. For each issue, we will consider the following:

- *Reason.* Why does the issue arise?
- *Effect.* What is the impact on E-Business implementation if the issue is not resolved?
- *Actions.* If the issue does arise, what are some suggestions as to what to do?
- *Prevention.* What can you do to prevent the issue from arising in the first place?

The issues are grouped into the following categories:

- *External Factors to the E-Business Effort.* These include other projects, the industry, competition, and factors beyond your detailed knowledge and control.
- *E-Business Management.* This includes both management of the E-Business effort and the team.
- *E-Business Implementation and the Plan.* This includes all facets of planning, analysis, and direction.
- *The E-Business Team and Resources.* This covers the management and coordination of all resources, including the core implementation team.
- *The E-Business Vendors.* Problems that arise relating to consultants and vendors supporting E-Business.

- *Methods and Tools.* This encompasses methods and tools employed in the effort.
- *The E-Business Work.* This is the direct management and oversight of the work.

EXTERNAL FACTORS TO THE E-BUSINESS EFFORT

1. **Delays in related projects impact tasks across the E-Business effort.**
   Reason: Dependencies between projects were not evident. No one was in charge of pulling together all of the projects.
   Effect: Tasks slip. The morale of the team may be lowered.
   Action: Managers should stop and define relationships between projects. A separate project for interfaces between projects should be set up under the umbrella E-Business project.
   Prevention: Implement overall project coordination within E-Business and between E-Business and other work.

2. **Too much of the E-Business project depends on external organizations such as suppliers or other parts of the company that cannot be controlled.**
   Reason: Since these organizations are not under the control of the team, team members feel powerless to implement plans to assist themselves in dealing with the external organizations.
   Effect: The team and leader feel helpless to remedy the situation.
   Action: For each organization, consider what its self-interest is; establish contacts to work with each organization on that basis.
   Prevention: Make a chart to map each organization in terms of the effect of E-Business work towards its self-interest.

3. **Competitors working on their E-Business projects are ahead of your E-Business work.**
   Reason: Beyond having more resources or a head start, the reason for this may also lie in the competitor's approach to E-Business.
   Effect: Pressure on your team will increase.
   Action: Try to determine how the competitor's project is organized and what the competitor's technical approach is.
   Prevention: While not preventable in every case, you can survey what other firms are doing in the area of your project at the start of your work.

4. **Nobody considered the impact of external factors at the start of the E-Business work.**
   Reason: This occurs in organizations that are internally focused.
   Effect: You may face one surprise or issue after another.
   Action: Refocus the work to deal with the impact of external factors affecting E-Business.

Prevention: From the beginning, consider the range of external factors and what their potential impact might be. Gather examples of each factor and its impact to instill fear and awareness in the team.

5. **There is no detailed initial competitive assessment effort to determine what existing and potential competitors are doing in E-Business.**
   Reason: The firm may be internally focused and is not familiar with competition assessment, or the competitive assessment may be assigned, but is not given a high priority.
   Effect: Without this information, it is likely that the web site will not be competitive.
   Action: Even if the E-Business effort has been started, you should get going on the assessment. This will be a continuing activity.
   Prevention: Assign someone at the start of the project to collect the information. Have them report back on what they find on a regular basis.

6. **No systematic method is in place for identifying and addressing external competitive, industry, and technology factors that can impact E-Business.**
   Reason: The team fails to address the need for a systematic approach to project management.
   Effect: Control of the schedules and work is taken over by events in a reactive mode. Work effectiveness is impacted.
   Action: Demonstrate to management the impact of not considering these external factors on E-Business.
   Prevention: Make the assessment of outside impact a natural part of the E-Business processes.

7. **There is no investigation of chat rooms and other bulletin boards that criticize similar web sites.**
   Reason: This is an area frequently missed. Chat rooms often contain gripes of customers about the web site. In some cases, customers are so angry, they set up a web site that attacks the firm.
   Effect: If you miss this information, you really have no idea how the firm's site is doing.
   Action: Like the competitive assessment, get started on this right away.
   Prevention: Have this activity start with the competitive assessment. If the person assigned to this task finds nothing soon, push them to continue searching.

E-BUSINESS MANAGEMENT

8. **Management does not make the effort to generate decisions related to the E-Business implementation.**
   Reason: People may assume that decisions will be made automatically on a timely basis.

Effect: Project work may continue based on a set of assumptions about a management decision. The decision may eventually be different from what was assumed, disrupting the work.

Action: Gently press for a decision. Indicate what direction the E-Business effort will take until the decision is made.

Prevention: Prepare managers for the pending decision required. Try to get acceptance of an informal decision in the interim.

9. **Decisions are being made ad hoc and not on an organized basis in response to E-Business pressures to implement.**

Reason: Management could be attempting to demonstrate that it is action-oriented. Any problem gets an immediate decision from management.

Effect: The decisions may be inconsistent with each other.

Action: Try to package a set of issues to obtain more systematic decisions. Point out alternative decisions and their impact on the project.

Prevention: Take a systematic approach to identifying and analyzing issues.

10. **Consistent project controls in the E-Business effort are lacking.**

Reason: The organization may never have taken the time to establish controls in terms of resource use and budgeting.

Effect: Each E-Business effort can end up having a slightly different set of controls based in part on the style of the participants.

Action: Establish controls for the E-Business project now.

Prevention: Use the first E-Business as a model of control for future projects.

11. **Some in the organization oppose E-Business—a factor not addressed by management.**

Reason: Upper management assumes that their endorsement is sufficient to make the organizations fall into line.

Effect: Management and the team are thinking one thing; others in the organization are working from another set of assumptions. Problems will arise in reviews and in getting resources.

Action: Attempt to get everyone on board. Use direct contact and market to these groups.

Prevention: Attempt to align the organization with the E-Business by explaining the roles of the various organizations and the benefits of the project, emphasizing the aspects that will appeal to the self-interests of the different groups. Always assume that there will be resistance.

12. **Actions that follow from decisions are not consistent with the decisions.**

Reason: No one thinks ahead as to how the decisions should be implemented. Faced with the actions, management reverses decisions.

Effect: The result may be loss of management credibility in the decisions.
Action: Begin immediately to identify actions and reconcile them with the decisions.
Prevention: Package the actions with the decisions.

13. **Followup is neglected after E-Business decisions are made.**
Reason: Decisions are made. Actions are taken. Management may go on to the next decision, assuming that no followup is needed.
Effect: Actions and decisions become ineffective.
Action: Make followup part of the actions.
Prevention: Include measurement of the actions in the decision process.

14. **The E-Business implementation has no organized forum to address issues with management.**
Reason: Management addresses each project and issue individually—including E-Business. This leads to an inconsistent approach to issues.
Effect: This creates the potential for conflicting decisions.
Action: Start categorizing the issues to show patterns.
Prevention: On a proactive basis, develop a consistent approach for the issues.

15. **Managers are dabbling in the E-Business.**
Reason: Managers may be attracted to the E-Business due to the fascinating technical aspects or the financial importance of the work.
Effect: The work may become micromanaged, holding up progress.
Action: Move to create summaries of the E-Business subproject and to reduce visibility of E-Business. Involve management in issue resolution.
Prevention: At the start, define management's role in the E-Business work. Management's major role is to help issues resolution.

16. **Management doesn't hold the E-Business team accountable.**
Reason: Managers take on too much responsibility and let the team off the hook.
Effect: The E-Business team may lose a sense of accountability.
Action: Instill more accountability with the team at the task level.
Prevention: Define accountability for the team and for management at the start of the work.

17. **Significant top management change occurs during E-Business implementation.**
Reason: This is a normal course of events since the E-Business schedule has a substantial elapsed time.
Effect: New leadership may slow progress on E-Business while learning their job and about the work. New management may have a different notion of E-Business.
Action: Try to work with the new management immediately by getting them on board with E-Business.

Prevention: Adopt the approach that the E-Business depends on a management team, rather than on any one person, and that the organization has a vested self-interest in E-Business.

18. **Even with a high priority, E-Business is unsuccessful in competing for resources.**

Reason: Due to political factors or the excitement generated by another project, the E-Business effort suffers. Maintenance and emergencies can also get in the way. This even happens if management sets a high priority on E-Business (e.g., Y2K work in the late 1990's).

Effect: E-Business will have to get by with fewer resources.

Action: Consider restructuring the work to a lower resource level.

Prevention: Begin with a smaller number of resources and don't count on many additional resources in the short term.

19. **Critical milestones are not reviewed in the E-Business work. They are taken for granted.**

Reason: A regular method of review may not have been instituted. Review may be seen as indicating a lack of trust in the team. Review may not occur due to pressure to implement E-Business.

Effect: The problem will surface when it becomes apparent that the work is not satisfactory. The entire E-Business effort may be questioned.

Action: If a review is not imposed by management, define your own review approach.

Prevention: Define a formal review method for critical milestones.

20. **Management is too formal and emphasizes E-Business status as opposed to content and issues.**

Reason: This often reflects the current management style.

Effect: Time for dealing with projects is consumed by concerns with status. Issues and substance are ignored. Later, crises arise that consume management attention.

Action: Begin to present issues as a part of addressing status.

Prevention: Try to institute a method in which status and issues are dealt with separately.

21. **The ability or desire to pull all of the projects including the E-Business work together for analysis does not exist.**

Reason: Perhaps no one thought of doing this. Also, the projects may be in different formats and structures, making summaries more important.

Effect: Managers lack an overall sense of how well projects are being managed, including E-Business.

Action: Create a summary plan of the subprojects of E-Business. This is a rollup of the subprojects into one overall E-Business plan. Then you will be able to see how all subprojects work together.

Prevention: Establish a summary reporting process for E-Business.

22. **There is a general lack of understanding of E-Business and its implications on the changes needed in the company.**

    Reason: People may assume that with the media attention, everyone knows what it is and how it is. This is a dangerous assumption.

    Effect: Misconceptions continue and spread unaddressed. They typically surface later in the project—potentially impacting the project deliverables and schedule.

    Action: If you sense this, then you should hold some meetings to share information with the staff.

    Prevention: E-Business orientation should begin at the start of the work.

23. **An organizational process for dealing with issues is missing.**

    Reason: Management may never have been comfortable with project management. Issues from projects are treated the same as those from line organizations. This surfaces with E-Business due to its size and visibility.

    Effect: Without a method, the issues are addressed one at a time and not systematically.

    Action: Propose developing a standard method for analyzing issues.

    Prevention: Develop the issues approach as discussed in the preceding chapter.

24. **Management changes its E-Business strategy in the middle of the E-Business implementation.**

    Reason: Management may think that the current approach is taking too long. They decide to shortcut and force a streamlined version of E-Business to be rolled out.

    Effect: It is likely that this streamlined version of E-Business will cause more problems than it solves.

    Action: If this occurs, prepare trade-off analysis to indicate the impact of change. Also, indicate several different strategies.

    Prevention: Management strategy changes should be pointed out as an initial issue in E-Business.

25. **Management overreacts to E-Business issues.**

    Reason: This may be a natural occurrence. The problem arises when management begins to overreact to many issues being brought in. Also, not all issues presented have obvious solutions.

    Effect: If the team members perceive the overreaction, they become reluctant to bring issues forward. The issues tend to sit until there is a crisis. This in turn feeds the overreaction.

    Action: Attempt to provide an overall perspective of each subproject in a summary mode. This can help managers step back from the detail.

    Prevention: Implement a structured approach for issue management that allows for escalation.

26. **Misunderstandings about E-Business are not corrected.**

    Reason: With communications extending over months, misunderstandings are likely to occur many times. This is made worse because people may have misconceptions about E-Business.

    Effect: Misunderstandings can make enemies of the project. Misconceptions can fester. These can then affect decisions related to E-Business.

    Action: Tackle misunderstandings head-on. Don't wait.

    Prevention: Establish regular communications with managers related to the work.

27. **There are too many changes in the project plan during E-Business implementation.**

    Reason: The leader may not keep up the detail in the E-Business plan. A surge of changes can come from management, vendors, marketing, other internal departments, and technology vendors.

    Effect: Failure to keep up with the changes puts the E-Business plan and work in jeopardy.

    Action: Review the plan and outstanding issues right away.

    Prevention: On a regular basis, check your progress on dealing with issues and see if these are reflected in the plan.

28. **Management fails to explain to employees the relationship and differences between normal and E-Business.**

    Reason: Management may assume that the employees do not need to know about the E-Business effort.

    Effect: Employees become confused and feel threatened. The E-Business work is threatened.

    Action: Begin to explain how the normal business and E-Business fit together.

    Prevention: Formally prepare materials and explain the relationship in the initial phase of the work.

29. **Marketing does not get creative and fails to change to address E-Business opportunities.**

    Reason: Marketing may not realize what the differences between E-Business marketing and that of regular business are.

    Effect: Marketing gets in a reactive mode so that even with wonderful software and a web site, the site traffic does not meet expectations.

    Action: It is hard to turn this around. Begin with tactical promotion planning.

    Prevention: Monitor and meet with marketing often.

E-BUSINESS IMPLEMENTATION AND THE PLAN

30. **A baseline plan for the E-Business is not created and does not exist.**

    Reason: A firm does not get in the habit of measuring actual vs. planned results for its projects. This is carried over to E-Business.

Effect: Without a baseline plan, the E-Business plan can shift and decay.

Action: Set baseline plans for all subprojects of E-Business.

Prevention: Implement the baseline vs. actual comparison as soon as work is performed on the E-Business.

31. **Resource consumption in the E-Business is too variable.**

    Reason: This occurs when the demand for resources varies with the types of tasks that are active.

    Effect: Management of the work is more difficult, since the E-Business manager must constantly adjust to the workload and staff members.

    Action: The variability may be planned, so adjust the approach for managing the resources.

    Prevention: Through planning, try to move task schedules.

32. **Team meetings for the E-Business effort lack focus.**

    Reason: This occurs when no standard method for handling meetings is in place.

    Effect: Issues remain unresolved meeting after meeting.

    Action: Step in and impose a standard format for meetings, and then control the meetings.

    Prevention: Establish standard meeting formats with sample agendas.

33. **E-Business is being treated too routinely, like past projects.**

    Reason: This occurs when people are too confident due to success on past projects.

    Effect: When you treat a project as routine, people don't take the issues seriously. This can lead to a crisis.

    Action: Try to put a spark of life in the project by emphasizing what is new and different about E-Business. Discuss what the competition is doing.

    Prevention: Clearly define what is new and what can be learned from past projects as well as other web sites.

34. **The E-Business plan lacks key resources despite upper management support.**

    Reason: The person creating the E-Business plan left out important resources. This is typically due to lack of experience.

    Effect: Resources must be requested on an ad hoc, disorganized basis.

    Action: Update the project plan with all of the resources that you require.

    Prevention: Assign people to review the list of resources that are in E-Business.

35. **Too much time elapses between milestones in E-Business.**

    Reason: This can be the result of inexperience, or lack of planning and review of the plan.

    Effect: With substantial elapsed time between milestones, one begins to wonder what is going on in E-Business. What is the status and progress?

Action: Find out what is going on. Then define more milestones to reduce the gap between the existing milestones.

Prevention: Attempt to reach a milestone every three to four weeks. Define interim milestones every two weeks.

36. **E-Business gets off to a slow start.**

    Reason: E-Business may have no early actions. The tasks may be related to purchasing and hiring.

    Effect: E-Business languishes, but management expectations are still in place. The risk is that progress will not resume.

    Action: Begin on parallel tasks. Demonstrate activity.

    Prevention: With a standard template and detailed tasks, many initial, parallel tasks should be scheduled.

37. **The E-Business plan is not kept up-to-date during implementation.**

    Reason: There are many parallel tasks in E-Business implementation. If there is a single leader, he or she may not have time to do updates. The leaders may also think that updating is not important.

    Effect: Without updates, the plan begins to lack credibility. Status is not changing; new, additional tasks are not updated. Things begin to fall apart when management notices that the project plan is out-of-date.

    Action: Unless the E-Business leaders have a regular pattern established for updating the plan, it will not get done. Take a snapshot of what is going on now to do an update and then do the updates on a regular weekly basis.

    Prevention: Require that an overall plan of E-Business subprojects be created and maintained. All plans and projects should follow a regular update pattern.

38. **The E-Business implementation plan is too detailed and difficult to use.**

    Reason: Some first-time project managers want to do the work "right" and define a great many tasks down to the level of a one-day or two-day duration. For an E-Business project, this is overwhelming. Alternatively, they may place all of the tasks in one plan without subprojects—the scenario for a disaster.

    Effect: Such a plan cannot be updated or changed without great effort. This may lead to the plan not being updated at all, or being ignored.

    Action: Cut back the detail in a new schedule. Make the shortest task at least two weeks in duration. If there is just one plan, chop it up into subprojects by areas of responsibility.

    Prevention: Use a template and instruct managers on rules relating to detail as discussed in previous chapters.

39. **The scope of the E-Business implementation continues to expand.**

    Reason: This may be due to a lack of management control as well as lack of planning and anticipation of potential issues. The phenomenon of "scope creep" is common in E-Business. Many individuals will want to add just one more requirement. Then previously unseen tasks appear.

Effect: The E-Business schedule slips and the budget balloons.

Action: Evaluate your plan to ensure that it is complete even if you have started work. Separate out the items that should be deferred. With the scope redefined, return to the plan and revise it to fit the scope.

Prevention: Impose rules at the start of the E-Business effort relating to any changes in requirements. Also, test your plan for completeness.

40. **Despite an expanding scope, no budget adjustments or resource additions are made to the E-Business effort.**

Reason: The people who approved the E-Business scope change are not often the ones who approve budget and resource additions. Thus, the resources and budget don't fit with the scope.

Effect: The E-Business project will grow out of control and is more likely to fail.

Action: After reviewing the E-Business scope, go to management with the choice of additional funding and resources or reduced scope.

Prevention: Impose a rule that all scope changes for E-Business of a certain level and above must have resource and budget review.

41. **The E-Business plan is not synchronized with the actual results of the work.**

Reason: The E-Business plan may not have been updated. The updates to the plan may not be complete. The additional out-of-scope and rework tasks are not added. There is additional work on E-Business tasks that are not reported to the managers.

Effect: People begin to ignore the E-Business plan since it is not realistic.

Action: Conduct a review of the status of the actual work. Go to each person working on E-Business and identify their active tasks. Then go to the plan and update this to fit the reality. You could find an iceberg situation where a higher percentage of tasks are untracked than tracked.

Prevention: The E-Business managers should verify that the plan matches the work that is being performed.

42. **E-Business issues are being addressed one at a time rather than in sets.**

Reason: No systematic, organized approach to address E-Business issues is in place. As a result, each one may be treated alone and inconsistently compared to others.

Effect: The resolution of successive issues may be contradictory. Issues may sit unresolved, while time is spent on analysis of past decisions. Decisions may be reversed—making management appear indecisive.

Action: All outstanding issues should be grouped and then organized for review. A standard review method for E-Business issues should be put into place.

Prevention: A method for identifying and dealing with issues should be included in the E-Business plan. This method should address issues that arise that involve regular work or other projects.

43. **The E-Business plan is changing too much and is not stable.**

Reason: The E-Business leaders may be attempting to have the plan reflect everyday events. They may lack experience in project management and so are making many changes.

Effect: With so many changes, the credibility of the plan is in doubt. This can occur when several versions of the E-Business plan are in circulation at one time, leading to more confusion. Loss of credibility in the plan may affect E-Business work.

Action: Procedures for updating and changing the E-Business plan should be put into place.

Prevention: Guidelines for changing the E-Business plan and for employing standard templates should be established. Changes should only be made when there is a major event. In general, you want to have at most three different versions during the life of the implementation work since some change can be tolerated.

44. **The level of effort required is consistently underestimated in the E-Business project.**

Reason: People on the team have never implemented E-Business. This can be due to inexperience or due to unrealistic target dates. They also do not think of all of the tasks that are required.

Effect: The E-Business schedule will immediately slip and continue to do so. The plan will lose its meaning. Management is now more likely to intervene in the work.

Action: All changes and updates to the plan should be stopped while people realistically estimate duration and effort. Also, an effort is needed to ensure that there is completeness.

Prevention: The best prevention is to have a detailed project review at the start and additional reviews periodically.

45. **Significant tasks in the E-Business effort are missing.**

Reason: Many team members and/or leaders have not done E-Business implementation before. Another reason for missing tasks is that events and elements of the plan are not within the control of the leader and team.

Effect: The schedule will stretch out as these tasks appear. If the tasks are not added to the plan, the plan will not reflect the work. The morale of the team will drop as more missing tasks surface.

Action: Review the plan structure with the additional past, present, and future work added.

Prevention: Schedule an extensive review of the initial E-Business plan prior to setting the baseline schedule.

46. **The wrong tasks are changed or deleted to try to meet the E-Business deadlines.**

    Reason: The E-Business leader may panic and try to cut tasks just to meet the deadline.

    Effect: Slippage will occur as the now missing tasks draw resources from the remaining tasks in the plan.

    Action: Revisit the structure of the E-Business plan and expand the tasks. Review the new schedule with management.

    Prevention: Draw up guidelines for revising the E-Business plan and for task deletion.

47. **The number and frequency of milestones in the E-Business plan are insufficient.**

    Reason: Inexperience is one cause. Optimism or relying on strategies from past successful work on smaller projects that had a reduced scope may lead people to create fewer milestones.

    Effect: The E-Business project will be more difficult to track. This means that quality of work will be an issue.

    Action: Revisit the E-Business schedule and identify additional milestones.

    Prevention: Using an E-Business template, assess the schedule to see if there are sufficient milestones. You can filter the plan for milestones and see how many and when they appear.

48. **The E-Business work is going on much longer than planned.**

    Reason: This is the nature of the work. Requirements could have been changed many times. The work may be hung up on a technical issue that cannot be resolved quickly.

    Effect: The schedule may begin to drift out of control. People may get caught up in the process of E-Business as opposed to the work.

    Action: Consider dividing the work into a number of separate parts.

    Prevention: At the start, divide the project into subprojects, each of which has separate milestones.

49. **The E-Business plan should be changed significantly, but it is not.**

    Reason: The leader may be reluctant to make changes that might disrupt the E-Business effort.

    Effect: The E-Business plan does not reflect what is going on in the work.

    Action: Make a general schedule change and then impose standard reviews.

    Prevention: Define guidelines for changing the schedule.

50. **The E-Business plan is not adaptive to results or events.**

    Reason: This may be due to a template or schedule that is too rigid. Too many dependencies result. If a template that has not been tested is used, then this problem is more likely to occur since you are more likely to make mistakes in planning the first time out of the gate.

    Effect: The plan may end up being obsolete and not used.

Action: Consider developing a new version of the E-Business plan that is more flexible, with summary tasks and fewer dependencies.

Prevention: The use of a template combined with tests of the template and lessons learned should make the E-Business plan more adaptive.

THE E-BUSINESS TEAM AND RESOURCES

51. **The single project leader cannot cope with all of the issues that arise in the E-Business implementation.**

    Reason: E-Business projects are composed of many diverse subprojects. It is highly unlikely that you will find one project leader who has the ability, let alone the stamina, to deal with the issues.

    Effect: Issues begin to remain unresolved longer. The implementation schedule may slip.

    Action: Try to get some of the work assigned to an additional manager.

    Prevention: Set up the implementation with multiple subproject leaders where one is the overall leader.

52. **Business employees claim that they are too busy to test the E-Business software and web site.**

    Reason: The business employees feel that their main role and rewards are in their departments and normal work. They may see E-Business as just another burden.

    Effect: If these people do not participate, then the E-Business is definitely going to be in trouble. You cannot think that the IT staff can do the testing.

    Action: The issue should be presented to the department managers. Here is one issue that you may need to appeal to upper management.

    Prevention: Anticipate that this will be a problem. Plan ahead with the users and get them involved earlier.

53. **Customer service fails to treat web visitors differently from standard customers.**

    Reason: They may not be directed by their management to address web customers differently in terms of attitude and speed of service.

    Effect: Web customers may start complaining about the web site.

    Action: You should meet with customer service management on the issue. Try to support implementation of new procedures.

    Prevention: Customer service should have their own subproject.

54. **One of the E-Business leaders lacks personnel skills.**

    Reason: The leader may have been assigned to E-Business based on availability, rather than necessary skills. Management may not realize the complexity of the E-Business work and the need for collaborative work.

Effect: The team and E-Business suffer while the leader goes through a learning curve.

Action: In extreme cases, the leader may be replaced. A less severe approach is to assign another leader of the team to be a mentor.

Prevention: This is another point in support of multiple project leaders.

55. **No organized approach for sharing of information has been formulated.**

Reason: People may mistakenly assume that information will be shared. They may see no need to share the information.

Effect: People may be working on E-Business in a vacuum. Without information sharing there will be less coordination.

Action: Consider having meetings in which information is shared relative to issues.

Prevention: Establish guidelines to support lessons learned and sharing of information.

56. **Too much bureaucracy rules the management of the E-Business effort.**

Reason: This may be due to the style of management or to the style of one of the leaders.

Effect: Bureaucracy puts measuring results in the back seat. The project looks good on paper. In reality, it may be falling apart.

Action: Without replacing the manager, move the emphasis of the project toward issues rather than status. Reduce the overhead tasks.

Prevention: Guidelines for the E-Business leaders should be in place.

57. **People are spread too thin in the implementation project.**

Reason: The E-Business work may depend on a few key people who are used in many tasks.

Effect: The plan may start to slip as the team members become stressed and overworked.

Action: Consider reassigning some of the tasks or dividing tasks up so that junior employees can do some of the work.

Prevention: In planning for E-Business, tentatively assign resources to the work, then filter the project to see how overcommitted people are.

58. **The E-Business leader fails to delegate to the team.**

Reason: The leader may be attempting to do too much of the work himself or herself.

Effect: The leader becomes a bottleneck and the team members get increasingly frustrated.

Action: Reassign some of the tasks to team members.

Prevention: Clearly define and review the role of the leaders. As a sidenote, this is another reason for multiple leaders.

59. **Team assignments in the E-Business are being changed too often.**

Reason: Due to the pressures of the work and outside influence, the team may be shifted frequently.

Effect: The team may lose faith in the project leader and feel that the project is in chaos.

Action: Revisit the E-Business project plan and assign areas of tasks to team members.

Prevention: Make team assignments to areas of tasks, not individual tasks. Change team assignments on an infrequent basis.

60. **People are kept on the E-Business team too long.**

Reason: Personal relationships may have been established so that the manager is reluctant to reassign the people. The leaders may want the same people because they are known and give stability to the E-Business effort.

Effect: Morale may suffer as some team members feel that others are dragging down the E-Business work.

Action: Review all roles and responsibilities on the team. Move to reassign or remove some team members.

Prevention: Explain clearly to each team member at the start when he or she will enter and leave the project team. Stick to the schedule.

61. **An E-Business manager is spending too much time on administrative work.**

Reason: This can occur in an E-Business effort that is large with many administrative tasks. It can even occur in smaller projects when the project leader prefers administrative tasks.

Effect: The management side of the implementation will suffer.

Action: The E-Business leader should be counseled and guided to spend more time on management.

Prevention: The role and duties of the leader should be clearly defined at the start.

62. **Miscommunications with line management occur.**

Reason: People spend too much time inside E-Business. The leaders are too internally focused.

Effect: Miscommunications can lead to misunderstandings, which in turn lead to resistance and hostility.

Action: Open up the lines of communications with line management by discussing issues and status of E-Business.

Prevention: The approach for working with line managers should be defined at the start of the work.

63. **An E-Business manager lacks management skills, and no team member fills the vacuum.**

Reason: While people realize the problem, they let this ride rather than cause additional problems by interfering. The leader may have been selected for his or her knowledge of E-Business or technical skills but not their management skills—which are severely lacking.

Effect: Management issues remain unresolved. The team senses a lack of management.

Action: Consider reassigning some duties to senior team members or adding a senior project leader to address issues.

Prevention: The lack of management skills known up front can be accommodated for in planning and staffing.

64. **The project suffers from uneven distribution of skills and knowledge.**

Reason: This is a natural occurrence in E-Business efforts where you are not likely to have highly skilled people in all business and technical areas.

Effect: The work may fall back and depend on the key people. The talents of the junior team members are wasted.

Action: Consider subteams within the project team to get people to work together.

Prevention: Pair junior team members with senior members.

65. **Team members fail to learn lessons during the E-Business implementation.**

Reason: Perhaps no process was instituted for collecting and using lessons learned. People are overly focused on the present.

Effect: People repeat variations of the same mistakes.

Action: Institute a review to gather lessons learned so far in the work. Update these on a regular basis.

Prevention: Guidelines at the start of the implementation should stress the importance of and the approach for benefiting from lessons learned.

66. **People are spread too thin between high-priority work in the E-Business effort and elsewhere.**

Reason: Different projects other than the E-Business may require the same set of skills and knowledge, placing stress and demand on key people. No one created a method to deal with resource allocation across multiple projects.

Effect: The worst case sometimes occurs—all projects suffer.

Action: Management from all projects should get together and set priorities.

Prevention: Draw up an overall summary project plan that links all projects, including the E-Business one. That will allow you to see where resources are scarce and assist you in allocation.

67. **Boundaries at the edge of the E-Business effort (indicating scope) are breaking down.**

Reason: People on the team are too helpful—they perform more work than that which falls within the scope of E-Business.

Effect: The scope is expanding, but the resources and schedule are not changing.

Action: The boundary of the E-Business effort needs to be firmly drawn and enforced.

Prevention: Establish rules for changing the scope and taking on more work at the start of the E-Business work.

68. **The anticipated resources fail to appear.**

Reason: People assigned to help you out when the work began are not available due to priorities of other projects. Similar problems can occur with equipment and facilities.

Effect: E-Business can slip due to the lack of resources. The effects can increase due to collateral damage to other tasks.

Action: Line up alternative resources.

Prevention: Check availability of resources at least one month prior to when you need them and then check weekly prior to the arrival of the resources.

69. **Management communications gradually deteriorate.**

Reason: This can be due to lack of contact and misconceptions. Management committed to E-Business and then moved on to some new subject.

Effect: Support for E-Business may be threatened. This can be due to fear, lack of understanding, or lack of sustained interest.

Action: Begin to re-establish communications on a regular basis. Focus on informal management communications.

Prevention: Establish a communications pattern early in the work to maintain regular, expected contact.

70. **Too much of the E-Business project is being done by one person.**

Reason: In many projects, one particular person tries to be helpful. This person takes on more and more work. On an E-Business project this dependency on the knowledge of the person occurs because people become dependent on someone with specific technical or business skills.

Effect: The first impact may be to delay the schedule. Another effect is to create a bottleneck. The work may suffer from that person being a single source of information. No backup is prepared to take over if this person becomes ill or leaves.

Action: Reassign the work and distribute it to more than one person to prevent recurrence of the problem.

Prevention: Establish clear boundaries at the beginning of the work concerning what people are to work on.

71. **Poor performance by some drags down performance by all.**

Reason: Uneven performance is frequent on E-Business implementation efforts due to size and complexity as well as time.

Effect: The other team members see that nonperformance or poor performance is not addressed. They may then have a tendency to slack off in their work.

Action: Performance of the entire team should be measured. At the same time as you are addressing poor performers, praise good performance.

Prevention: Indicate the policies related to performance review and follow up with statements about performance on a regular basis without mentioning names.

THE E-BUSINESS VENDORS

72. **A regular flow of end products from contractors is not occurring.**
   Reason: This may be due to poor planning on the part of the project leader, as well as to inexperience in dealing with contractors. It may be due to the vendor staff being diverted into other activities away from their core role in E-Business.
   Effect: Project control can shift from the leader to the contractor.
   Action: Sit down with the contractor and define a new subproject plan for work with this contractor. Then merge this with the current plan.
   Prevention: In defining milestones, make sure that the work of the contractors can be tracked. Filter all milestones in the plan to see if there is a regular flow of milestones.

73. **The consultants receive work from other companies. They are spending less time on your firm's E-Business effort.**
   Reason: E-Business is hot. Experienced vendors may find that they have more work than they can handle. They don't want to give up so they continue to spread their employees thinner.
   Effect: Your E-Business work suffers.
   Action: Raise hell. Arrange a meeting with the consulting manager to review the plan and their tasks.
   Prevention: Bring this up as an issue with the consultants at the beginning of their work. Determine how this can be prevented or minimized.

74. **The consultant/contractor team is not managed well.**
   Reason: This can occur when the leader does not provide supervision. The leader of the consultants may be out hustling more E-Business contracts —not unusual.
   Effect: The lack of organization and management among the subcontractors may impact the project negatively. You may have to divert your effort to do the contractor's management job.
   Action: Contact the manager of the subcontractor and negotiate rules.
   Prevention: Prior to the start of work, establish policies on how the contractor's staff will be managed.

75. **Without knowing it, you have become dependent on the specific software tools used by the vendor. These are not part of the contract.**
   Reason: The vendor staff employ their own tools to improve their productivity. However, the firm does not make a point of this. It suddenly is revealed in later stages of their work.

Effect: You have signed up the vendor for an indefinite period but you did not know it, and you really didn't want to subcontract them indefinitely.

Action: Try to negotiate the use of the tools and the transfer of some basic knowledge associated with the tool.

Prevention: Have the vendor identify all of their tools in the planning stage. If they have tools that your people do not know, then arrange for a familiarity session and some training.

76. **The consultants maintain their own separate project plans for their E-Business work.**

Reason: Separate project plans are what they are used to. Your firm did not insist on a common plan.

Effect: The coordination effort increases as meetings are necessary to reconcile their plan with yours. If the situation continues, it becomes extremely difficult to reconcile the plans later.

Action: Try to force the issue and have them integrate their plan with yours.

Prevention: Set a common plan as a requirement for the vendor work.

77. **There are several consulting firms involved. They are stepping over each other.**

Reason: E-Business may require several consultants for process improvement, marketing, web development, and other activities. These activities interact and interface with each other.

Effect: Lack of coordination means that the firms are working independently—probably impacting the project schedule in a negative way. You cannot assume that just because they are paid all of that money, that they are coordinating their efforts.

Action: Set up a separate subproject for coordination with E-Business.

Prevention: Set up the subproject for coordination and identify a number of issues related to this.

78. **Vendor work is not reviewed sufficiently.**

Reason: There is much pressure in the E-Business work. Since the vendor is being paid a great deal of money, there is sometimes a tendency on the part of management to assume that the work is OK without review—a bad idea.

Effect: Without review, the quality of the work is unknown. If the quality is poor, then the work must be redone—adding more time and cost.

Action: Start reviewing the vendor work right away.

Prevention: Determine which milestones of the vendor work have risk.

79. **No one made provisions for ongoing vendor involvement and support for E-Business.**

Reason: It was thought that the E-Business work would end so that the need for the vendor evaporates. Any other work would be handled by internal staff.

Effect: Loss of vendor support when they find other work means that you must find a new vendor—you incur a learning curve and higher cost. Thinking that internal employees can rapidly pick up on what the vendor staff took several years to learn is a little optimistic.

Action: Try to negotiate an extension with the vendor.

Prevention: Be flexible at the start of the work to keep your options open. Make sure that you have the option to have the vendor continue work.

METHODS AND TOOLS

80. **Performance of the web site suffers due to undersized hardware.**
    Reason: The IT group may not realize the severity of the peak loads that can occur on the web site due to peak customer demand.
    Effect: Performance suffers and customers complain. Business may be lost. What is worse, it may not be easy to fix the problem through a simple upgrade due to the hardware, network, and system software configuration.
    Action: Review the hardware performance and determine corrective measures for both the short and long term.
    Prevention: Establish a subproject for performance measurement as an ongoing activity.

81. **Even though a method or tool has proven to be a failure, it is not discarded or replaced. It continues to be used in later E-Business efforts.**
    Reason: People may not want to acknowledge failure or problems. They may still pay lip service to the method or tool.
    Effect: A method or tool gap is being addressed on an ad hoc basis by each person. This leads to reduced productivity as each person struggles separately.
    Action: Announce the replacement method or tool at the same time that you kill off the old method or tool.
    Prevention: Carefully evaluate and select the methods and tools at the beginning.

82. **Different people are employing different, incompatible tools.**
    Reason: If no standards are established concerning the tools at the start of the work, people often employ the tools that they have used before. The situation may also be that different consultants and contractors are employing incompatible tools.
    Effect: Incompatible tools mean that a person may have to understand multiple tools that do the same thing. Additional work may result from trying to make one tool work with another.
    Action: Review the existing tools and implement a phaseout of some tools. Conduct this review with the vendors.

Prevention: Identify the tool set at the start of work. Reinforce proper use of the tools with training.

83. **Staff members are resistant to the methods or to the tools required for E-Business.**

    Reason: If training is not good or not provided, or documentation is poor, staff may get a bad impression of the methods and tools.

    Effect: If staff members are resistant, they may not use the methods or tools properly. They may resist using the methods and tools at all.

    Action: Meet with the resistant people and identify why they feel uncomfortable about the methods or tools. Take steps to rectify the situation.

    Prevention: Having announced and reinforced the methods and tools at the start of the work, follow up by monitoring their use.

84. **The work suffers from a lack of experts in the E-Business methods and tools.**

    Reason: This may occur if the E-Business implementation is the first in the company to use the method or tool.

    Effect: Productivity falls as people attempt to use the method or tool for the first time.

    Action: Appoint someone to learn how to use the tool and then have him or her train the others.

    Prevention: Identify the future experts in tools at the start of the work.

85. **No one took enough time to learn the method or tool to a point of proficiency due to the time pressure of implementation.**

    Reason: The pressures of the schedule precluded any substantial learning.

    Effect: The team is not able to take advantage of the features of the method or tool.

    Action: Prepare basic guidelines for the method or tool. Circulate these at the start of the work and gain concurrence and commitment.

    Prevention: Add tasks related to learning the method or tool to the plan and template.

86. **Bad habits in using tools and methods are not addressed or unlearned.**

    Reason: Bad habits can happen because of laziness or because they are what the people knew before, and E-Business managers failed to give them any direction with respect to tools and methods.

    Effect: Poor tool use reduces productivity and may affect the schedule. It also adds to complexity given the number of individuals involved in the work.

    Action: Have people share experiences and lessons learned on how to employ tools on a regular basis.

    Prevention: The use of the tool expert and mentor, along with reinforcement training, can help keep bad habits from forming.

87. **Given the dynamic nature of E-Business, it is possible to have a new tool inserted into the implementation without planning.**
Reason: Some manager gets excited about a tool and buys one without accompanying planning and training. There is no information sharing.
Effect: No one knows the learning curve or how people are going to integrate this new tool with other tools.
Action: Stop the use of the tool and assess its role and learning curve.
Prevention: Implement a planned approach for tool evaluation, selection, and implementation at the very inception of the E-Business effort.

88. **No one knows whether the methods and tools being used are really helping to improve efficiency and productivity.**
Reason: No organized approach is taken to measure the project internally. People are just rushing around trying to implement the project.
Effect: Doubts may arise about the company effort in E-Business itself.
Action: Institute a review of methods and tools by having the team share lessons learned. Document these lessons learned and update them.
Prevention: Make measurement of the methods and tools a regular part of the E-Business effort.

THE E-BUSINESS WORK

89. **Setting up product information takes too long for the Web.**
Reason: People underestimate what it takes to get the description, pictures, and other product information set up. This delays getting the products on the Web.
Effect: Business sales are impacted.
Action: Review the resources that are assigned to this work.
Prevention: Try to find out what other firms have done with staffing for these activities.

90. **Data quality for the products on the Web is not good.**
Reason: There is a lack of review of the web content.
Effect: Problems are discovered by customers. The burden falls on customer service to manually fix each problem.
Action: The current web site should be reviewed in terms of the most popular items.
Prevention: Make web content review a part of the E-Business plan.

91. **There remain too many exceptions and manual steps in the processes even with the new E-Business processes.**
Reason: There was not sufficient time to make all of the changes. There may have been resistance to change as well. The person analyzing the processes may have missed some exceptions.

Effect: The efficiency of the E-Business may be impacted. Gains in revenue are now offset by higher costs due to workarounds and shadow systems.

Action: Begin an effort to identify these exceptions and deal with them.

Prevention: Track the exceptions and manual steps through the entire implementation or expansion effort.

92. **The E-Business effort requires too much rework.**

Reason: This can be due to poor quality or lack of training. It can also be because of the rush to implement. Examples of rework are software, procedures, and web content.

Effect: The schedule will slip and the credibility of the team will suffer.

Action: Investigate where the rework needs to be done, then work backward to find out where the problems are.

Prevention: Keep an eye on quality and review of work. This can translate into an analysis of rework. The rework should also be measured closely.

93. **No one is looking for improvements. They are rushing to implement the new E-Business software.**

Reason: In some projects the actual techniques related to work are frozen in time at the start of the project to achieve better stability. Management is saying, "Just get it installed and we'll fix the rest later."

Effect: The opportunity for change and the benefits that could result from the changes are lost. The likelihood of major problems will rise.

Action: People on the team should meet to discuss how they do their work at the start and where there is an absolute necessity not to rush.

Prevention: Incorporate improving the work as a regular task in the schedule.

94. **Too many tasks are unplanned.**

Reason: An E-Business effort is very large in scope. After work gets started, unplanned additional tasks will appear. Rather than include these in the subprojects people attempt to do the work, but not record it. This can also be due to the lack of planning at the start.

Effect: Unplanned tasks make the schedule extend in time and create more resource conflicts. The schedule is not reliable since it does not reflect the tasks or the status of the work.

Action: Start by dealing with the unplanned tasks that occurred in the past. Then expand your energy into tasks in the near future.

Prevention: The best prevention is to gather people together to identify possible issues that may arise. Do this at the start of the project. By identifying issues, you can determine related tasks.

95. **Quality of the E-Business work is an issue.**

Reason: Management may put too much emphasis on schedule and not enough on quality especially given the time pressure for going live with E-Business.

Effect: Poor work leads to rework and extra work, affecting the schedule. Poor work may mean that errors are left untreated. These then blow E-Business transactions out of the water later when you go live.

Action: Make quality an important part of reviews. On the systems side emphasize quality assurance.

Prevention: Spell out quality standards at the beginning of the project. Give regular examples of disaster stories of when a web site fails and customers complain loudly in a web chat room.

96. **The E-Business effort is hit with compound issues and crises and does not recover.**

Reason: The E-Business can be hit by manager turnover, increased competitive pressure, demands for changes from marketing, and complaints from other departments at almost the same time.

Effect: The work may grind to a halt while a new leader is found. Momentum is lost and the entire effort is in jeopardy.

Action: Identify and assess the outstanding issues. Then address these issues.

Prevention: Warn people that crises may come in bunches and that they should be ready to address these through issue management. Give them examples of groups of issues to instill a realistic attitude.

97. **What has been accomplished is not reviewed even though it has a high priority.**

Reason: People may be in a hurry. The review will cause the schedule to slip. People also may be scared of what might be found. Better to push it under the rug, they think.

Effect: E-Business is exposed because of the lack of review. Additional rework may be needed later.

Action: The level of review should be set ahead of time. This is a planned trade-off to determine how much to do with available resources.

Prevention: Schedule reviews for all significant milestones. Assess the level of effort needed vs. the risk and exposure.

98. **Information on how to evaluate the work is lacking.**

Reason: Without preparation for doing a review, the review of the work may accomplish very little.

Effect: The major impact is that management gets the impression that the review was complete, when it was only superficial. This is deadly in E-Business where errors and mistakes may be noticed externally and taken advantage of by competition.

Action: Distribute packets of material prior to the review. Follow up with visits to the recipients.

Prevention: Include preparation for reviews as tasks in the plan.

99. **One issue dominates the work in the implementation or expansion—leading to problems with other tasks.**
    Reason: This is natural when one issue is dominant financially or politically. It occurs also for organization reasons and resistance to E-Business.
    Effect: Other issues may be lost in the shuffle.
    Action: Include the other issues in an issue summary. Allocate time to a group of issues separate from the main issue.
    Prevention: This will occur. You can only mitigate the impact with an organized prioritization of issues.

100. **Issues surfacing around the work are not taken to the E-Business leader and team.**
    Reason: People may be reluctant to bring problems to management.
    Effect: The issues tend to fester. They are unlikely to diminish. The issues then can impact the schedule and work—making action more complex and difficult.
    Action: Spend time getting acquainted with the day-to-day work being performed in the subproject. Gather up issues and match those with the plan and the issues list.
    Prevention: Initiate more regular communications between the team and any other workers related to E-Business. Encourage and monitor open communication.

101. **IT creates too many web sites for E-Business.**
    Reason: Marketing generates many promotions. The quick approach is to implement these on separate web sites.
    Effect: Confusion among web visitors reigns. People find the best web site discounts—negating the other promotions.
    Action: You should probably cut back on the number of web sites and promotions until promotions are better organized.
    Prevention: Plan ahead for the extent and range of promotions.

CONCLUSION

E-Business is a major force for building, expanding, and maintaining the competitive position of your firm. Implementing E-Business consists of implementing many complex, interrelated subprojects under the umbrella of the E-Business effort. E-Business implementation projects are not one-shot affairs. E-Business projects are ongoing as the firm responds and takes initiatives to respond to customer, supplier, and competitive pressures and to proactively take advantage of new business opportunities and technology.

Generally, experience has shown that E-Business implementation fails if all of the traditional project management methods are used. In a nutshell, E-Business is multifaceted and is a multiple-program effort that includes many discrete projects. E-Business management is most successful if carried out following modern techniques. These include:

- Dynamically managing issues to control the schedule and reduce costs
- Multiple project analysis and coordination
- Resource allocation across E-Business, other projects, and regular work
- Capability to adapt to new conditions and change the E-Business implementation direction
- The use of templates, issues and lessons learned databases
- Gathering experience through lessons learned to improve performance and the chances of E-Business success
- Collaborative management in which team members and managers play active roles in E-Business management and in which information is shared
- Breaking up the E-Business effort into subprojects, each with an accountable team leader
- Designation of several individuals as leaders of the E-Business effort

Appendix 1

E-Business Implementation Templates

A project template consists of standardized high-level tasks together with general resources (not specific people) and dependencies. Since dependencies are subject to conditions within an individual company, our attention will be on tasks and resources. As was stated in chapter 2, project templates serve as the basis for developing detailed implementation plans for E-Business. Templates also help in planning, dealing with issues, analyzing schedules and work, and lessons learned.

E-BUSINESS IMPLEMENTATION RESOURCES

A general list of resources is shown in Figure A-1. These include business, contractor, and IT resources. You should establish a blank schedule with no tasks, but with these resources as a resource pool. You can then add specific resources in terms of individual people to the resource pool. All E-Business subprojects would then draw upon this resource pool. This gives you several benefits.

- There is a consistent use of resources across all E-Business efforts as well as regular work. This supports consolidation and analysis.
- To use these resources, you can simply replace general by specific resources when you develop a detailed plan.
- You can determine where you are in a project in terms of detail by considering where the detailed resources end.

IT resources

- Systems analyst
- System designer
- Network specialist
- IT planner
- Systems programmer
- Application programmer
- Quality assurance staff
- System operator
- IT help desk
- IT project managers
- IT system supervisors

Business unit resources (indicate department manager, supervisor, and business staff for the following)

- Business Planning
- Auditing
- Warehouse
- Procurement
- Distribution
- Shipping
- Accounts Payable
- Accounts Receivable
- General Accounting
- Order Processing
- Customer Service
- Supplier Relations
- Marketing
- Sales

Contractor/consultant resources

- Contract programmer
- Network installer
- Network tester
- Systems programmer
- Systems analyst
- Project leader
- Database designer
- System designer
- Business analyst

Figure A-1: General Resources for an E-Business Implementation Template

Tasks belong to specific departments, consultants, or other entities in terms of responsibility and ownership. You should use a text field to indicate responsibility. This is different than resources. The text field answers the question, "Who is responsible?" The responsibility field answers the question, "Who will do the work?"

E-BUSINESS IMPLEMENTATION TASKS

For the tasks, you will first chop up the overall E-Business implementation into subprojects. There are several reasons for doing this, including:

- Schedules tend to grow over time as more tasks are added. This makes a single schedule unmanageable.
- By assigning subprojects to specific leaders you obtain more accountability and visibility for the project parts.
- Using subprojects allows you to create a separate subproject that relates to integration and interfaces among subprojects.

Figure A-2 gives a list of subprojects for an E-Business implementation. Feel free to add to this list. Figure A-3 gives higher level tasks for each subproject in the E-Business implementation. You will want to use Figure A-3 as a starting point and not as a final list. These tasks have been numbered for ease of use. Note that in these figures many subprojects are worked on in parallel. Do not infer a sequential relationship based on the task numbering.

1000	Develop E-Business strategy and identify business activities
2000	E-Business implementation plan and external resource requirements
3000	Systems and technology architecture
4000	Software package evaluation and selection
5000	Software development
6000	System integration and testing
7000	Technology infrastructure implementation
8000	Data conversion and setup
9000	Business activity analysis and definition
10000	Conducting competitive and industry assessment
11000	Organization roles and responsibilities
12000	Marketing campaign for the web site
13000	Data warehouse, data mining, and data analysis
14000	Credit card processing
15000	Rollout of E-Business
16000	Expansion planning and measurement

Figure A-2: Potential Subprojects for the E-Business Implementation

1000   Develop E-Business strategy and identify business activities
1100   Identify E-Business strategy alternatives
1200   Assess alternatives and arrive at strategy for E-Business
1300   Identify business activities that are affected by E-Business strategy
1400   Determine which organizations are involved in these activities
1500   Identify systems and technology that support the activities
1600   Identify business and technical issues that inhibit E-Business implementation.
         Milestones: E-Business strategy in place, related business activities and organizations are identified; inhibiting issues are identified.
2000   E-Business implementation plan and external resource requirements
2100   Identify initial team members
2200   Develop detailed implementation plan
2300   Identify available resources
2400   Perform analysis to determine where consultants are needed
2500   Define management approach for consultants
2600   Develop statements of work
2700   Identify vendors and solicit proposals
2800   Proposal evaluation and selection
2900   Contract negotiations
         Milestones: Completed E-Business implementation plan; consultant requirements defined; consultants and contractors on board.
3000   Systems and technology architecture
3100   Assess current architecture
3200   Define new E-Business architecture
3300   Identify hardware, system software, and network components
3400   Identify database management systems, development, testing, and other tools
3500   Procure hardware, software, and network components
         Milestones: Elements of the supporting hardware, software, and network architecture are identified and obtained.
4000   Software package evaluation and selection
4100   Identify functions and transactions required to be supported
4200   Identify potential software packages and vendors
4300   Evaluate and select software packages
4400   Procure software packages
         Milestones: E-Business software is identified, selected, and contracted for.

Figure A-3: High Level Subproject Template Tasks

5000 **Software development**
5100 Define development approach
5200 System design
5300 Interface design
5400 Programming and unit testing
5500 Programming and unit testing-interfaces
5600 System security
5700 Operations backup, recovery, restart
        Milestones: Individual programs are completed and tested.
6000 **System integration and testing**
6100 Generation of test scripts
6200 Perform integration of software programs
6300 Performance testing
6400 Function testing
6500 Error correction
6600 System testing
        Milestones: System is integrated and tested; system is ready for production.
7000 **Technology infrastructure implementation**
7100 Upgrade and install of hardware and system software
7200 Upgrade of network components
7300 Training of staff
7400 Network and hardware integration
7500 Network and architecture testing
        Milestones: Infrastructure is in place for E-Business.
8000 **Data conversion and setup**
8100 Assess current data
8200 Determine data cleanup approach and perform cleanup
8300 Develop conversion programs and test as needed
8400 Convert data and setup system for production
        Milestones: Data is converted for E-Business.
9000 **Business activity analysis and definition**
9100 Evaluate current business activities
9200 Identify new business activities needed to support E-Business
9300 Define new and modified business activities
9400 Determine requirements for software
9500 Determine benefits for E-Business
9600 Develop procedures for activities
        Milestones: Current processes evaluated; new business activities are defined and documented.

Figure A-3: continued

10000   Conduct a competitive and industry assessment
10100   Select companies and sources
10200   Perform data collection
10300   Data analysis and documentation
          Milestones: Competitive assessment is completed.
11000   Organizational roles and responsibilities
11100   Determine organizational roles for E-Business
11200   Evaluate current organization structure
11300   Define new E-Business oriented organization structure
11400   Plan for the migration of the organization
11500   Carry out the organization change
          Milestone: Organization is E-Business ready.
12000   Marketing campaign for the web site
12100   Define marketing objectives in general
12200   Develop plans for discounts and promotions
12300   Design marketing campaign
12400   Continue to do competitive assessments
12500   Implement marketing campaign for E-Business
12600   Measure results of marketing
          Milestones: Marketing campaigns are designed and implemented.
13000   Data warehouse, data mining, and data analysis
13100   Determine data warehouse and data analysis approach
13200   Identify and procure software tools
13300   Install and test the software
13400   Construct interfaces to the data warehouse
13500   Test the interfaces
13600   Begin to fill the data warehouse on a production basis
          Milestones: Data warehouse setup and analysis of E-Business data
          are completed and underway.
14000   Credit card processing
14100   Identify potential banking and other suppliers of credit card services
14200   Acquire and install credit card interface software
14300   Test the credit card processes and software
14400   Place the credit card process and systems into production
          Milestone: Credit card interface systems are completed.
15000   Rollout of E-Business
15100   Training of staff for E-Business
15200   Final overall testing of E-Business
          Milestone: E-Business is live.
16000   Expansion planning and measurement

Figure A-3: continued

Appendix 2

The Magic Cross Reference

The letters "ff" indicate the reader should also see the following pages.

Area	Topic	Page Numbers
Communications	Communications planning form	122
	Meeting guidelines	124–125
	6 actions	119ff
E-Business	Characteristics	3
	Technology dependence	3
E-Business budgeting	Budget creation	82
	Necessary resources	81
	Resource strategy	83–84
E-Business implementation	Changing requirements	86–87
	Characteristics of failure	18
	Characteristics of success	17–18
	Critical success factors	6–7
	Leader duties	49
	Leader selection, responsibilities	47, 48
	Plan elements	11–12, 17
	Problems	9–10
	Project templates	13
	Two project leaders	45
E-Business issues	Alternatives to solution	260–261
	Common mistakes	255
	Crises	263–264
	Guidelines	267–271
	Issue assessment	249
	Issue management form	258
	Issues data base	251–252
	Issues graphs	254–255
	7 steps in managing issues	257–260

Index